Human Rights along the U.S.-Mexico Border

HUMAN RIGHTS
ALONG THE U.S.-MEXICO BORDER

GENDERED VIOLENCE
AND INSECURITY

Edited by
Kathleen Staudt, Tony Payan, and
Z. Anthony Kruszewski

The University of Arizona Press   Tucson

The University of Arizona Press
© 2009 The Arizona Board of Regents
All rights reserved

www.uapress.arizona.edu

Library of Congress Cataloging-in-Publication Data
Human rights along the U.S.–Mexico border : gendered
violence and insecurity / edited by Kathleen Staudt,
Tony Payan, and Z. Anthony Kruszewski.
    p. cm.
    Includes bibliographical references and index.
    ISBN 978-0-8165-2805-9 (hard cover) – ISBN 978-0-8165-2872-1 (pbk.)
    1. Women—Violence against—Mexican–American Border
Region. 2. Poor women—Violence against—Mexican–American
Border Region. 3. Human rights—Mexican–American Border
Region. 4. Crime—Mexican–American Border Region.
5. Violence—Mexican–American Border Region.
I. Staudt, Kathleen A. II. Payan, Tony, 1967–
III. Kruszewski, Z. Anthony.
    HV6250.4.W65H85 2009
    303.60972′1—dc22   2009033168

Publication of this book is made possible in part by a grant
from the College of Liberal Arts and the Lineae Terrarum
Fund at the University of Texas at El Paso.

Manufactured in the United States of America on acid-free,
archival-quality paper containing a minimum of 30 percent
post-consumer waste and processed chlorine free.

14 13 12 11 10 09   6 5 4 3 2 1

Contents

Preface

As we complete the final preparations for this volume, the borders between and among twenty-seven countries in Europe have opened. In the European Union, people cross without documents and without the presence of national military or law enforcement forces. U.S. policies run counter to the European trend. A wall is being built ("the wall of hate," as described in some Mexican media); political campaign sloganeering about immigrants and Mexico is at an all-time hateful high; violence is rampant in northern Mexico; and official national armed forces are positioned at or near some parts of the border, on both sides.

At the U.S.–Mexico border, gender-based violence is also rampant, but it has fallen through the cracks of scholarly and official writing, with the exception of the infamous femicide in Ciudad Juárez, centerpiece of the border. Femicide has taken a horrifying toll on over four hundred women since 1993, many of them raped and mutilated before being dumped in the desert periphery. Everyday domestic violence continues, unabated, and desperate people trek northward from Central America and Mexico to escape poverty, including gender-based poverty, in lives filled with many kinds of violence.

We coeditors are compelled to analyze these everyday realities at and from the perspective of borderlands, the frontlines of the global economy and the places where nationalists aim to draw (but could erase) deeper lines and higher fences in the desert, mountain, and urban terrains. Political scientists with interdisciplinary specializations on different world regions, we teach and research in comparative politics and international relations. Oscar Martínez's *Border People* (1996, 60) would categorize us as transnational borderlanders, with ties to the neighboring nation. Together, we have lived and worked in the U.S.–Mexico borderlands for eighty-two years—an area we view as our beloved home. We have many people to thank for assistance and insights in the development of this volume.

Scholarship on the U.S.–Mexico border, once colonized from afar, is now shared among border-based and mainstream people. Z. Anthony (Tony) Kruszewski cofounded the Association of Borderlands Scholars, and Tony Payan has been the president of this organization. Kathleen Staudt took the lead in this volume.

This volume is Kathleen's sixth book on these fascinating borderlands, with their compelling issues of human rights (and wrongs) in border spaces. She thanks coauthors, like Irasema Coronado, David Spener, and Susan Rippberger, and coresearchers, like Alejandro Lugo, Cheryl Howard, Howard Campbell, Beatriz Vera, and Gregory Rocha. After nearly thirty years of teaching, research, and activism at the borders, Kathleen counts herself privileged to have the opportunity to live at this crossroads of comparative politics and international relations, also a crossroads of class, gender, and ethnicity. As good friend and comparative politics colleague Jane Jaquette once said, "Lucky Kathy. . . . She can do comparative research, yet still live at home." Kathleen acknowledges support from another good friend and colleague, Irasema Coronado, with whom she has shared many research adventures.

The study of international borders now blossoms, augmented with comparative perspectives from Europe, Latin America, and Asia. For this we thank those who participated in the 2006 Lineae Terrarum Conference, located in El Paso–Ciudad Juárez, with its more than six hundred scholarly participants from over thirty countries. Tony Kruszewski and Tony Payan (fondly known as the "two Tonys" around this conference) co-organized these pioneering meetings over four days in March 2006, as participants crossed institutional and national borders at the rotating locations of cosponsoring higher education and research organizations: the University of Texas at El Paso (UTEP), La Universidad Autónoma de Ciudad Juárez (UACJ), New Mexico State University (NMSU), and El Colegio de la Frontera Norte (COLEF). Authors of two chapters in this volume presented their papers at Lineae Terrarum and the International Studies Association conference (Staudt and Mueller, et al.). The two Tonys will publish Lineae Terrarum papers in future volumes that embrace international borders in other locales besides North America.

Kathleen would like to thank others associated with the preparation of this volume. First and foremost, the reviewers provided excellent comments that helped to sharpen the focus. Second, Jaime Ruiz and Terrah Thomas, two UTEP students, ably assisted in communicating with authors and formatting this volume. Third, Beatriz Vera contributed her excellent translation skills for two chapters. Fourth, dedicated investigative journalists—such as Kent Paterson, of the online Frontera News Service, and the *Rio Grande Guardian*, a daily subscriber online newspaper—covered events in our 14-million-person border zone and among the 80 million residents who live in the ten Mexico–U.S. border states. And finally, community activists provided ongoing inspiration for action and policy change: the Coalition Against Violence toward Women at the Border, Casa Amiga, the Border Network for Human Rights, Border Interfaith (affiliated with the Industrial Areas Foundation, or IAF), and the Paso del Norte Civil Rights Project. They/we envision a world without violence and poverty, an equitable world with living wages, social justice, human rights connected with law enforcement, genuine democracy, and civil rights.

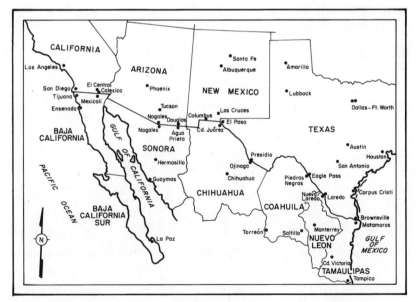

The U.S.–Mexico border region (Map courtesy of Oscar Martínez)

Violence at the Border

BROADENING THE DISCOURSE TO INCLUDE
FEMINISM, HUMAN SECURITY, AND DEEPER
DEMOCRACY

Kathleen Staudt

OVER THE LAST TWO DECADES, a host of social scientists, literary theorists, novelists, and filmmakers have titillated people's imaginations with their portrayals of the U.S.–Mexico border region. One can visualize the border in concrete terms: corrupt, drug-trafficking hellhole (*Traffic*) and/or gritty, seedy pathology of big-city femicide (from Lourdes Portillo's *Señorita Extraviada* to the Hollywood-produced *Virgin of Juarez* and *Bordertown*). On a more philosophical level, poets and literary analysts discuss the hybridized borders as "in-between places" (Bhabha 1994) and border crossroads as "open wounds" (Anzaldúa 1987) where multiple cultures are described less with museum-like, static metaphors and more with "garage sale" metaphors (Rosaldo 1989). Violence, vacuum, and/or chaos are prevailing themes in these portrayals.

Violence and fear also pervade official portrayals of the border, but they are narrowly conceptualized. In the United States, early twenty-first-century national policy seems fixated on border security designed to keep out undesirable people (Brotherton and Kretsedemas 2008). Officials declare "wars" on drug dealers, immigrants, and terrorists, blurring distinctions among them and proposing control solutions focused on a narrow set of "crimes" using "hard" tools: fences or walls and sophisticated technological surveillance. In bureaucratic space, immigration enforcement has moved from its initial birthplace in the Department of Labor (1925) to the Department of Justice (1940) and more recently, the Department of Homeland Security (2003). The international border is a legal boundary, and unauthorized movement across it has become a criminal offense.

Consider the language used to describe immigration and border cross-ing. Across the long, invisible line in the desert through the Rio Grande/ Río Bravo, Mexicans "invade" the United States. "Border Security" has become the watchword phrase of fear and of bureaucratic and bipartisan political campaign sloganeering, with a private industrial and commercial sector eagerly seeking contracts to work in public-private partnerships to "control" the border. The process strengthens nationalist rhetoric, even as globalizing economies tend toward more open borders, at least for capital, goods, and services, if not yet for the movement of people.

Mexico is not immune from punitive solutions to controlling its bor-ders (Martín Alvarez and Fernández Zubieta, this vol.). Globally gener-ated inequalities and instability south of Mexico's border produce con-ditions that propel people northward—conditions parallel to Mexico's interior. The length of the trek for Central American immigrants makes their trips even riskier, subject as they are to crimes, including those insti-gated by policing authorities. Nationalist rhetoric trumps practices that are respectful of human rights, both to citizens and immigrants.

Meanwhile, producers and consumers in the United States—and increasingly in Mexico—blithely depend on labor in foreign-owned industry labor enclaves known as *maquiladoras* with their shockingly low wages or on immigrants for their price-sensitive marketplace decisions. All of us are implicated in the crime, insecurity, and violence present on and at borders—regions shaped by national, binational and trinational public policies that backfire. We all help generate new problems, espe-cially at the U.S.–Mexico border.

Superimposed on the border threat and border security lingo that per-vades the airwaves and daily talk is the discourse of international human rights, seemingly guaranteed by international and inter-American trea-ties. International and regional agencies issue reports about and/or chal-lenge practices that violate human rights, including women's rights, but their bite dissipates or disappears once they enter the bowels of national bureaucracies. National and state human rights commissions lack author-ity to compel changes in Mexico, as is the case with critiques of femicide on the border (though see Aiken Araluce, this vol.). Transnational activ-ist pressure and advocates of good governance norms transmit growing human rights awareness and, perhaps, the spread of international norms: life with dignity, living wages, and community and human security in the form of food, shelter, and freedom from violence (see Mueller, et al., this vol.). Yet the driving forces are economic in nature: neoliberal global economies promote competitiveness, low prices, high profits, and comparative advantage in limited-government, free-trade regimes, whatever the consequences for *human* security and rights and for environmental well-being.

Border security should encompass life with dignity, living wages, and basic human security. Narrow rhetoric hardly engages the United Nations' eight *Millennium Development Goals* (United Nations 2000; United Nations Development Programme 2009), which include the eradication of extreme poverty and hunger and the promotion of gender equality and women's empowerment. These are goals around which international feminists cohere.

Framing the Volume

In this volume, I thread an amalgam of feminist theories and perspectives through issues such as border security, border insecurity, violence, and human rights. After all, much of the focus on violence at the border has addressed gender-based variants: femicide, rape, and everyday domestic violence, so normalized already that it is hardly noticed at the border (or in the mainstream). Antiviolence activists have problematized such border violence, as is well justified, but doing so risks reinforcing anxiety-producing, yet narrow border security discourses and practices that justify a more militarized border that, in fact, devotes limited attention to eradicating violence against women. Thus, we are all engaged in a violence-condemning cycle in which activists reinforce the very images that are used to justify further "official" violence. Yet the irony is that the voices against violence go unheard in the chambers of power that determine border security policy. Violence against women alone is all too real, yet it is un- or underreported in official statistics on both sides of the border. On one side, government bureaucrats ostensibly address such violence but hardly diminish everyday violence, though, I acknowledge, their fragmented responses include murders, including domestic violence homicide, another form of femicide.

We need to understand violence, security, and human rights from the perspective of those who live with violence day in and day out.

In so doing, it will also be necessary to expand narrower conceptions of human rights to include women's perspectives (Bunch 2006, 67).

Gayle Binion takes the conjuncture of women's rights and human rights one step further: "a feminist perspective on human rights has implications for *all* human rights, not just those of women" (Binion 2006, 75). Binion continues by saying that feminist approaches lead us to ask new questions, to challenge existing institutions, and to utilize inductive methodologies for answers. Such is the approach in this volume, drawing on voices from both sides of the border that understand the difference between discourse and practice (Merry 2006).

Former U.S. congressman Tip O'Neill once said that all politics is local, but international feminist theorist Cynthia Enloe goes a step further, saying that she sees "the 'international' as embedded in the national and in the local" (Cohn and Enloe 2003, 1188). This is, of course, particularly true for any border. Those of us who live on the U.S.–Mexico border know that Enloe trumps O'Neill.

In their analysis of the parallels between Bush and bin Laden, postcolonial (also internationalist) feminist theorists Anna Agathangelou and L.H.M. Ling conceptualize the differences between common hegemonic masculinity, a preference of superimposed traditions that shape institutions and society, and hypermasculinity, a reactionary stance which "arises when agents of hegemonic masculinity feel threatened or undermined, thereby needing to inflate, exaggerate, or otherwise distort their traditional masculinity" (Agathangelou and Ling 2004, 519).

At the U.S.–Mexico border, I argue, two hypermasculinity variants collide and collude: one related to national security and the consequent militarization of everyday life (as others have well argued: Tickner 2002; see also Dunn 1996) and the other related to a backlash against real and perceived threats (men's backlash against women, and xenophobes' backlash against immigrants). Rather than producing security, the results of these forces aggravate human insecurity in terms of everyday violence, sporadic violence, and policy-induced deaths at and near borders, as well as lingering poverty from policy-generated, market-based inequalities that fester from free-trade regimes.

The inspiration for this volume was born from frustration with the narrow terms of security debates. Living in and knowing the border region, *fronterizos y fronterizas* (borderlanders) are familiar with crossing for

work, visiting relatives and friends, going to school, working or shop-
ping. And increasingly, many are wary of the human costs associated with
border control: separated families, fearful lives, policy-induced intimidation, muted public voices—a kind of quiet desperation. Hundreds of
people die annually crossing a harsh border (Dunn 2009; U.S. GAO
2006; Eschbach, et al. 1999). Noncitizen residents lay low, exhibiting
lower crime rates than the citizen population (Martínez and Valenzuela 2006; Rumbaut and Ewing 2007), but they experience harassment,
detention, and deportation. Politicians use hateful rhetoric in political
campaigns and debates about immigration reform, most notably the 2005
failed Sensenbrenner bill, which would have criminalized millions—not
only undocumented residents but those, like teachers and clergy, who
help them in any way, even in time of need (Staudt 2008a). Border residents' fatigue with the persistent neglect of gender-based violence is now
evident everywhere, as the gruesome femicides of Ciudad Juárez stimu-
lated awareness of misogyny and everyday ineffective law enforcement
institutions that are hardly touched by border security wars. The official
security discourse completely ignores the terror of everyday lives amid
violence and poverty (see both Staudt and Aiken Araluce, in this vol.).

In *Policy Paradox*, Deborah Stone discusses symbolic representation
as central to defining problems in politics, with symbols as ambiguous
metaphors, both numeric and narrative (Stone 1997). Ambiguity allows
people to agree, Stone says, "because they can read different meanings
into the words" (Stone 1997, 161). A cacophony of voices uses and challenges border security discourses, some at the power core, such as capital
cities and centers, others at the border itself, where democracy is shallow
(Payan 2006) and power is expressed more in the form of resistance than
in engagement to frame debates.

In spatial and power terms, borderlanders are located at the periphery; their voices are sporadic and muted, rarely reaching the core. For
border twin cities, economic lifelines depend on movement and economic interactions, as does commerce for the mainstream, although in
less visible ways. Border voices are rarely engaged in the framing of border security and insecurity, in what I theorize later in this chapter as
spatially disadvantaged "third-tier pluralism" in shallow democracy (an
insight from Hero's 1992 conception of two-tiered pluralism). Rather,
border security concepts and tools emanate from the centers of power,

with multiple practices, policies, and discourses, but little consultation with border voices. One telling quote comes from Michael Chertoff, former secretary of homeland security, in his remark at a Border Security conference in 2007—a remark reminiscent of the destruction of villages in Vietnam: "We don't want to destroy the border in order to save it" (in Hsu 2007, A1). Another one comes from Ralph Basham, of Customs and Border Protection, who, when asked about the tiresome lines to cross the international bridges in El Paso, Texas, replied, "A safer border is well worth the wait" (in Preston 2007). He, of course, has never had to wait two to four hours in line just to cross a highly interdependent border. U.S. citizens in border communities rushed to get passports to return to their own country, complying with a new rule after January 31, 2008, and local public officials challenged these new crossing obstacles. Chertoff responded to concerns with the patronizing comment: "Grow up" (Grissom 2008).

This volume identifies problems associated with violence at the border, in everyday gender, immigration, and crime dimensions. As such, authors raise critical questions about the meaning of border security and its connection to human rights, and even ask: who benefits from or is burdened by the current discourse? The authors raise questions about criminalization approaches without accountability and broad-based voices that include all stakeholders. Whose security are we addressing? Do we focus on terrifying episodic events or everyday realities? And what insights do ethnicity, class, and gender bring to discussions of security and insecurity? This volume also addresses potential solutions for these problems, ranging from social movements and policy changes (from local to global) to institutional reforms and to the "arts of everyday resistance" (Scott 1990). Chapter contributors look toward a future when perhaps genuine border security can include decent living standards, honest law enforcement institutions, and freedom from everyday violence—a future when border security is equivalent to human and community security.

The remainder of this chapter is divided into three sections, as follows. First, I examine border security from narrow and broad perspectives. Next, I develop the theoretical perspectives from feminism and social democracy, briefly alluded to earlier, that comprehensively embrace the diverse chapters of this volume. And finally, I outline the chapters, previewing how each connects with the framework.

Border Security: Narrow Perspectives and Solutions

The events of September 11, 2001, tragic as they were, mobilized U.S. public opinion against the enemy "others": immigrants, foreigners, and non-English speakers. The language of security is persuasive: Who can be against security? Yet it is important to unpack the security discourse in its narrow versus broad dimensions. In so doing, one must engage with figures and trends about crime at the border, however inadequate and noncomparable they are, because most policy analysis, including security analysis, begins with numbers and narratives (Stone 1997).

Crime Statistics: Caveats and Numeric Metaphors

There is power in defining, measuring, and reporting crime. The notion of what crime is, both in legal terms and people's perceptions, changes over time and does not mean the same thing on both sides of the border. Crimes come in many categories: property crimes, injuries and murder, and victimless crimes. Over the past century, massive perceptual shifts have occurred concerning recreational alcohol and drug use: prohibition, dry and wet counties (that still exist in some Texas locales), and zero-tolerance enforcement for possession of various quantities and types of drugs. Whether actions are legal or criminal depends on the country: prostitution is legally regulated in Mexico, but outlawed in the United States (except some Nevada counties); first-trimester abortion is a crime in Mexico, but not in the United States.

Official sources differentiate crime statistics as serious or nonserious. Using Federal Bureau of Investigation (FBI) figures, *Congressional Quarterly* ranks the ten safest big U.S. cities and ten most dangerous big U.S. cities. Two border cities with populations over five hundred thousand, El Paso and San Diego, fall within the ten safest cities, at second and sixth respectively (*CQ Press* 2007). (Detroit, technically a border city with Windsor, Canada, is the most dangerous big city.) But only "serious" crimes are counted in those rankings, such as murder and assaults with a weapon, rather than misdemeanors like most domestic violence. As such, domestic violence is not computed in this measured ranking; the El Paso Police Department reported thirty-one thousand domestic violence calls in 2006 (El Paso Police Department, personal communication, 2007).

National and Border Crime Rates

Trend data are revealing, and many studies show declining crime rates in the United States since 1991. The fall has been even faster at the border—with some caveats. Coronado and Orrenius report that "border crime was 30 percent higher than the national crime rate in 1990," but that a decade later, only 12 percent higher (2006, 38–39). In 1990, there were 650 offenses per 100,000 people at the border (versus 500 nationally). By 2000, both border and national crime rates fell to under 400 offenses per 100,000. Coronado and Orrenius attributed drops at the border to a reduction in property crime, to urban Border Patrol initiatives known as Operation Hold the Line (El Paso) and Operation Gatekeeper (San Diego), and to a 10 percent rise in job growth (predicted to produce a 6.7 percent reduction in crime). The exception to their analysis occurs in rural counties such as those in southern Arizona and southwestern Texas, east of El Paso (2006, 46). Neither these authors nor I have comparable, reliable figures from the Mexico side of the border.

Border Misery and Deaths: Not Official Crimes

From the perspectives of those outside the state, who lack the power and authority to define and measure crime, official figures do not count what might be termed policy-induced deaths and misery. Since the start of border blockades and heightened enforcement at cities near ports of entry, migrants have crossed in treacherous desert areas, dying from "natural" and human causes: thirst and bandits, for example (Eschbach, et al. 1999). Based on the number of bodies that were located, there were 421 border-crossing deaths in 2006 (U.S. GAO 2006). Over the 1994–2007 period, Dunn counts 4,600 crossing deaths reported from official and academic sources (Dunn 2009), more among women than men (see Ochoa O'Leary, this vol.). The suffering associated with those deaths for the victims and relatives is, of course, untallied. Is this a crime? And if so, who is responsible? Who is accountable for policies and practices that result in such deaths among North American people? The state would never accept responsibility for these deaths.

FIGURE 1.1. Dangerous terrain for immigrants crossing near the U.S.–Mexico border in southwestern Arizona. The sign posted by Mexico's Instituto Nacional de Migración warns of the danger of extreme temperatures. (Photograph by Tony Payan)

Many crimes go unreported, thus not appearing in official reports and counts. In the United States, it is estimated that half of the crimes are reported (Orrenius and Coronado 2005, 6). But crimes like sexual assault and domestic violence have particularly high underreport rates, a result of shame, intimidation, and fear. Another large category of nonreporters would include undocumented immigrant victims, anxious about calling attention to their status. Poverty and policy-induced family breakups, what Vélez-Ibáñez calls the "distribution of sadness," are analyzed as individual rather than public problems (Vélez-Ibáñez 1996).

Immigrant victims' concerns have been aggravated with the increasing use of monetary incentives from national and state government sources to local law enforcement agencies to engage in activities that impact federal immigration law and deportation. In 2006, the El Paso Sheriff's Department, working with federal incentive money passed through state government, set up frequent road checkpoints in outlying areas, known

TABLE 1.1. Crime Rates in Border Cities, per 100,000 People

	United States	Mexico
Murder	5.62	13.04
Murder with firearm	3.25	2.58
Aggravated assault	310.14	86.86
Rape	32.99	14.26
Theft	2,445.80	112.47

Source: Data from United Nations 2003.

as *colonias*, to check for licenses, insurance, social security, and citizenship documents. This program, known as the terrorism- and drug-fighting Operation Linebacker, resulted in the deportation of over eight hundred residents. No terrorists were located, and deputies made minuscule drug confiscations (Staudt 2008a). An alliance of human and civil rights organizations filed lawsuits and pressured the sheriff's office to desist, with some success. Local democratic achievements, however, go unmatched at the state and federal levels—the sources of the monetary incentives.

In Mexico, people express massive distrust in criminal justice systems and anxiety about police impunity. While police corruption is difficult to erase in any country, Mexican police are reputedly complicit with or even responsible for crime, leading to reluctance to report (Zepeda Lecuona 2002; Magaloni and Zepeda 2004; selections in Cornelius and Shirk 2007; Staudt 2008b). One research source on Mexico City reports that over 80 percent of crimes go unreported due to mistrust in the police (Giugale, Lafourcade, and Nguyen 2001, 729).

Given these caveats—which collectively show that no one has any idea of the real crime and delinquency picture on the border—the tables included here should be examined with caution. From the *Eighth United Nations Survey on Crime Trends and the Operations of Criminal Justice Systems, 2001–2* (United Nations 2003), the most recent U.N. data available, we can compare overall crime rates in Mexico and the United States, per one hundred thousand people. (Data are reported by government agencies, rather than independently verified.)

Property crime and rape seem more extensive in the United States, but based on the discussion above about report rates, such crime is also more likely to be reported in the United States than in Mexico.

The Drug Connection at the Border

In the 1990s, the U.S.–Mexico border corridor became a gateway for trafficking drugs from southern suppliers to high-demand northern consumers. Organized criminals (drug cartels) engage in ruthless competition in major northern Mexican border cities where gang-style and drive-by shootings increase murder rates (Payan 2006). Richard Nixon declared a "war on drugs" in 1969, and nearly forty years and five hundred billion dollars later, there is little evidence of its effectiveness in terms of demand reduction (Nadelmann 2007; Wallace-Wells 2007). War casualties are numerous, from those in the business, killed execution style or "disappeared," to consequences that spill over to family members and innocent victims. Tobar and Sánchez report on expendable workers who "toil for traffickers . . . [and] often die in obscurity," some five thousand in the last two years (2007). One wonders how and where these crime figures are counted.

The most reliable crime figures come from homicide and femicide rates, at least for corpses that are found. Pedro Albuquerque analyzes a "universal fall" in homicide rates per 100,000 population from 1985–2001, both in Mexico and the United States and in border rates compared with national rates (2007). From tables in his analysis, I have constructed table 1.2 for

TABLE 1.2. Homicide Rates in Border Cities in 2001, per 100,000 People

Cities of less than 500,000 people	
Matamoros	10.1
Brownsville	4.9
Nuevo Laredo	15.4
Laredo	4.4
Reynosa	9.4
Cities of 500,000 people or more	
Ciudad Juárez	19.3
El Paso	3.5
Tijuana	17.6
San Diego	4.0

Source: Data from Albuquerque 2007.

border cities for 2001. Mexican border cities always report higher rates than U.S. cities (except for Detroit, the most dangerous border city in the north, with 41.3 homicides per 100,000 people).

Albuquerque also analyzes the volatility in Mexico homicide rates, noting alternative cities as "homicide rate leaders": Matamoros in the 1980s, Nuevo Laredo in the early 1990s (the highest at 41.0), Ciudad Juárez in the mid 1990s (but surely peaking again in 2008 with its cartel war), and Tijuana in the late 1990s. Nuevo Laredo peaked again in 2005. Such rates coincide with drug cartel territorial competition, with many execution-style murders in either intra- or inter-cartel violence (Payan 2006). Julia Monárrez Fragoso provides murder rates for Ciudad Juárez that show femicide rates peaking at different years: 1995 and 2002, with 41 and 42 cases respectively, or leading rates of 8.1 per 100,000 (2005, 279).

Private industry threat specialist Chris Parkerson estimates the kidnapping totals for major northern Mexico cities in 1999/2000 (Parkerson 2007). Totals range from a high of 114 and 84 in Tijuana and Ciudad Juárez, respectively, and a low of 17 in both Nuevo Laredo and Nogales.

In a comparison of the two cities that make up the largest metropolitan region at the border—Ciudad Juárez and El Paso—official statistics using 2001 figures show striking differences in violent crimes against people and in property crimes. One of the safest cities at the border (and in the United States), El Paso records 3.1 murders for every 100,000 people, while Ciudad Juárez has 28.5 murders per 100,000 people (Payán Alvarado 2004, 224, different from Albuquerque's figures but both from different official sources). However, property crime (robbery) totals are far higher in El Paso than in Ciudad Juárez that year: 27,203 compared to 14,511 (Payán Alvarado 2004, 222). Although the city of El Paso is half the size of Ciudad Juárez, it is a city where crimes are more likely to be reported.

Whatever the reliability and comparability of these figures and trends, figures that Deborah Stone would call "numeric metaphors" in her chapter on U.S. policy discourse, crime and insecurity seem daunting, yet puzzling. There are simply too many unexplained observations. U.S. border big cities seem relatively safe, using official crime (murder) data, but Mexico's border big cities, quite dangerous. Coupled with 9/11 anxiety and figures that suggest 12 million immigrants live in the United States illegally (but see discussion in Staudt 2008a), the border is officially constructed as one long security risk in the media and elections.

Little effort is made to make a distinction between national security and public safety. For everyday lives, public safety concerns match those of national security, each of which can result in death and injury.

U.S. politicians cannot afford to "look weak" on border security, a form of political suicide, as twenty-first-century state and national elections show. With the "Culture of Fear" (Glassner 1999) so prevalent in the United States, politicians exploit fears with spatial metaphors, focusing on, even demonizing, borders, especially the two thousand–mile border separating Mexico and the United States, and its migrants and immigrants, drug dealers and consumers, and outlaws who cross north or south to elude their national authorities. However, poverty, inequalities, and harsh treatment have become the screaming silences in border security rhetoric.

No doubt, border zones can become magnets for violence. The presence of multiple national sovereignties and multiple rules of law create conditions in which outlaws flourish in the North American free-trade zone. There seems to be a third space, seldom explored but often used, that is a veritable no one's land. For example, drug dealers escape through border crossing, north to south or south to north, as do serial domestic-violence batterers (see details in Staudt 2008b). After killing a spouse, the perpetrator can drive through the border port of entry with far greater speed than on foot or horse, as in Hollywood images from "wild west" frontier history and tales.

Narrow Problem Definition and Solutions: Criminalization, Enforcement

Officials' solutions center on control and interdiction strategies, through physical barriers like walls or fences, bureaucratic patrols, and technological surveillance. Laws, policies, and enforcement criminalize the movement of unauthorized border crossers. Once apprehended, some crossers sign voluntary departure papers and are moved across the border, while others increasingly are put in detention camps awaiting deportation. The harsh conditions of these detention centers turn them into internment camps of the twenty-first century. In late 2007, 27,500 immigrants lived in such camps, including the futuristic tent city in Raymondsville, near the south Texas border, where local incentives in a high-unemployment poverty-stricken area resulted in four hundred jobs and $2.25 per detainee

FIGURE 1.2. This border wall has been augmented in height. Some sections are blank, others have pictures, and still others sport graffiti. (Photograph by Tony Payan)

to the county government (Hsu and Moreno 2007; Democracy Now 2007). At the south Arizona border, with the massive infusion of Border Patrol and other officials in a sparsely populated area, one Cochise County official said residents live in "occupied territory, with one agent for every 20–30 residents," producing unintended consequences (Newman 2007).

A military-industrial complex—or law enforcement–industrial complex—fully blooms, but in spatialized border terms, fifty years after President Eisenhower's prophetic warning. In the closing chapter, we refer to this as the Border Security Industrial Complex (BSIC) (Staudt, Payan, and Dunn, this vol.). Nearly all solutions to the "border problem" further militarize the environment with increasingly stronger forms of what Timothy Dunn called low-intensity conflict (1996). This spatially specific, narrow security agenda does not address airborne trafficking, visa overstays (such as the perpetrators of 9/11), homegrown terrorists like those who bombed the Oklahoma City government building, leaky sea ports of entry (Nordstrum 2006), and bureaucratic backlogs that turn law-abiding residents into outlaws.

Border security analysts seem deaf to the growing calls in international relations approaches for "soft power," that is, persuasive and emulative power that comes from modeling collaboration, negotiation, and good-neighbor practices (Nye 2005). This may be in part because such solutions may demand some resource-sharing schemes, unacceptable to a population that seems to be losing a grip on its own material well-being and to politicians who may have a tough time convincing them. If and when laws pass that enable Mexicans to work in the United States, or if and when the countries of North America develop into deeper collaborative status, as in the European Union, the harsh, criminalization approaches to narrow definitions of border security will be viewed, in hindsight, as extraordinarily counterproductive.

Border Security: Broader Perspectives and Solutions

Comprehensive border security involves a wider problem agenda than that proposed in intelligence, defense, and security agencies—one that includes solutions that safeguard human rights (including women's rights), provide open and full employment, reduce inequalities within and across borders, and generate living wages.

Comprehensive border security also involves job creation at living wages in interdependent borderland communities and metropolitan regions. The United States is Mexico's largest trading partner, and Mexico is the United States' second-largest trading partner. As Jason Ackleson establishes, the scope of cross-border interaction in North America is huge: "More than 100 million people cross the United-States–Canadian frontier each year; over 300 million pass annually through the United States–Mexico border" (from Papademetriou and Meyers 2001, cited in Ackleson 2005, 139). Open commercial borders in a liberal trade regime, whether from the 1980s General Agreement on Tariffs and Trade (GATT) or from the North American Free Trade Agreement (NAFTA), create risks and facilitate the movement of illegal goods (such as drugs) and the movement of people. Ackleson argues that the inherent risks must be weighed against benefits: information technologies, screening, and

FIGURE 1.3. The border *colonia* of Sunland Park, New Mexico, is across a fence and a Border Patrol road from the colonia of Anapra in Ciudad Juárez. Colonias are unplanned settlements in or near urban areas. (Photograph by Tony Payan)

biometrics themselves have problems that potentially become counter-productive for border residents (Ackleson 2005). One wonders not only about the effects of securitization on border economies, but also the effects of high-tech surveillance on freedom and civil liberties.

Those living in close proximity to the border can visualize the stark and obscene inequalities that government policies generate on a daily basis. Although U.S. border residents are among the most poverty stricken in U.S. terms (the exception being San Diego, seventeen miles from the border), U.S. borderlanders' earnings seem high compared with Mexican border residents—even as the Mexican borderlanders' standard of living is relatively high compared with the rest of Mexico. Legal minimum wage rates, in U.S. dollar terms, amount to a ten-times differential: nearly $50 daily for U.S. borderlanders versus $4.50 daily for people in the Mexican borderlands. The second rate falls well below Mexico's poverty line. In actual wage terms, the differential is sixfold. Legal minimum wages, in a 1990s study, fell well below informal earnings, with the informal sector being a rough measure of real market value (Staudt 1998).

Domestic violence and femicide subject women to abuse and death; they are insecure in their own homes and neighborhoods. Comparable proportions of women in the United States and in Mexico, "one in four," experience physical violence at the hands of a partner in their lifetimes, but both poverty and migration make survivors more vulnerable—unable to exit dangerous relationships, unable to draw on social support networks nearby (Staudt 2008b; Staudt and Montoya 2009). Gender wage gaps are ubiquitous on both sides of the border, but when one adds race/ethnicity into the equation, the disparities are even more visible. Romero and Yellen, using census data, report that female Hispanic workers earn 37 percent of what male white workers in El Paso earn—annual salary differences that amount to $11,314 versus $30,594 (Romero and Yellen 2004, 16). Against these figures, stack an estimated six- to tenfold differential across borderlines to paint a numeric picture of economic desperation. Male homicide rates are high, and lacking decent pay alternatives, many men turn to everyday drug trafficking (Campbell 2005).

Away from these urban situations, with walls and fences, migrants cross inhospitable desert regions, risking their very lives. Prior to the harsh border enforcement, people returned to Mexico often in circular migration patterns (Massey, Durand, and Malone 2002; also see Cornelius and Lewis 2007). As noted earlier, annual death rates for recovered bodies total three to four hundred. Women face special threats in crossing in terms of sexual assaults (both Marrujo and O'Leary, this vol.). Crossers often depend on smugglers/*coyotes*, in what was once a low-cost, casual enterprise that has now turned into risky business, both for the suppliers and consumers of this high-profit market. Some undocumented residents are increasingly "entrapped" in U.S. enclaves, living lives in fear (Nuñez and Heyman 2007) and enduring assaults on human dignity. Many are now afraid to go out of their dwellings, even for exercise, sports, or to visit friends. From deep ethnography with New Mexico residents comes a report of an informant hiding from Border Patrol vehicles or trying to out-run them, calling "these vehicles *perreras* (kennels) because they put you in them just like dogs" (ibid., 358).

A lack of dignity also extends to those who disrespect human rights. I remember a middle-income neighbor who joked about employing an undocumented person all day on a landscaping job and then calling the Border Patrol to avoid paying the worker, resulting in the worker's deportation. These kinds of practices are all too common. In Austin, Texas, nonprofit organizations work with the undocumented on "wage recovery" issues, as employers sometimes refuse to pay or to pay what had been promised, knowing well that the undocumented worker is unlikely to complain. In Nicholas de Genova's analysis of how policies "produce" migrant illegality, he says employers discipline subordinates, making them vulnerable workers (de Genova 2002, 439).

These examples bring to mind J. M. Coetzee's apartheid-era allegorical novel on the frontier, with transcendent implications for other borders, *Waiting for the Barbarians* (1982). By the close of the novel, readers can only wonder who are "the barbarians": Officials and those complicit with them, or the "other" supposedly invading the frontier?

The grim everydayness of poverty undermines people's ability to live their lives to fuller capacities. The border separates and perpetuates inequalities of great magnitude, so much so that the inequality undermines reigning policies, whether focused on free trade or border control, as Erfani's (this vol.) analysis shows. Public policies, like NAFTA, make it difficult for farm families to survive, pushing migrants on desperate treks northward to sustain themselves and their families. Some 1.3 million Mexican farmers are thought to have been displaced by NAFTA (Carlsen 2007; Polaski 2006). A broader approach to security should examine what pushes migrants on dangerous northward treks.

Solutions in Broader Perspective

Broad-based solutions involve short- and long-term strategies. Living wages on both sides of the border should be a priority. Mexico's minimum wage rates must at least triple, with foreign assembly plants at the lead, followed by other employers. The rise in the cost of living has not been matched with equivalent wage increases, especially with periodic peso devaluations (Staudt and Vera 2006). This is particularly true for the lower socioeconomic strata of the Mexican society. State policy interventions should be geared to reducing and ultimately eliminating the huge wage differentials across borders. Organizations seeking to renegotiate NAFTA should address the destruction of small-scale agriculture in Mexico and the way that drives migrants northward. As the agricultural chapter of NAFTA enters into full effect in January 2008, small farmers in

Mexico will likely be worse off than before, increasing pressure on them to migrate. Perhaps the worst in border-crossing-related deaths is yet to come. Even the data from this chapter's first section illustrate the positive effects of job expansion on lowered crime rates. With decent wages, wages worth the value of workers' contributions, would-be migrants who desire to stay in their own country could do so and live lives with dignity.

At this point, nongovernmental organizations (NGOs) have risen to the moral challenge to provide water, shelter, and food to sojourners across the desert, particularly in the months of June, July, and August. One, Humane Borders, has developed a map that notes crossing death points. The U.S. Border Patrol launched the Border Safety Initiative (BSI) in response to the hundreds of annual deaths, aimed at prevention, search/rescue, identification, and data tracking. An evaluation of BSI's effects shows that it "has not reduced migrant deaths overall" (Guerette 2007, 254). Yet the Border Patrol and vigilante groups like the Minutemen oppose humanitarian assistance, criminalizing some and pursuing occasional prosecution, against, for example, No More Death volunteers who medically evacuated three migrants in critical condition from the 105° desert (Guerette 2007, 261). Others have criticized NGOs for providing incentives for migrants, among them the American Border Patrol, an anti-illegal immigrant group based in Sierra Vista, Arizona, and the U.S. Border Patrol itself. Most analyses of ethical and moral development, along with most human rights and faith traditions, deem that saving lives trumps obedience to the law. NGOs must be able to work freely to save lives, and official rescue operations should continue to prevent annual death counts from rising higher.

Antoine Pécoud, with the International Migration Section of UNESCO, summarized the emerging debate over the future of human mobility in "Toward a Right to Mobility: International Migration, Border Controls, and Human Mobility" (2008). He argued that the globalizing trends in the world economy imply that human mobility is increasingly viewed as a human right, rather than a privilege bestowed on individuals by centralized governments.

For these changes to occur, however, deeper democracy must be in place, a democracy with process and vision. In process terms, women and economically marginal men require space and voice in public institutions. In vision or outcome terms, active governance must ensure security in

FIGURE 1.4. Migrant pathways through the desert are littered with drinking containers, jackets, and other personal belongings, such as this toothbrush discarded near Naco, Sonora. (Photograph by Tony Payan)

food, shelter, and health terms so that all can participate in both process mechanisms and the fruits of public governance. The theoretical perspectives below embrace these themes.

Theoretical Perspectives: Deeper Feminism, Deeper Democracy

Thus far, my analysis has examined narrow and broad perspectives about violence, security, and human rights at the border, the spatial periphery of mainstream societies. A core focus is on everyday insecurity, whether from crime, unreported gender-based violence, poverty, or life without dignity and public voice.

Feminist theories have the potential to embrace these core comprehensive issues, although singly, they have not yet done so (for overviews, see Tong 1998; Jaggar 1983). Instead, feminisms have been sorted and categorized with numerous modifiers: initially, variants of liberal feminism, socialist feminism, and radical feminism have blossomed into a dizzying array of labels that include postmodern and/or French feminisms, postcolonial and/or global feminisms, identity feminisms such as Chicana and Black/African feminisms, lesbian feminism, maternal and/or conservative feminism, and libertarian (antistate) feminism. Liberal feminism is peculiarly a product of the United States, calling for a proactive state amid a capitalist market economy—an understanding quite different from the limited-government meaning of liberalism in the non-United States, 95 percent of the world's population.

It is time to locate convergence and morph consensus among feminisms, and the place to do so is at borders where the transnational meets the local race/ethnicity, class, and gender constructions. This I do in the following theoretical conjuncture.

Feminism has always had an uneasy relationship with the state and state institutions, most all of which encompass hegemonic masculinity norms and allow only thin democracy to the majority (most women and economically disadvantaged men) in the name of "pluralism" with women as one of many "interest groups." Feminists who address the state as shaper of social constructs view gender and class as core organizing concepts in state institutions, privileging male elites (Charlton, Everett, and Staudt 1989).

Although the terminology is now passé, socialist feminism maintains its special edge. However, the post-1980s "triumph of capitalism" (Heilbroner 1989) requires new terminology like social democracy, critiques of crude neoliberal economic practices, redistributive practices within and across national boundaries, and alternative economies. I call this Social Democratic Feminism.

Radical Feminism, once the only version that prioritized violence against women, finds itself in league with institutional reformism, once called liberal feminism (United States), in the search for justice, safety, and shelter for survivors of violence. Such feminists are unwilling to wait for the dismantlement of hegemonic masculinity and heterosexuality in future generations, beyond this lifetime, for safety and security; they do not seek to become a vigilante force in lieu of state law enforcement institutions with such functions. Old-style radicals and liberals converge with some mainstreamers (see selections in Rai 2003) who seek coalitions between those inside and outside the state around demasculinizing institutional culture and making it more responsive and accountable to the broader public. And old-style reformists find common ground with critical legal theorists in a contemporary "rights-based feminism" that seeks legitimacy and authoritative legal tools from international treaties, human rights, and law (AWID 2002; Kerr, Sprenger, and Symington 2004). Yet case-by-case approaches to address individual and local justice are costly and time-consuming, relying on justice institutions that often reflect still-remaining hegemonic masculinity embedded in state institutions and neoliberal assumptions about efficient markets.

Social Democratic Feminism with an edge, from forty years ago until now, focuses on class, income, and the distribution of resources and opportunities at local, state, and transnational global levels. That sort of feminism relies on active, rather than limited, democracy and public institutions to address gender inequality and dismantle the hegemonic masculinity embedded in our day-to-day institutions. It is a feminism that is wary of crude, market-driven neoliberalism (Tickner 2002). This feminism uncovers the ways in which "neoliberal pluralism" and market-driven concepts atomize the individual and weaken her/his power to change the forces that shape the social environment. It is an approach that challenges social constructions in the form of class, race, ethnicity, and nationality that intersect to sustain privilege for the few (on intersectionality in feminist analysis, see Weldon 2006).

Feminists, such as the internationalists earlier who use a global-to-local lens, problematize the militaristic security discourse to reassert masculinity and elite control—a discourse that is sometimes evoked out of concern for or protection of women, home and family, whether in Afghanistan, Iraq, or the U.S.–Mexico border region (Cohn and Enloe 2003; Tickner 2002).

In the U.S.–Mexico border context, postcolonial feminism, with which Agathangelou and Ling (2004) identify, might seem more appropriate to Asia and Africa, or to an historic Latin America, in the once colonized (now neocolonized) global south. However, the reference is more than adept at the U.S.–Mexico border for it conveys the historical colonizing and recolonizing core-periphery spatial relationship between the centers of power and capital and their distant frontiers, the borderlands and their residents whose voices are muted and prevented from developing their own security discourse and practice.

Decisions are made away from the border, in the national capitals—principally in Washington, D.C., even more so than Mexico City—obeying a strong-to-weak hierarchy. Border political voices have been marginalized in many ways. Even the infrastructure was built to connect the colonized frontier outposts to the centers of capital and power in state and national capital cities, rather than to one another, at the borderlands. Whether traveling by land through the interstate highway system or by air, especially in Texas, which constitutes half of the borderlands, infrastructure connects the border to the center. In Mexico, the roads run north to south with huge gaps in infrastructure between border-states. In the United States, congressional district gerrymandering manipulates border cities and towns, stretching them northward to the center and nonborder populations, thereby muting border voices. Of 435 congressional districts, 11 with a Southwest border boundary, there is but one solely in a border zone, less than sixty-two miles from the international line (the traditional 100 km definition of the border zone from the 1983 binational La Paz Agreement).

Vulnerable people, whether vulnerable from poverty, lack of citizenship or civil rights, intimidation, or fear, do not operate in a level playing field in the political realm. Modern-day borderlanders may be worse off than before, whereas historically, people at the frontier asserted a once-vibrant political culture with border-crossing ideologies and practices in Spanish and English for many decades (Romo 2005). The border has experienced a "closing" that has increasingly divided people into "those in" and "those out." Over a century, a combination of fear and intimidation, poll taxes, literacy tests, and monolithic assimilation has marginalized the majority of Mexican Americans at the border and rendered their skills into deficits. Many survive by assimilating into American identity.

Marginalization processes in the mainstream worked in parallel fashion for Latino populations, leading Rodney Hero to develop the concept of "two-tiered pluralism," sustaining privilege and advantage for the top tier (including the assimilated) but opening limited access and political opportunity for those at the second tier (Hero 1992). Some political opportunities go unused, given the production processes in place that "apprentice" people for subordination for the workplace (de Genova 2002) and, I argue, civic subordination. Hope and opportunity do exist, albeit in limited spaces for voice, accountability, and change.

Extending Hero's tiered analysis and joining it with feminist theories that are cognizant of the postcolonial world, I contend that a "three-tiered system" is in place at the borderlands, a spatial periphery that marginalizes people in deeper ways than ethnicity, class, and gender. This volume elaborates on the insecurity and violence at borderlands, using feminist, institutional, and social democratic lenses.

It is one thing to democratize national politics, a feat that Mexico is trying to achieve, but another to activate accountable democracies at state and local levels (see both Aiken Araluce and Staudt this vol.), an area where much is left to be desired not only in Mexico and parts of the United States, but also along the border. Whether in Mexico or the United States, the lives of local people transcend the borderline and have thereby legitimate stakes and rightful voices in decision-making processes about their environment. The federal systems of both countries virtually ignore these voices in efforts to preserve the integrity of their nationhoods. Consider what Winders (2007) calls *Nuevo* South and its attempts at restrictions against immigrants in a U.S. region of "paternalism, dependency, and coercion that have always characterized labor relations . . . being transferred to a new group of workers" (McDaniel and Casanova in Winders 2007).

All along the Border: An Outline of the Chapters

The border region is large, home to 14 million people living at or near the border or, counting the ten border states of Mexico and the United States, 82 million people (Staudt and Coronado 2002, using census figures). Until the middle of the nineteenth century, the border region was part of northern Mexico. Since 1848, after which most of northern Mexico became the U.S. Southwest, the border has undergone transformations through several regimes, from the frontier regime until 1910, to the customs regime of 1920–80 and the law enforcement regime of 1980–2001, and finally the security regime from 2001 onward (Payan 2006, 6–15.) Contributors to this volume propose a new regime: broad-based human and community security focused on human rights, one that de-links and de-borders violence and militarization.

Living and climatic conditions along the border vary enormously, ranging from urban to rural, desert to river areas, and dense to sparsely populated. This volume addresses violence, security, and human rights abuses all along the two-thousand-mile border, with specific chapters on points in between, including places along the Arizona-Sonora border and Ciudad Juárez–El Paso.

Authors write from vantage points both south of and north of the U.S.–Mexico borderline, yet with understanding of the border as a region. Contributors to this volume use concepts and methods from multiple disciplines, from anthropology and international relations to political science, law, geography, criminal justice, and sociology, conveying a complex and comprehensive picture of the region. In readable, yet multifaceted and substantive analyses, chapter writers report on contemporary field research that utilizes transparent methods.

The volume is divided into two parts. The first part, Framing the Problems: Violence, Security, and Immigration, addresses the problems of multiple types of violence at the border, focusing on gender, economics, immigration, and crime. The second part, Toward Action in Civil Society, Policy, and Transnational Policies, connects analysis with solutions in the forms of institutional change, social movement activism, policy reforms, and the spread of international norms that respect human rights and good governance. Yet global inequalities and the national or regional policies that sustain them hover heavily over the potential solutions.

Part I begins with social anthropologist Olivia Ruiz Marrujo in "Women, Migration, and Sexual Violence: Lessons from Mexico's Borders." She analyzes the routine sexual violence that migrant women face along Mexico's northern and southern "borders [which are] violent places for women." Ruiz outlines practices that make women vulnerable to abuse, from sexualizing and eroticizing non-native "others" to the limitations of gendered judicial institutions. Her chapter offers chilling commentary on women's migrant travels and their routine assaults.

In "Human Rights Violations: Central American Immigrants at the Northeastern Mexico Border," political scientist Alberto Martín Alvarez and sociologist Ana Fernández Zubieta tap interviews with over six hundred migrants coming through or to Mexico, along with faith-based shelter staff and the Tamaulipas human rights agency. Migrants are subject to great risks for robbery and gender-based violence, both from municipal police and railroad "security" workers and from guides, ranging from *polleros* to "false *coyotes*" and coyotes. While Mexican laws subject immigrants to punitive treatment, partial reforms are underway that may not make a dent in the "pockets of local authoritarianism" in northeastern cities.

Julie Murphy Erfani, also a political scientist, takes on economic inequalities and a wide array of crimes in "Crime and Violence in the Arizona-Sonora Borderlands: NAFTA's Underground Economy as a Source of In/security, with Comparisons to the EU." Erfani argues that global markets accelerate underground economies and illegal commerce (counterfeit pharmaceuticals, official corruption, intellectual piracy, among many others) in regions like North America and the European Union, focusing on southern Spain for her comparisons.

Anthropologist Anna Ochoa O'Leary's chapter, "In the Footsteps of Spirits: Migrant Women's Testimonios in a Time of Heightened Border Enforcement," focuses on the humanitarian crisis in the borderlands. With testimonies from three women, she shows how poverty and violence drove their journeys, but how close to death their movements brought them in the context of current border enforcement policies.

Part II also contains analyses of violence, but with greater attention on resistance to and pressure on governments to change policies and practices. In "Violence against Women at the Border: Unpacking Institutions," I begin with a focus on femicide in Ciudad Juárez, where over four hundred women were murdered from 1993 to 2006. In approximately one-third of the cases, the murderers mutilated and raped young women victims, with the other two-thirds victimized primarily in domestic-violence and routine opportunistic murders. After analyzing data from domestic violence surveys, I focus on institutions, both law enforcement and nongovernmental organizations (NGOs), comparing them from both sides of the border in mirror-like ways with an aim to inspire both government and NGO changes to eradicate the epidemic of violence against women.

In "Femicide on the Border and New Forms of Protest: The International Caravan for Justice," sociologists Carol Mueller, Michelle Hansen and Karen Qualtire map the wide array of social movement organizations that spread awareness about femicide. Specifically, they trace the innovative efforts of the Mexico Solidarity Network and its International Caravan of Justice, which visits the heartlands and mainstreams of both countries and takes testimonials from victims' mothers.

From yet another angle, international relations specialist Olga Aikin Araluce examines "Transnational Advocacy Networks, International Norms, and Political Change in Mexico: The Murdered Women of Ciudad Juárez." Her global focus addresses how transnational pressure triggered socialization toward international rights standards, examining the federal attorney general's office in particular.

In political science and law respectively, David Shirk and Alexandra Webber tackle the topic of "Human Trafficking and Protections for Undocumented Victims in the United States." After defining the problem in its multiple dimensions, they assess the complications of the law that focuses more on traffickers than on the victim-survivors.

Sociologist Timothy Dunn and political scientists Tony Payan and I bring closure to the volume, focusing on violence, security, and human rights problems and solutions in the context of United States and Mexico policies that generate contradictions, despair and hope at the still-less-than-democratic borderlands region. The chapter, "Closing Reflections: Bordering Human Rights, Democracy, and Broad-Based Security," summarizes other volume chapters and connects them with this chapter's social democratic feminism in future broad-based border security.

Acknowledgments

Thanks to Tony Payan and Timothy Dunn for their comments on this chapter.

Framing the Problems

VIOLENCE, SECURITY, AND IMMIGRATION

Introduction to Part I

The four chapters in Part I set the stage for a broad, gender-based perspective on violence, security, and immigration. As the introductory chapter discussed, the aim of this collection is both to understand and to act on human rights problems and solutions in everyday life. Women are at the center of such conceptions.

In the first chapter of this section, "Women, Migration, and Sexual Violence," Olivia Ruiz Marrujo analyzes routine horrors of sexual assault at Mexico's borders, both north and south. Deeply entrenched masculinist ideologies appear to give some men license to treat women as less-than-human, eroticized beings. Alberto Martín Alvarez and Ana Fernández Zubieta, in the second chapter on "Human Rights Violations," focus on Central American migrants at Mexico's northeastern border. Crimes, few of which are reported to the authorities, are a routine part of immigrants' journeys. In "Crime and Violence in the Arizona-Sonora Borderlands," Julie Murphy Erfani provides comparative perspectives on both the U.S.–Mexico and Spain's borderlands in the context of global neoliberal economic inequalities. Free-trade ideologies—mentalities and behaviors that value short-term profits over other principles, including human rights, decent jobs and pay, and safe goods in more regulated and accountable capitalism—produced consequences for illegal production and consumption that make us all complicit in immigrant-driven cheap labor and counterfeit goods. Finally, "In the Footsteps of Spirits" anthropologist Anna Ochoa O'Leary offers compelling *testimonios* of migrant women's efforts to escape poverty and violence in the harsh desert journeys through Sonora.

Women, Migration, and Sexual Violence

LESSONS FROM MEXICO'S BORDERS[1]

Olivia T. Ruiz Marrujo

IF RISK PLAYS a role in most international undocumented migration, along the U.S.–Mexico and Mexico-Guatemala borders, for example, the focus of this chapter, it underlies the experiences of undocumented women migrants.[2] To be sure, like their male counterparts, women face the possibility of robbery, assault, extortion, and mistreatment at the hands of authorities. Likewise, in search of less costly ways to travel, women risk falling from freight trains, tumbling off the backs of trucks, and drowning in rivers and oceans.[3] Still, among the dangers undocumented women face, sexual violence sits foremost in their minds when they leave their countries without documents (Azu 1997; Amnesty International 2000; Adital 2002).

Along the U.S.–Mexico and Mexico-Guatemala borders, sexual violence has become of fact of life for migrant women. The Procuraduría de Derechos Humanos y Protección Ciudadana de Baja California states that, among undocumented migrants both in California and Baja California, women are especially vulnerable to mistreatment by authorities and frequent victims not only of robbery and extortion but also of sexual aggression (*La Opinion* 1997, April 16, May 2; *Reforma* 23 July 1997). According to some estimates for Mexico's northern border, between 80 and 90 percent of migrant women have suffered sexual violence (*La Jornada* 2003). Rape has become so prevalent that, in the words of one regional director of the UN development fund, some women consider it "the price you pay for crossing the border" (*San Diego Union-Tribune* 2006).

Women fare no better at Mexico's southern border. According to a director of Beta Sur, the Mexican police force charged with protecting the rights of migrants, sexual assault of migrant women is part of the modus operandi of bandits and gangs who carry out frequent attacks on migrants in the region. Indeed, hardly a day goes by without a report in the local newspapers of an attack on a woman or group of women crossing through the region. In one incident, not atypical in the number of women affected nor its savagery, twenty-two women, three of them fifteen years old, were raped by twenty-four men carrying guns and knives, who later robbed their victims of their belongings (*Tertulia* 2000).

Furthermore, we can expect more of this violence in years to come, judging from the growing numbers of women leaving their homes without documents—95 million at this writing or almost half of the world's immigrant population, according to a report by the United Nation's Population Fund (*La Jornada* 2006). While estimates for Mexico's borders appear to be lower, they also reveal a growing number of women: approximately 20 percent of all migrants along Mexico's northern border, with even higher averages, about 30 percent, for the country's southern divide (*La Jornada* 2003). Yet despite the reality of sexual violence, it is a poorly documented risk, if and when it is registered at all. Indeed, not until the 1990s, when "the physical, sexual and emotional violence—that many women experience because of their gender" was added to the long list of officially recognized human rights violations, did the plight of women migrants draw any attention at all (Maier 2001, 122). Notwithstanding cautionary advice about sexual abuse and rape told by migrants (both male and female) to warn women and their companions of the dangers ahead, relatively little attention has been paid to the subject. As such, any effort to bring this violence to light, to understand why and against whom it occurs presents a difficult challenge.

What follows are some initial observations on sexual violence and undocumented migration at Mexico's northern and southern borders. To be sure, the areas' size and complexities make generalization difficult. As such, the discussion will focus largely on the Tijuana–San Diego area in the north, and the western coastal strip known as the Soconusco in the state of Chiapas to the south. The chapter draws on testimonies of migrant women and men; participant observation, especially in missions in Tijuana, Baja California; Tapachula, Chiapas; and Tecún Umán, Guatemala; and interviews with individuals, groups, and organizations dedicated to helping undocumented migrants in the regions; it draws on secondary sources as well.[4] In the end I hope to contribute to an understanding of sexual violence against women migrants, suggesting why it occurs and why it does so with such frequency along Mexico's borders. By way of a conclusion, I propose ways to address the issue.

Defining Sexual Violence

While the subject of sexual violence appears infrequently in the literature on undocumented migration, it occupies an important place in women's and gender studies. With its emphasis on sexuality and the role men play in the subordination of women, radical feminism, in particular, places the issue at the center of its analysis (Tong 1989, 9–123). Kate Millet, for example, suggests that sexual violence is intrinsic to patriarchy, which "relies on a form of violence particularly sexual in character and is realized most completely in the act of rape" (1970, 44). Later studies, widening the scope of analysis, have focused on the political character of sexual violence and its diverse and complex origins (Bergareche 2002). Underlining the need to situate its occurrence in historical, sociocultural, political and economic perspectives, on the one hand, and the configurations of class, race and ethnicity, on the other, they examine how different contexts, from the individual to the institutional, give rise to patriarchal ideology and, by implication, to sexual violence (Bergareche 2002).

Sexual violence against undocumented women reflects much of what characterizes this aggression against women in general. Consequently, the definition proposed here reflects issues germane to its occurrence in society at large. As defined here, it refers to an act that is physical or psychological in nature—a sexual assault as well as a threat of sexual assault, for example—aimed at the sexuality of the woman migrant, at attacking her physical, emotional, and psychic integrity. More specifically it has the following characteristics.

First, to repeat, sexual violence refers to a physical and/or symbolic affront, which a migrant woman identifies as an offense to her sexuality and, by implication, her physical, psychological and emotional constitution as a woman. When classifying acts as expressions of sexual violence, we must always keep in mind these women's points of view.

Second, it refers to abuses aimed at the body of a female migrant. It is an aggression directed at those parts of the body that physiologically distinguish her as a woman—her breasts and genitals—and lie at the heart of her identity as a woman (Schafer and Frye 1986, 195). As such, sexual violence includes physical attacks to her sexuality as well as verbal assaults, such as a threat of rape.

Third, sexual violence is an aggression that transgresses norms (whether set down in law or daily practice), themselves socially and culturally configured, that shape behavior, especially sexual behavior, towards the feminine body. In the life of a woman, these norms determine which man or men can (or can not) approach her body; they also influence how, if, when, and where he or they may do so. In other words, if cultures develop and establish an array of standards to treat women's bodies and conventions of respect as well as rules governing the transgression of female bodies, sexual violence involves a violation of one or more of them.

It is important to note that a migrant woman's interpretation of a specific act or event as sexually violent is socially and culturally configured. It will reflect how the cultures and societies in which she first became aware of her sexuality define transgressive and nontrangressive sexual behavior. Consequently, the place (or places) where a woman has lived, the sociocultural landscape where she developed as a woman, necessarily influence her interpretation of an act or event as sexually violent or not. If a woman has rarely had consensual sex, she may consider a coyote's demand for sex in exchange for assuring her "safe" passage a repulsive kind of hounding, but not necessarily deviant behavior. Indeed, she may even consider it "expected" or "usual" adult male conduct, "what one can expect from a man if you are a woman."[5] In other words, a woman will (or will not) define an experience as sexually violent depending, to an extent, on whether her culture of origin has equipped her to identify that experience as such.

In that process, the degree to which a woman understands her personal, civil, and human rights plays a crucial role. Preparing for the worst, a possible sexual assault on the journey north and the additional hardship of a forced pregnancy, a woman migrant may take birth control pills. She may not consider this decision (acquiring and taking birth control pills to avoid a pregnancy in the event that she is raped) a form of "sexual violence," but from the standpoint of human rights, it is difficult not to see it as such. In the end, whether or not she recognizes this psychological terror and the choice it imposes as sexual violence will depend to a large extent upon the degree to which her society of origin has encouraged the education and socialization of human rights, especially her civil and gender rights as a woman.

Explanations of Sexual Violence

The literature on sexual violence offers a number of explanations for aggressive behavior toward migrant women. One approach suggests that sexually abusive behavior has clearly defined motives and occurs in specific and recurrent situations—the rape of women during a robbery, for example. Assailants rape women, according to this explanation, to "reward" themselves for a successful robbery or as a "gratification" after the assault. Likewise, some forms of male-bonding or rites to establish loyalties and hierarchies in a group of boys or men include, may even require, the sexual abuse of women (Segal 1990, 246). Initiation rituals of some gangs involve the collective rape of a woman.

Coyotes, or migrant traffickers, insofar as they have almost exclusive control over the people who have paid them, often gain access to the bodies of women migrants by default. Coyotes may refuse to take a woman with him, threaten to turn her over to unknown men or abandon her midway if she refuses his advances. Aware of the possibility of such a demand and seeking to avoid a confrontation and possibly greater risk, a woman may "agree" from the beginning of her negotiations with a coyote to have sex with him in exchange for his "help" or "protection."

There also exists a trafficking of women and girls. They are purchased and sold, often for sex work. Those who buy and sell women may or may not abuse the women themselves; however, they force their hostages into a cycle of abuse—the sale of their bodies for the sexual gratification of customers. U.S. Department of Justice estimates for the number of female victims of trafficking in the United States range from 14,500 to 17,500, while estimates for Mexico run higher, perhaps up to 18,000 (Fuentes 2005).

Sexual Violence and Immigration

Yet the question remains: why are women migrants along Mexico's northern and southern borders so vulnerable to this form of aggression?

Parting from the premise that the number of men who sexually abuse women varies from society to society, we need to ask what, if anything, in societies where this aggression occurs frequently, produces sexual aggressors or permits men with a predisposition towards this kind of behavior to act on it. More specifically, what permits men in these border regions to commit acts of sexual violence against women migrants?

While there are no easy answers, an explanation might begin by examining what makes this kind of violence not just permissible but gratifying or even rewarding. Specifically, and following the advice of much of the literature on sexual violence, I propose we look at a number of local realities, which, combined, render migrant women vulnerable to this kind of abuse. These include: practices and legacies of domination, constructs of "native" and "foreign," practices of violence, judicial rights of women, and gender and erotic culture (Scully 1990; Segal 1990).

Practices and Legacies of Domination

As behavior that subordinates women, sexual violence is an act of domination. MacKinnon states that in incidences of sexual violence "a man takes possession of the sexuality of a woman, as it is mediated by her body" and, by way of this act, proclaims that her sexuality "belongs to him, is subordinated to him" (MacKinnon 1982, 532–534). I suggest that sexual violence reflects a more general exercise of domination, and gains acceptance, if not legitimacy, from that practice in society at large.[6] Domination of another is, almost by default, conduct that reflects and determines who is vulnerable (women, children, the aged, the infirm, and the poor, for example) and institutionalizes that vulnerability. Societies where subjugation and exploitation are rampant will most likely give rise to and allow the abuse of women.

Although an analysis of the institutions and practices of domination along the U.S.–Mexico and Mexico-Guatemala borders lies beyond the scope of this chapter, suffice it to say they have played a decisive role in the history of these regions, as sites of conquest, colonization, ethnic and racial conflict, territorial dispute, migration, and capitalist growth. Mexico's southern border, an area par excellence of colonial domination, has some of the highest degrees of social, economic, and political marginalization, especially of indigenous and, increasingly, migrant peoples.

Chiapas, with the heaviest traffic of migrants and some of the oldest immigrant settlements, registers some of the highest rates of socioeconomic inequality in Mexico. It is also the second poorest state in the country. Likewise, areas adjacent to the international line in the United States have some of the highest levels of poverty and political disenfranchisement in the country. One in four border residents lives at or below the poverty line, two times the national average for those living in poverty (MPI Staff 2006). Although the Mexican side of the U.S.–Mexico divide has enjoyed more prosperity than its counterpart to the south, it is an area of enormous socioeconomic inequalities and marginalization, populated increasingly by growing numbers of poor.

The Definition of "Native" and "Others"

If domination renders undocumented migrants vulnerable and exposes them to risk, it often does so by invoking binary oppositions of "native" and "foreign" and enlisting resources (the Border Patrol, for example) to sustain their differences. Foreign subjects by degrees lose power; subordinated subjects are made foreign, their "otherness" spotlighted. Undocumented women, I suggest, due to their national origins, undocumented status, poverty, and gender, embody what is foreign, its "otherness," in both border areas. Remanded to the perimeters of hegemonic notions and forms of "civilized" life, they live at risk, easily subjected to violence.

Definitions of "otherness" and the enforcement of rules governing those definitions (immigration laws, for example) lie at the heart of modern nation-states and conceptions, often idealized, of community and peoplehood. They underlie official discourses of citizenship and sovereignty and give meaning to ideas about national identity and cultural authenticity. They offer answers to the questions: "Who is and what does it mean to be American or Mexican?" and "Who should be allowed into Mexico or the United States?" By implication, they rely on a continual and vigilant classification and control, if not subjugation, of people, especially of those crossing a nation's borders.

Immigrants, to be sure, while almost always foreign, embody varying degrees of "otherness." The measure of their difference, furthermore, depends on much more than what their passports state. To borrow from Omi and Winant, nation-states emerge out of the "interpretation, representation or explanation of the racial [ethnic] dynamics" (1994) within relations of domination among peoples and communities— between those of the Soconusco and the peoples of Central America or between those of the U.S. border and migrants from Mexico and Central America, for example. Both in the United States and Mexico, notions of "native" and "foreign" are ethnically and racially cast. At the same time, these notions are mediated by legal and class attributes. The proper immigration documents and a sufficient amount of money may well earn an immigrant citizenship in the country of his or her choice, regardless of national (ethnic) origin.

Mexicans and Central Americans have been a ubiquitous foreign presence in the complex intersections of ethnicity, race, class, and gender as well as in constructions of nationhood and "otherness" along the U.S.– Mexico and Mexico-Guatemala borders. Since the late nineteenth century, rural laborers and domestic workers, many indigenous from Guatemala, have crossed Mexico's southern border to look for work in the Soconusco. Today, the migration of seasonal agricultural workers, engineered by Mexico's and Guatemala's governments and institutionalized in the immigration laws of both countries, constitutes a continual replenishment of the Central American population in Chiapas. By extension, many residents in the state identify Central Americans, especially if poor, indigenous, and female, with rural and domestic labor. They are by definition of their employment, national and ethnic origin, and migrant status— and in the case of women, their gender—a socially marginal group. Also, most sex workers in the region come from across the border; not surprisingly, the association of Central American women with sex work is entrenched in the region. In short, popular images of Central American migrants portray them as low-wage, if not poor, expendable agricultural laborers, domestic workers, and prostitutes.

For students of the U.S.–Mexico border, this history seems almost too familiar. Like their Central American counterparts, since the nineteenth century Mexican migrants have crossed the border into the United States in search of jobs in the country's railroads, agriculture, mines, and, especially since the latter half of the twentieth century, towns and cities. Similarly, agricultural work in the southwestern United States is still performed largely by Mexicans (even if the majority of migrants from Mexico work elsewhere), as is domestic service. As recent debates in Congress make clear, Mexican migration remains a subject of intense interest in the United States and Mexico, the shortcomings of the Bracero Program notwithstanding. Given these realities, the mistreatment of undocumented migrants from Mexico and Central America should come as no surprise.

In few places do notions of "native" and "foreign" acquire such significance as they do along international borders. In this respect, Mexico's northern and southern borders provide no exception. On the contrary, they are emblematic. As areas where the practice of exclusion occurs daily—indeed, as areas maintained for that purpose—they are places of risk for undocumented migrants, especially women.

The exercise of domination shapes daily life at Mexico's northern and southern borders. It does so officially at the international lines and ports of entry, where people are admitted into the country or removed, and unofficially, in debates concerning who should or should not enter and how to enforce the rules of entry and residence. In this respect, patrolling borders involves much more than territorial disputes or registering passports. It involves concentrated efforts to shape and enforce rights and obligations of citizenship and to fix ideas about the nation-state and national identity, whether Mexican or North American. We need only witness the appeal of legislation hostile to migrants, the orchestration of efforts to apprehend migrants at their work places, and the mobilization of groups like the Minutemen along the U.S.–Mexico border area.

The ambiguity of borders, the meeting, mixing, and colliding of peoples of different national and cultural origins and identities, complicates the development of a consensual understanding of everyday life at the border. Definitions of "foreign" and "native" and the enforcement of those benchmarks are never easy. Despite efforts to seal borders, they remain porous and people slip through. Because of the tension involved in determining who is "native" and who is "foreign," who must leave and who can stay, borders are neuralgic centers of vigilance, exclusion, coercion, and control and, by extension, places of explicit and latent violence. Along both of Mexico's borders, this has led to growing numbers of immigration and customs officials, as well as police forces and military personnel. The result has been an escalating militarization of both regions, which has, not surprisingly, further entrenched, if not institutionalized, the exercise of violence (Andreas 2000).

The Practice of Violence

Historically, vulnerable groups have been dominated through various forms and degrees of violence. By implication, sexual abuse of women migrants cannot be understood outside the perimeters of violence as a social practice. Studies show that generalized use of violence, as a tool of domination and response to conflict, corresponds to a high incidence of sexual aggression (Lorber 1994, 76–77; Segal 1990, 238). In other words, it accompanies a predisposition towards aggression in a society and most likely belies a high incidence of abuse of women.

In this light, an explanation of sexual violence needs to determine if, and to what extent, violence in general constitutes culturally appropriate, accessible, and permissible behavior. Regarding its practice we should ask whether people employ it frequently and whether it is tolerated or punished. We need to know if it is used in a wide range of situations or limited to specific and controlled circumstances. In other words, we should ask if and to what extent, in the words of Bandura, there exists a "social learning of aggression," that is, a reinforcement and reproduction of aggressive behavior in the repertoire of acceptable social behavior. We also need to examine whether there exists a "social learning" that represses violence, a social and self-condemnation of it (Bandura 1975; Dobles Oropeza 1990).

As areas of conquest, colonization, and ethnic conflict, Mexico's northern and southern borders have been the scene of violence for centuries. In both border regions, those on the losing side, the most vulnerable, have been subjected to acts of terror, what Bakare-Yusef calls "the logic underpinning the creation of colonial reality and identity" and Taussig identifies as "the mediator par excellence of colonial hegemony" (Taussig cited in Bakare-Yusef 1999, 317) of most structures of domination. According to two historians of the area, the northern border's heritage is one of violence characterized by rampant racism and cultural chauvinism (Acuña 1972; de Leon 1983). Likewise, Mexico's southern border continues to reel from a legacy of colonial conquest, the subjugation of indigenous peoples, and the socialization of violence as a tool of social order. Indeed, today Chiapas registers some of the highest incidences of human rights violations, among them violations of Central American migrants.

It is important to point out the complex ways in which women have been used in this generalized abuse of power, since sexual violence may reflect inequalities of power among men and the attempts of one group to dominate another. History documents how groups of men have strategically employed sexual violence to humiliate and demoralize the "other." Since women—exclusive access to them as well as treatment and control of their bodies—are symbols of honor and shame in many societies, sexual violence against them, especially when carried out collectively, may reflect other kinds of societal violence, such as ethnic cleansing or war (Friedman 1992, 67). The collective rape of women migrants, a not-uncommon practice in the border region between Mexico and Guatemala, degrades and humiliates its victims; if carried out in the presence of husbands, boyfriends, brothers, or sons, it humiliates them as well.

The Judicial Rights of Women

The degree to which a society accepts or condemns sexual violence also depends on its judicial system's definition and defense of women's rights. More specifically, it depends on the extent to which laws will support a woman who says she has been sexually mistreated and facilitate or hamper the apprehension and punishment of her abusers (Scully 1990, 163). In addition, that commitment will most likely vary according to the judicial system's ability to accommodate migrants, particularly when they have crossed international boundaries without documents.

In light of the dynamics of migration and the Guatemalan, Mexican, and U.S. judicial system's limitations, it should come as no surprise that so few cases of sexual violence appear in official records. Women migrants, like their male counterparts, avoid public institutions and places where they must go if they want pursue a claim. Most women prefer to continue their journey unless a lack of money or an accident or disease makes traveling north impossible. In addition, women face the rigidity and complexity of the judicial systems. A case of rape on the Guatemalan side of the border takes three months to expedite; processes on the Mexican and U.S. sides also require extended lengths of time. Furthermore, despite the frequency of abuse, few of the perpetrators have been convicted. The case of one U.S. immigration agent is telling. Although arrested, tried, and convicted, after a woman migrant identified him as the man who had raped her when she attempted to cross into the United States, he received a sentence for another, lesser charge (AFSC 1999).

On a related note, immigration laws should be constructed with the gender of migrants in mind. Deporting women migrants across the border in the early hours of the morning, a practice still common among U.S. immigration officials at the U.S.–Mexico border despite the efforts of human rights organizations in the area, exposes women to risk. Alone in dark city streets, they are easy victims of assault.

The Culture of Gender

As codes and behavior that order and give meaning to relations between men and women, gender culture necessarily influences the degree and frequency of sexual violence. According to Scully, sexual violence occurs more frequently in societies where women are portrayed as property and relations between the sexes are marked by extreme distrust or hostility (1990, 163). It reflects a recurrent absence, often associated with a propensity for violence in general: the incapacity to identify with the "other," to feel empathy for her or him (Butterfield 1996, 103). By implication, in societies where images of women as property predominate, where an acute and generalized distrust of women prevails and hostility marks relations between the sexes, men are, in general, less likely to identify with women as equals—as people who feel and suffer as they do—and to feel less empathy for them when they do suffer.[7]

While an analysis of gender cultures at Mexico's northern and southern borders requires more space than is available here, it might begin by examining the degree of control men have over women, especially over their bodies and sexuality. What do women reveal about gender relations in the Soconusco, for example, when in daily conversation they refer to sexual relations with their partners as "cuando hace uso de mi" ("when he makes use of me")? Likewise, emergency rooms of local hospitals attend daily to women who arrive unconscious after suffering "fainting spells," the result, often, of disagreements or conflicts with a spouse or partner. In other words, what reception and treatment can Central American migrant women expect in a society that has built a culture of gender around the appropriation of women's bodies and sexualities by the men closest to them or where women "faint" when faced with an angry mate or husband?

One of the most telling and harrowing pieces of evidence regarding the configuration of gender cultures along Mexico's northern and southern borders is femicide. Along with the murdered women of Ciudad Juárez, many of them former migrants to the city, hundreds of women have been killed violently in Chiapas and Guatemala, fueling an outcry in local, national, and international human rights circles. There is evidence, also, that the assault on women in Ciudad Juárez is moving across the border. If, in the words of Brickman, acts of violence against women are "social statements [which] embody central themes and tensions of the civilization" in which they take place (1996, 16), the gender cultures of both border regions may prove to be some of the most dangerous for migrant women.

Erotic Culture

In a society's configuration of gender, erotic culture—how women and men imagine, construct, and live sexual desire—plays a definitive role. Following Tong's advice, assessing erotic culture requires looking for the balance between sexual impulse and Thanatos, or death instinct, in local sexual practices; that is, between a sexuality characterized by the full participation of two people as opposed to one shaped by subordination and domination (Tong 1989, 113). In this respect, even a cursory observation of public practices of erotic life in the Soconusco, especially, but in the northern border as well reveals troublesome signs. Bars along Mexico's borders, especially in the south, are places of male recreation and predominately masculine domains, except for the waitresses and dancers (who often double as sex workers). Men go there, most often in groups of friends and acquaintances, to talk, drink, play pool, watch sports, and amuse themselves with table dancers, who in the south come almost exclusively from Honduras, El Salvador, Guatemala, and, to a lesser extent, Nicaragua. Indeed, on the border between Mexico and Guatemala, men go to bars expecting Central American table dancers to entertain them. In a similar vein, young men in the Soconusco will often seek out Central Americans for their first sexual experiences, due to the ease and impersonality of those encounters. In short, Central American women play a singular and important role in male erotic life in the region, in so far as they occupy a central place in the development of personal

FIGURE 2.1. On the border in Ambos Nogales (Both Nogales). The United States, with its Border Patrol agents, is on the left. On the right is Mexico, with a stairway leading to modest homes and Cherry's Ladies Bar, its beer sign eroticizing a near-naked woman. (Photograph by Tony Payan)

sexual behavior and norms of conduct—toward a sexuality of subordination or full participation—that shape men's erotic relations with women.

What to Do

What can we do and how do we proceed in light of the consequences and ramifications of this abuse, both in the immediate present, in the day-to-day of women's migrations, and in the future, as these women begin to settle and participate in society, be it of their birth or of another country? What is to be done in the worst cases of sexual violence, such as rape, that can so damage a woman's sense of self she may feel stigmatized and marked for life (Brison 2002, 49)? To be sure, recent research on the consequences of sexual abuse of minors, young victims of rape, for example, is especially alarming, since it indicates that severe abuse may provoke irreversible neurobiological damage (Teicher 2002). The growing numbers of women migrants along Mexico's borders, a reality reflected worldwide, makes sexual violence against women an urgent issue for migration policy (CNN.COM U.S. News 2000; *La Jornada* 2000). I make the following proposals, taking into account the seriousness of the injury, the lack of information, and the need for a prompt response.

To begin, though elementary, when an abuse occurs we need to know what happened. This should be done, primarily, to assist the victim. Documenting abuse is also necessary to bring to light the causes and consequences of sexual violence for the victims and society. In addition, it will aid in better understanding the relationship between sexual violence and migration—whether or how migration gives rise to and permits abuse and whether it leads to migrant women's future disempowerment.

Documenting violence involves preparing people who are knowledgeable, helpful, and nonjudgmental about human sexuality, sexual violence, and migration. In general terms, since a migrant woman who has suffered abuse is more likely to seek help from individuals, groups, and organizations dedicated to helping migrants, those who want to help need more information about this form of violence. Programs need to be set up to prepare people to attend to women migrants who have been mistreated. They should provide guidelines indicating what legal and medical measures to take and how to address the psychological and emotional needs of women. This requires adapting procedures, which were designed to address the needs of local victims of sexual abuse, to the special requirements of undocumented women migrants who are probably unfamiliar with local Mexican or U.S. culture and are only temporarily in the area (that is, en route to somewhere else). This may require arranging to send victims of abuse home or putting them in touch with services for victims of abuse in their countries of origin.

In addition, help should be available for male victims of abuse, who may have suffered some form of sexual violence themselves or had to witness the assault on wives, mothers, sisters, daughters, girlfriends, friends, or companions. The availability of this care should be well publicized and accessible in centers dedicated to providing medical, legal, and psychological attention to migrants.

At the same time, taking into account the social and cultural roots of sexual violence, an effort needs to be made to disseminate in society at large knowledge about this form of abuse. Those most knowledgeable about the local reality of sexual violence can educate and sensitize the local population to the causes and consequences of this abuse; they might begin with local authorities, such as immigration officials. To emphasize, sexual violence is not only an individual act, but a social and cultural expression of a deteriorated image of women that permits abusive treatment of women in general and especially of the most vulnerable among them—undocumented migrants, for example.

Since most of the affected women travel without documents and with few resources (money or family, for example), which precludes them from staying for any length of time in the area (they may, of course, also fear being apprehended if they remain in one place for too long), those women who do decide to take legal action against their abusers should be able to do so with the least amount of difficulty. This requires making the legal process more agile. Legal action should not take months to process and resolve. Women should not have to fear deportation or prosecution for their undocumented entry while awaiting the resolution of a claim of sexual abuse. This is especially urgent in border areas where a case may entail working with two legal systems. Such incidences may require exchanging information across international lines between authorities responsible for managing or prosecuting the case in their respective countries. This occurs, for example, when the event took place on one side of the border and the victim seeks legal action on the other.

One of the most difficult issues surrounding sexual violence is the conception itself of sexual violence. As mentioned in the first part of this chapter, when identifying what is and what is not an act of sexual aggression, it is crucial to listen to the victims. As such, programs established to respond to sexual violence against migrant women need to be framed around what women migrants identify as sexually violent behavior. It is they who decide over what parts of their bodies they believe they should have or want to have control. At the same time, sexual violence and abuse are, to a degree, culturally construed. Both of these proposals carry risks. A woman who is unaware of her civil and sexual rights may not recognize an aggression as such. If she did not grow up in a society and culture that educated her about these rights, she probably will not recognize or defend them in the judicial system. That leaves the international human rights community to uphold them, a weighty and complicated task. Unfortunately, this complexity—a consequence of multiple readings and understandings, themselves reflections of local and regional social, cultural, and political constraints— may prove to be one of the most difficult obstacles to overcome.

Notes

1. This chapter builds on a previous essay, "The Gender of Risk: Sexual Violence Against Undocumented Women," in *A Promised Land, A Perilous Journey: Theological Perspectives on Migration*, eds. Daniel Groody and Gioacchino Campese, 225–239 (Notre Dame, IN: Notre Dame Press, 2008).

2. Throughout the text the U.S.–Mexico and Mexico-Guatemala borders will also be referred to respectively as Mexico's northern and southern borders.

3. On Mexico's southern border migrants frequently ride in the backs of trucks already loaded with bags of coffee beans, regularly piled seven to eight meters high.

4. The missions are the Casa del Migrante of Tijuana, Baja California; Tapachula, Chiapas, Mexico; and Tecún Umán, San Marcos, Guatemala, established and run by the congregation of the Fathers of St. Charles Borromeo, otherwise known as Scalabrinians.

5. This is not meant to imply that she is unaware or insensitive to the hostility in the behavior. Rather the aggression is understood as a common expression of a type of normal behavior (sex), which, in turn, is considered intrinsic to relations between men and women in general.

6. Drawing on a modified reading of Hartmann's concept of patriarchy, domination refers to here "a set of social relations, between [those in power] which have a material base, and which, though hierarchical, establish or create interdependence and solidarity among [the powerful]" that make it possible for them to control or subjugate others (cited in Tong 1989, 180).

7. It should be noted that women in such a society are also less likely to see men as their equals or to see themselves as men's equals; by implication, they may not identify with men's suffering.

3

Human Rights Violations

CENTRAL AMERICAN IMMIGRANTS AT THE
NORTHEASTERN MEXICO BORDER

Alberto Martín Alvarez and
Ana Fernández Zubieta

Translated by Beatriz Vera and Tony Payan

THE CONFLICT THAT DEVASTATED the Central American region in the 1980s and created a dramatic population movement had an effect on the migration patterns of the people in the area and the evolution of self-sustaining social processes. This generated new regional migration systems, according to Castles and Miller (2003, 26). In turn, these processes turned Mexico into a transit country—and in a very minor way a destination—for the thousands of migrants coming from Central America and moving to the United States.

An interest in understanding the dynamics of the migratory flows has led numerous academics to center their attention on the conditions of the journey and on the risks migrants face in trying to reach their destinations, including violations of their human rights. Such human rights violations, which migrants suffer along their route through Mexico, have been noted by several international organizations as well as by national and international nongovernmental organizations and spokespersons from the Catholic Church. However, and because of the particular characteristics of the undocumented migration phenomenon, there is an absence of quantitative information that would allow more precise knowledge of the nature and extent of the problem of human rights violations of Central American migrants crossing Mexican territory. This research modestly intends to fill that void.

Nature and Characteristics of the Study

This chapter gathers the results of the first phase of a field research project conducted between February and April 2007 in the cities of Nuevo

Laredo, Reynosa, and Matamoros, main border sites in the state of Tamaulipas (Mexico). It constitutes the preliminary phase of an exploratory, descriptive study, which offers a tentative diagnosis of the human rights situation of the target population comprised of Central American migrants in transit through Mexican territory.

The work includes an analysis of the data gathered through 650 questionnaires (635 valid) and 20 in-depth interviews with in-transit migrants to the United States. The objective of the interviews was to complement the quantitative information as well as to obtain a deeper understanding of it. Interviews were also done with officials in charge of local offices of the Human Rights Commission of the state of Tamaulipas and with personnel from organizations for the protection of human rights in the region. The administration of the questionnaires and a fair portion of the interviews was done in three shelters that provide assistance to migrants in all three border sites. These shelters are frequently used by Central American transit migrants—and less frequently by Mexican migrants and migrants from other nationalities—as places of rest, shelter, and protection while they make contacts to cross the Rio Grande or simply as safe places where they can eat and continue their journey.

Mexico as a Place of Transit and a Destination of Central American Migration

Until the 1960s, as stated by Olmos (2003, 3), Central American migration was basically internal and intraregional and composed of temporary movements. The migratory flows between El Salvador and Honduras, Nicaragua, and Costa Rica, or between El Salvador and Guatemala, traditionally served to satisfy the seasonal labor needs of the agro-industrial model on which, until recently, the regional economies were based. The Soconusco in Chiapas was equally a part of this seasonal labor market, which explains the long tradition of labor migration of the population from Guatemala who worked in the coffee, sugar cane, and banana harvests in Mexico (among others, García 2006, 45; Ruiz 2003, 5).

The armed conflicts that have devastated Central America since the end of the 1960s changed the displacement patterns of the population in the region. The civil war in El Salvador, the insurgency against the Somoza dictatorship and the ultimate aggression of the Contra in

Nicaragua, and the different phases of the guerrilla war in Guatemala caused a massive wave of refugees and internally displaced people. Between 1974 and 1996, more than a million people had to abandon their places of residence and seek refuge outside of the region (García 2006, 1). Due to the connections previously cited, as well as its proximity, cultural affinity, and geographic accessibility, southern Mexico became a natural destination for refugees from Guatemala who fled the strategy of land devastation implemented by military governments in places where the guerillas had certain support from the population in the early 1980s. In the same manner, the Mexican territory turned into the place of permanent residence or a transit zone for thousands of refugees from El Salvador and Nicaragua who sought refuge in the United States or Canada (García 2006, 45).

At the end of the crisis, a great number of refugees who had integrated into the receiving societies decided not to return to their places of origin, consolidating large numbers of groups of Central Americans in the receiving countries, notably in the United States, but also in Mexico, Canada, and Belize. As stated by Castillo, these nuclei were the basis upon which the social networks, which sustain the current migration flows, were built (2003, 3).

Since the 1990s, Central American migration has economics as its principal motivation—but not exclusively, as demonstrated in the work of R. Casillas (1996). To the destruction and the economic difficulties brought about by the civil wars, a process of productive restructuring was added, which generated important labor surpluses in the region. This process, as Castillo has pointed out, has shown signs of growth in the past years, as shown in the number of Central American migrants "secured" (held for deportation) by the National Institute of Migration in Mexico (2003, 5).

The Risks of the Journey: The Extreme Vulnerability of Migrants

The journey of Central American migrants through Mexican territory on their way to the United States is a highly risky undertaking (Ruiz and Scalabrini 2001; Ruiz 2003). As Ruiz points out, there are numerous risks that migrants face derived from the characteristics of the territory they

TABLE 3.1. Central American Citizens Secured in Mexico, 2002–2006

Year	Guatemala		Honduras		El Salvador		Nicaragua		Other		Total	
	Number	Percent	Number	Percent	Number	Percent	Number	Percent	Number	Percent	Number	Percent
2002	67,336	48.8	41,801	30.3	20,800	15.1	1,609	1.2	6,343	4.6	137,889	100
2003	86,023	45.9	61,900	33.0	29,301	15.6	2,150	1.1	8,255	4.4	187,629	100
2004	94,404	43.8	72,684	33.7	34,572	16.0	2,453	1.1	11,651	5.4	215,764	100
2005	100,948	42.0	78,326	32.6	42,674	17.8	3,980	1.7	14,166	5.9	240,094	100
2006	84,523	46.3	58,001	31.7	27,287	14.9	3,590	2.0	9,319	5.1	182,720	100

Source: Compiled by researchers based on data from the National Institute of Migration.

must travel through, especially in the first phases of their trip in the areas surrounding the southern border. Additionally, they face the possibility of becoming victims of abuse from civilians as well as public officials. The recent reinforcement of border controls in the traditional transit areas of the Chiapas-Guatemala border has diverted migration flows to less frequented and more inhospitable areas (Kauffer Michel 2003), considerably increasing potential risks. The frequency with which Central American transit migrants are victims of crime or abuse by authorities is a consequence of their extreme vulnerability. The profile of the migrants places them in a position of extreme weakness, of power asymmetry, in the face of the native population and the agents of the different police forces of the territories through which they travel. The fact that they are poor, are often ethnically differentiated, and lack migratory documents places them in a position of structural and cultural vulnerability (Bustamante 2006).

According to Jorge Bustamante, the differentiation that all states make between nationals—with the recognition of full citizenship rights and access to the state's resources that this entails—and foreigners imposes on migrants an asymmetrical power relationship between them and the native population of the receiving country (2006). This structural inequity becomes an accepted value and an element that permeates the cultural baggage of both sides. As a result, the migrants end up internalizing a notion of inferiority to the native population. People who violate the migrants' human rights use this vulnerability, which Bustamante calls cultural, as the ideological justification for their actions. This rationale connects, in the case of authorities, with a rooted tradition of discrimination against poor people among Latin American police (Pinheiro 1996, 19). Both prejudice and the migrants' lack of power contribute to reducing undocumented migrants to a status of inferior human beings, susceptible to be abused with impunity.

The condition of structural vulnerability that Central American migrants in Mexico suffer is the result of the conjunction of normative, geopolitical and institutional elements.

The normative factors include the existence of specific legal rules which, in Mexico, severely penalize undocumented immigrants, forcing them to stay underground throughout their journey and to avoid any contact with the authorities. This contributes to their reluctance to report

FIGURE 3.1. A broken fence along a pathway through which migrants cross south of Bisbee, Arizona, and north of Naco, Sonora. Discarded plastic water containers, artifacts of the dehydrating journey through harsh deserts, litter the route. (Photograph by Tony Payan)

the crimes and violations of human rights they suffer. As an example, it is worth citing Article 118 of the General Population Law, which defines fines of up to five thousand and two hundred pesos to those foreigners who, having been expelled from Mexican territory, come back repeatedly without having obtained a readmission agreement and to those who enter the country illegally (Cámara de Diputados del H. Congreso de la Unión 2009). It is true that, as pointed out by the Special Rapporteur on the Human Rights of Migrants after her visit to Mexico in 2002 (CDHNU 2002), the above-mentioned articles are usually not applied to undocumented migrants, and they are usually deported without subjecting them to prosecution. However, certain authorities still use this as a threat, taking advantage of the lack of knowledge of their victims as a form of pressure for extortion and other abuses.

The fact that the majority of Central Americans who cross over Mexican territory do so illegally may also be explained by the regulations of the General Population Law in Article 161, which demands that migrants in transit have an entry visa from their country of destination to obtain a transit visa in Mexico (Cámara de Diputados del H. Congreso de la Unión 2006). It is evident that very few Central American citizens who migrate can fulfill this requirement given the restrictions that the United States—country of destination par excellence—imposes on them to enter its territory. The geopolitical factors refer to questions such as the increasing politicization of migration and its characterization as a matter of national security in the United States since the Reagan era (1981–1989), but increasingly also in Mexico. The criminalization of unauthorized persons, the increasing penalization of those who help them, the reinforcement of border controls, the implementation of special operatives, and the militarization of the U.S.–Mexico border, as well as the hardening of the penalties against repeat undocumented migrants, are some of the effects of that politicization and "securitization" of migration affairs. All of this increases the migrants' vulnerability, because they must try crossing borders underground and through more remote areas. Also a consequence of this is the increasing use of intermediaries (*polleros* or *pateros*) by inexperienced migrants, and the probable increase of the costs of these smuggling services (from *coyotes*). As Spener (2001) has demonstrated, migrants who are members of communities with fewer social networks in the place of destination frequently resort to smugglers (*polleros*) who are not trustworthy, which exposes them to crimes such as fraud, robbery, and even rape.

Finally, there are factors related to the dysfunction of Mexican institutions, such as corruption, the broken accountability systems, and the existence of authoritarian enclaves. The consolidation of democratic practices in all levels of government is still a pending task in Mexico due to the persistence of strongly established authoritarian practices in certain governmental areas, especially in the police forces. Abusive practices by the police are not directed solely at Central American migrants on their way to the northern border, but also against Mexican migrants who are on their way to the U.S. border or have been deported recently from the United States. This indicates that the condition of vulnerability is associated in general with the interactions of citizens with security forces, the lack of power, poverty, and ethnicity.

TABLE 3.2. Migrants Who Have Suffered Aggression, by Gender

| | Suffered Aggression | | | | | |
| | No | | Yes | | Total | |
	N	%	N	%	N	%
Men	280	56	217	44	497	100
Women	26	68	12	32	38	100
Total	306	57	229	43	535	100

Source: Survey conducted by the author in Nuevo Laredo, Reynosa, and Matamoros, Tamaulipas, Mexico, February–April 2007.

Violations of the Human Rights of Migrants in Transit

An analysis of the results obtained through our sample shows that, at the time of our data collection, migrants transiting through the northeastern border were primarily male—92.9 percent to 7.1 percent female—and that they were mainly young, with an average of 28 years of age. By nationality, Hondurans made up the main group—84 percent of all Central Americans surveyed—followed by Salvadorans (7.11 percent) and Guatemalans (5.85 percent), while the presence of citizens from Nicaragua was extremely small. A large percentage of migrants had been victims of some type of human rights violation by civilians as well as by some authorities. The results show that 229 (42.8 percent) of the 535 migrants acknowledged having suffered some kind of aggression or had been victims of abuse or crime in their migratory process, whereas 306 (57.2 percent) had not.

Analyzing the gender distribution (table 3.2), we observe that women showed a lower percentage of abuses and aggressions than men (32 percent to 44 percent). However, as will be demonstrated further on, women suffered more serious crimes associated with gender. It is also possible that, because of their characteristics, these types of crimes (such as sexual abuse) are not reported frequently in surveys.

By type of crime, the most frequent was robbery, which constituted 69.4 percent of the total (table 3.3). Beatings and injuries were experienced by 7.4 percent. Other more serious crimes like kidnapping and rape were reported by 4.8 percent and 1.7 percent, respectively. Aggressions

TABLE 3.3. Frequencies of Abuse by Type of Crime Suffered
by Migrants

Crime	Frequency	Percent
Robbery	159	69.4
Other	38	16.6
Beating and injuries	17	7.4
Kidnapping	11	4.8
Rape	4	1.7
Total	229	100.0

Source: Survey conducted by the author in Nuevo Laredo, Reynosa, and
Matamoros, Tamaulipas, Mexico, February–April 2007.

classified as "other," which included threats and assaults, were reported
by 16.6 percent. Another type of abuse that migrants suffered throughout their journeys was extortion.

If the types of crimes are analyzed by gender (table 3.4), it is clearly
evident that two of the most serious crimes that are committed against
migrants (rape and kidnapping) have a higher incidence in women.

Of women surveyed, three acknowledged having been raped, which
represents 25 percent of the total offenses suffered by migrant women.
It is often not possible to obtain a clear trend through the gathered data
in regard to the identity of the aggressors because "coyotes" as well as
unknown persons are reported. These events happen more frequently in
uninhabited areas. Near the Rio Grande, where female migrants await
the precise moment for their crossing, seems to be an especially dangerous place. Additionally, we ascertained from the interviews that women
must endure sexual harassment by civilians as well as by government
officials in their journey to the northeastern border. Although women
seem less exposed to offenses such as robbery, they are more susceptible
to becoming victims of more serious crimes than men, because of the
high probabilities they will suffer sexual aggression.

The Aggressors

We found that 45.4 percent of migrants assaulted or abused declared
having been victims of some police group (table 3.5), while 11.8 percent

TABLE 3.4. Frequency of Type of Crime by Gender

	Beating and injury		Robbery		Rape		Kidnapping		Other		Total
	N	%	N	%	N	%	N	%	N	%	
Men	16	7.4	153	70.5	1	0.5	10	4.6	37	17.1	217
Women	1	8.3	6	50.0	3	25.0	1	8.3	1	8.3	12

Source: Survey conducted by the author in Nuevo Laredo, Reynosa, and Matamoros, Tamaulipas, Mexico, February–April 2007.

TABLE 3.5. Distribution of Frequencies of Migrants
Assault by Type of Aggressor

	Frequency	Percentage
Police	104	45.4
Civilians	54	23.6
"Garroteros"	27	11.8
"Coyotes"	23	10.0
Immigration Agents	8	3.5
Others	6	2.6
No Answer	7	3.1
Total	229	100.0

of migrants have been victims of *garroteros*—security personnel from the railroads—and 10.0 percent by coyotes. In 23.6 percent of cases, the migrant was robbed and/or beaten and/or assaulted by civilians.[1] According to information obtained in the interviews, the majority of cases were perpetrated by groups of attackers or robbers.

Also, the interviews allowed us to know some of the most frequent abusive behaviors of the different police groups. In many of the robberies, the men in uniform do not return part of the migrants' belongings after searching them, especially their money. In other cases, police agents extort the migrants, demanding an amount for not detaining them or presenting them to the National Institute of Migration (INM). Sometimes when the migrants resist, the officer beat and threaten them. Collusion between police and groups of "coyotes" in the kidnapping of migrants has been reported in border cities.

Certain railroad security guards behave in a similar manner, demanding money from the migrants in exchange for not throwing them off the trains or reporting them to the INM. These trains are cargo and not passenger trains. In other instances, these security personnel have been pointed out as the perpetrators of assaults, beatings, and threats when the migrants refuse to accept their proposals.

The data reveal that among the people who interact with the migrants along their long voyage, in general the coyotes, do not present a high risk for them, something one might think a priori. However, a more frequent occurrence is that organized groups of criminals—false

TABLE 3.6. Distribution of Frequency of Migrant Victims of Police Abuse, by Type of Group of Force

	Frequency	Percent
Municipal	40	38.5
State	8	7.7
Federal	11	10.6
No answer	45	43.3
Total	104	100.1

coyotes—deceive, rob, or kidnap the migrants. Some testimonies describe people who "hook" migrants in bus stations or in the public square of the border cities by offering to take them to the other side of the border. Instead, though, they take them to a "security house," with the excuse that they are keeping them in a safe place until the appropriate moment comes to make the trip. In reality, the migrants will not be liberated until their families in the place of origin agree to a pay a certain amount.

According to the data about human rights violations committed by the police, the organization that commits abuses most frequently is the municipal police force, with 38.5 percent (table 3.6). The federal police and the state police follow with much lower percentages: 10.6 percent and 7.7 percent, respectively. However, these data must be taken with extreme caution because the migrants had trouble during the interviews distinguishing the different security forces with which they interacted along their journey. In fact, more than 43 percent of those interviewed could not identify the body in question. In spite of this, evidence allows us to conclude, at least in the case of the border cities, that there are police officers who on a more or less continual basis commit extortion or robbery against undocumented transit migrants—a fact confirmed by human rights officials.

The most common site in which these abuses occur is the street or other open spaces not specified, with a total of 52.0 percent of cases (table 3.7). The train is the second most frequent place abuses occur, making up 22.7 percent. The bus is the site of 3.1 percent of cases, and 7.0 percent of cases occur in "other places." The most frequent locations among the "other places" category were bus stations and open fields.

TABLE 3.7. Acts of Aggression by Place of Occurrence

	Frequency	Percentage
Street	119	52.0
Train	52	22.7
Other	16	7.0
Bus	7	3.1
No answer	35	15.3
Total	229	100.1

TABLE 3.8 Assaulted Migrants and Filing of a Complaint

	Frequency	Percent
No	219	95.6
Yes	10	4.4
Total	229	100.0

Impunity

The majority of migrants, 95.6 percent, decide not to make a formal complaint before the police, but 4.4 percent do file some type of complaint to a human rights organization (table 3.8). In the interviews, migrants were asked why they would not file a complaint regarding events in which they had been victimized. The most frequent reason was fear of being detained or deported if they went to the police, since they had entered the country illegally. The futility of the complaint to a human rights organization, wanting to avoid problems or delays in their travel, and the impossibility of filing a complaint against the police itself were also cited as reasons. Also, in the interviews with human rights organizations, an additional problem was brought up. When migrants file complaints before these organizations and an investigation is pursued, migrants are often no longer in the country and cannot be located when needed. This makes it extremely difficult to pursue an investigation. Migrants themselves are usually the principal witnesses in these cases, because the events usually happen in remote places, but when they are no longer present, the evidence against aggressors disappears. All of these factors come together so that the human rights violations of transit migrants are surrounded by almost total impunity.

Tentative Conclusions

The preliminary analysis of the data offers some interesting initial results. First, it confirms that the travel of Central American transit migrants is a high-risk enterprise; almost 5 out of 10 migrants suffer some type of aggression or abuse on their journey through Mexico. Notable are the number of abuses perpetrated by the police, which were found to be significantly higher than reported in other border studies—45.4 percent compared with 37 percent at the border with Chiapas (Ruiz and Scalabrini 2003, 13). This could indicate that comparatively in the first stages of their journey through Mexico, migrants are exposed to being victims of aggressions and theft by civilians. As migrants continue their travel and as they interact with different police groups, these become the principal risk factor to the welfare of migrants and to the continuation of their journey. Municipal police officers and railroad security guards are two of the main violators of human rights of undocumented transit migrants. The places most frequented by the migrants and the transportation methods they use are the sites where these events happen; that is, in bus stations or on cargo trains.

The majority of abuses and crimes that migrants suffer remain free from punishment. They are not formally reported to the police and therefore they will never become part of official statistics or the registries of human rights groups or commissions. Therefore, these crimes—some of which are very serious and fall within federal jurisdiction, having been committed by organized groups—will never be officially recorded. The extreme vulnerability of the migrants leads them to avoid almost any contact with authorities and to distrust practically everyone except religious personnel, who are in charge of the shelters where they find refuge, or the fellow nationals they meet on their way or who are their travel companions. In these conditions, both the groups of attackers and thieves they will have contact with during their route, as well as the corrupt elements from the security forces who abuse their situation, will have total impunity assured.

As stated above, there are normative, geopolitical, and institutional factors that explain why this situation does not change, despite having been denounced by human rights organizations and specialized agencies of the United Nations (CDHNU 2002; United Nations Committee 2006). The "securitization" and politicization of the border are a consequence of the global flow of people and of the corrupt political responses with which states confront them. These movements of people are closely related to the transnationalization of the labor flows in the United States–Mexico–Central America axis and with the consolidation of social networks that provide a self-sustaining dynamic to the current population movement. The geographic situation of Mexico turns it into a strategic point in the route for irregular flows of labor toward the labor market in the United States. This market has a structural need for this type of labor in some of its productive sectors.

Finally, there are the institutional elements mentioned above. It seems clear that the Mexican public security system is corrupt, especially those belonging to municipal governments. Together with this, we would have to cite the corruption that frequently is found in these same levels of government, and the structural problems of the Mexican political system that do not allow accountability mechanisms to work. All of these elements point to the need to evaluate the quality of the Mexican polyarchy in some important dimensions, especially regarding the effectiveness of the law in relation to those excluded, to the functioning of law and order, and to the exercise of horizontal accountability mechanisms. Without improvement in these, it is not clear that the human rights situation of Central American transit migrants through Mexican territory will improve in the short term.

Acknowledgments

The authors want to acknowledge the invaluable help of Marisol Vargas Orozco, Father Francisco Pellizzari and all the staff from the shelters Nazareth, Guadalupe, and San Juan Diego.

Notes

1. It must be pointed out that on occasions migrants are objects of several crimes at one time. For example, robbery and beatings go together frequently, as well as threats and extortion. We also detected that some migrants have suffered several episodes of robbery and extortion along their trip to the border.

4

Crime and Violence in the Arizona–Sonora Borderlands

NAFTA's UNDERGROUND ECONOMY AS A SOURCE
OF IN/SECURITY, WITH COMPARISONS TO THE EU

Julie A. Murphy Erfani

UNDERGROUND ECONOMIES AND TRANSNATIONAL criminal networks have mushroomed in North America and the European Union (EU) as the national economies of Mexico and Spain have undergone rapid internationalization since the 1980s and 1990s. Mexico's integration into North America via the North American Free Trade Agreement (NAFTA) in the 1990s and Spain's integration into the European Economic Community (EEC) and the EU since 1986 accelerated the growth of black markets in both countries (Fuentes 2005, 10). Instead of shrinking illicit commerce, the regional integration of Mexico and Spain into global markets has accelerated the rise of smuggling, trafficking, intellectual piracy, counterfeiting, money laundering, official corruption, and organized crime. Unauthorized migrant labor in North America and the EU is only one component of the booming underground economies of the two regions. To emphasize exclusively the illegality of migrant workers, as recent anti-migrant policies tend to do, is to ignore that regional economic integration has dramatically expanded illegal commerce as a multifaceted component of the economies of both regions. In fact, the integration of North America and Europe has helped spawn transnational black market networks that overwhelmingly dominate the music, movie, and software industries in Mexico and the construction, real estate development, and banking sectors of southern Spain.

As one component of North America's underground economy, Mexican migrant remittances have indeed become Mexico's second largest source of foreign exchange after oil. At the same time, Mexico has also become one of the world's largest distributors of counterfeit, pirated, and knockoff name brand goods. In Spain, migrant arrivals by boat have made Spain the EU's principal frontline state for unauthorized migration to Europe via Africa. At the same time, Spain has also become a key base for money launderers worldwide as well as home to almost five hundred different international organized crime rings (Jones 2004; Tarvainen 2006). This chapter demonstrates that (a) many types of unauthorized commerce, not just undocumented migration, are prevalent in North America and the EU; (b) black market operations within Mexico and Spain thrive off regional and global disparities in wealth; (c) organized crime engaged in black markets generates violence and human insecurity for borderland residents; and (d) policies to ameliorate the growth of black markets in North America and the EU should focus on decreasing intraregional disparities in wealth rather than on scapegoating unauthorized migrant workers as "criminals."

Pirates of North America: Snapshots of NAFTA's Underground Economy

Counterfeit Lipitor, lacking any medicinal ingredients to reduce the cholesterol of unsuspecting customers, has been sold by drugstore merchants in multiple Mexican border towns. Counterfeit pharmaceuticals cross the border into the United States with relative ease while unauthorized migrant workers are aggressively intercepted and detained as criminals. In fact, bogus pharmaceuticals, counterfeit products and knockoff name brand goods cross the U.S.–Mexico border on a daily basis, transported by U.S. visitors returning from Mexican border towns. In 2005, a U.S. visitor to Agua Prieta, Sonora, across from Douglas, Arizona, could buy counterfeit versions of Evista, a drug to fight osteoporosis—with no active medicinal ingredients—and carry the bogus prescription drugs across the border to Arizona with minimal, if any, regulatory intrusion (*FDA Consumer* 2005). Similarly, in 2006, tourists from Phoenix visiting the Sonoran beach town of Puerto Peñasco (Rocky Point) could purchase for only $50 a nearly perfect knockoff of a Louis Vuitton Papillon 26 handbag that costs $815 in shops in Scottsdale, Arizona. While truckloads full of such knockoffs are likely to be intercepted by U.S. Customs at U.S. points of entry, tourists visiting Mexican border towns can easily smuggle such counterfeits in by simply driving across the border with

FIGURE 4.1. A pharmacy and ophthalmologist's office in Tecate, Baja California, for cross-border shoppers and other customers. (Photograph by Tony Payan)

the purchases. As recently as mid-March 2007, U.S. Customs officials at the Lukeville crossing station were asking Americans returning from Puerto Peñasco if they had any drugs, firearms, or fruits and vegetables from Sonora: in other words, counterfeit goods are not part of the interrogation process.

Americans who frequent Mexican border towns, as well as nearly all U.S. citizens, are, in some respects, smugglers and pirates in North America's black market economic space: that is, we all benefit from unauthorized use of undocumented Mexican labor or from use of counterfeit goods. We eat in restaurants where undocumented workers cook and serve the food and clean the dishes; we purchase beef from Kansas where unauthorized migrants work the slaughterhouses; we live in houses built by undocumented construction workers; we eat fruits and vegetables harvested by undocumented laborers. All U.S. employers of undocumented workers are essentially engaged in piracy of unauthorized Mexican labor as well. Intentionally or not, U.S. employers and consumers almost inevitably make unauthorized use of undocumented workers' labor without public authorities' legal authorization to do so.[1] In sum, U.S. employers and consumers and Mexican workers alike are all making unauthorized use of North American labor markets. In this regard, this chapter interrogates the tendency within the United States to construct undocumented laborers as the singular agents of illegal activity.

North America's underground economy is, as suggested above, much broader than the underground economy of work performed by migrants residing within the United States without authorization. Commerce in counterfeit goods, copyright piracy, money laundering, smuggling, and trafficking are pervasive throughout North America, and Mexico is not the exclusive source of the traded contraband. In fact, the United States is the source of a variety of contraband merchandise smuggled into Mexico. Most notably, used clothing is smuggled and sold in Mexico in such large quantities that contraband clothing has effectively undermined the emergence of a high-quality garment design and manufacturing industry in Mexico (O'Day and López 2001, 235). Researchers Patrick O'Day and Angelina López estimated in 2001 that approximately 325 million contraband garments per year were being smuggled from the United States into Mexico—in other words, three garments for every man, woman, and child in Mexico per year. Other products commonly smuggled from the United States into Mexico include firearms and ammunitions, electronics, alcoholic products, frozen chicken, and satellite antenna dishes (O'Day and López 2001, 236–237).

The underground economy of North America also consists, of course, of extensive smuggling and trafficking of people and goods from Mexico into the United States. Narcotics and arms trafficking by organized crime and intellectual property rights piracy and money laundering associated with the underground economy of drugs, arms, and pirated goods in Mexico have large social and business costs on both sides of the border. For example, music piracy is so high in Mexico that local record companies in Mexico are going out of business, and, as a result, young musicians' careers are threatened or cut short (Gori 2002). In fact, more than 60 percent of all CDs sold within Mexico are pirated. What used to be the world's eighth largest market for music, including U.S. music, has been eroded by counterfeit CDs (Kelly, Smith, and Wonacott 2005). Such music piracy is fueled by the fact that many ordinary Mexicans earning a minimum wage of $5 per day can better afford a pirated CD-R for $1.35 than a legal CD costing about $12 (Kelly, Smith, and Wonacott 2005; see also Gori 2002). Ethnomusicologist Jack Bishop points out that the high numbers of CD-Rs in circulation that duplicate music stem, in large part, from the vast differential in wages between Mexico and the United States. Bishop argues further that U.S. music industry executives engage in price gauging by selling music to developing markets at the same price as in the advanced industrial world: "When you have a predatory price policy incompatible with the economic reality of a country, then you are simply paving the way for piracy" (Bishop 2004). In a broader sense, the lack of deepening integration processes that would shift investment flows from wealthy to underdeveloped areas of North America has left great wage differentials between Mexico, the United States, and Canada. As a result, North America's black market in pirated music has become a subsidy to ordinary Mexicans who would otherwise lack access to music CDs.

For ordinary Mexicans, pirated movies and other pirated copyright material serve an economic purpose similar to that of counterfeit music—namely, affordability. In Mexico, many residents would have to spend a full day's pay to see a film, so bootleg copies of movies that are affordable have dominated the video market (Bensinger 2003). Across all copyrighted products, Mexico is often designated as one of the world's top five markets for pirated copyright materials (Bensinger 2003). In fact, the head of Mexico's copyright regulatory agency, the Mexican Institute for Industrial Property (IMPI), recently remarked that, "For the amount of money it generates, piracy [in Mexico] could be considered as large a business here as the drug trade" (Bensinger 2003). Vigorous sales of black market goods derive, for instance, from the release of new movies by major U.S. studios: in fact, bootleg DVD-Rs of new movies appear for sale in Mexico City's Tepito market before the film ever reaches theatres (Bensinger 2003). According to the International Intellectual Property Alliance (IIPA), the Tepito street market is "one of the world's largest centers of pirate product and contraband sales (as well as drugs and weapons)[;] Tepito is well organized and politically protected" (IIPA 2006, 319). The Tepito street market is responsible for 65 percent of the pirated music products manufactured and sold in Mexico (IIPA 2006, 318). Pirated business software and video games undergo burning and assembly at Tepito, thus making the street market a major manufacturing and assembly hub as well as a sales and distribution center (IIPA 2006). Burning of counterfeit CDs is a major business in Mexico. In June 2004, for example, customs officials in Mexico City confiscated seventy-six hundred CD burners originating from China (IFPI 2005).

Table 4.1 presents the IIPA's estimates in U.S. dollars of the trade losses due to copyright piracy in Mexico from 2002 to 2006. The high percentages of estimated piracy of music, films, video games, and business software in 2005 are indicative of the degree to which black markets dominate key sectors of the North American economy as it operates within Mexico. These high piracy levels reflect, in part, ordinary Mexicans' inability to afford legal music CDs, movie DVDs, and optical disk products. In a North American economic space lacking deepened integration that distributes wealth to the most impoverished areas of the region, real and black market iPod prices tell the same story of price differentials characterizing the formal and underground economies of North America. A counterfeit 80GB iPod in Mexico City reportedly costs $130, whereas the legal article costs $350 (Demos 2006). The black market of counterfeiting and piracy flourishes in Mexico, in part, because of North America's maldistributed wealth that cripples Mexican consumers compared with their U.S. and Canadian counterparts.

In effect, black market commerce in Mexico subsidizes ordinary Mexicans' standard of living in a regional context in which the formal market economy fails to deliver and widely distribute sufficient wealth. North American businesses tend to impose high prices for consumer goods for Mexicans in a regional economy that thrives off low wages in Mexico. Since most Mexicans cannot afford to consume legal products, they consume cheaper bootleg products. Just as U.S. employers use undocumented Mexican labor to subsidize U.S. company profits and consumer lifestyles, ordinary Mexicans' pirate music, movies, games, and software and trade in counterfeit goods to subsidize Mexicans' consumption.

Clearly, there is high demand for people—and product—smuggling and high demand for counterfeit and pirated goods in North America. Pervasive throughout the North American economy are massive underground economic profits, black market subsidies to employers and consumers, and illicit profits and illicit wages all deriving from or related to piracy, smuggling, and money laundering. Money laundering basically

TABLE 4.1. Estimated Trade Losses due to Copyright Piracy (in Millions of U.S. dollars) and Levels of Piracy, 2002–2006

Industry	2006 Loss	2006 Level	2005 Loss	2005 Level	2004 Loss	2004 Level	2003 Loss	2003 Level	2002 Loss	2002 Level
Sound recordings and musical compositions	486.6	67%	376.5	65%	326.0	60%	360.0	61%	459.0	68%
Entertainment software	182.0	85%	137.7	75%	132.2	76%	136.9	66%	NA	NA
Business software	296.0	63%	263	65%	222.0	65%	220.0	63%	168.9	55%
Motion pictures	NA	NA	483.0	62%	140.0	70%	50.0	45%	50.0	40%
Books	41.0	NA	42.0	NA	42.0	NA	40.0	NA	40.0	NA
Total	1,005.6		1,302.2		862.2		806.9		717.9	

Source: International Intellectual Property Alliance 2006.

constitutes the financial platform that sustains black market commerce and the illicit profits derived from North America's underground economy. Counterfeiters, smugglers, traffickers, unauthorized workers, unauthorized employers, and other actors engaged in various sorts of piracy and smuggling constantly convert income from illicit commerce into legitimate assets and bank accounts. For instance, North American narcotics traffickers have laundered illicit drug money by purchasing invest-grade life insurance policies and later cashing in the policies (Lichtblau 2002). Other money laundering occurs via cross-border transport and deposits of cash in banks and cross-border wire transfers via agencies like Western Union and Moneygram (Timewell 2006). In certain respects, U.S. employers engage in money laundering of the profits they reap from the use of undocumented labor: through formal payrolls, such employers essentially engage in illegal accounting procedures that bolster their bottom line by accepting fake social security numbers from unauthorized workers.

U.S. employers' gains from the use of undocumented workers are as much a form of piracy as the sale of unauthorized CD-Rs by Mexican street vendors. In the past ten to fifteen years, definitions of money laundering in the United States have expanded beyond a focus on organized criminal money laundering to include any financial transaction generating a value or asset as the product of illegal action, including fictitious accounting and tax evasion.[2] Employer profits derived from use of undocumented labor and migrant remittances derived from unauthorized employment technically constitute financial gain from illegal action and can therefore be said to involve the laundering of illicit money. In 2007, the Arizona Legislature passed a bill that imposes sanctions—fines and licensure revocation—on employers of undocumented workers: the bill revokes the business licenses of employers who repeatedly hire undocumented workers (Small 2007). Nevertheless, such employer practices as well as migrant worker remittances have been increasing in size and financial importance in North America and worldwide during the mid-2000s such that even the world's largest commercial banks wish to expand into and profit from migrant remittance transactions (Timewell 2006). Mexico, along with India and China, was one of the top three recipient nations for remittances in 2004 (Timewell 2006). Beginning in 2006, large commercial banks, such as Bank of America, Citibank, and HSBC Bank U.S.A., have endeavored to claim market share in the remittance industry away from the informal wire agencies, such as Western Union (Timewell 2006). If, as some analysts predict, traditional banks succeed in competing with Western Union and in meeting all Financial Action Task Force (FATF) U.S. bank requirements, this then would be the ultimate money laundering operation—wherein "legitimate," U.S.-based commercial banks systematically cleanse remittance money as a transparent business function (Timewell 2006). Given that migrant remittances sent from the United States back to Mexico are often employed by Mexicans to build schools and clinics in the emptied-out, rural villages from which they emigrated, large commercial banks could conceivably one day become conduits of capital flows to rural Mexico.

In summary, North America's underground economy extends well beyond unauthorized work by Mexican migrants in the United States. Black market operations in North America essentially take off where the formal economy of NAFTA-style integration fails. To the extent that NAFTA's underground economy bolsters and subsidizes company profits, worker wages, and consumer lifestyles in the United States and Mexico, the underground economy of unauthorized labor and nonmedicinal counterfeit consumer goods constitute an informal source of economic subsidy and security to many people in the region. The next section examines the costs to human security of the underground economies of drug, people, and gun smuggling.

Whose Prosperity? What Security? Crime, Violence, and Assaults on Human Rights in the Arizona–Sonora Borderlands

Posited as a neoliberal economic agreement to promote region-wide prosperity, NAFTA had the unintended consequence of fueling massive human, drug, and gun smuggling and money laundering along the U.S.–Mexico border and across North America. NAFTA's burgeoning underground economy set the stage for a rapid escalation of organized crime and violence in the borderlands of Arizona and Sonora, the current main corridor for human and drug smuggling into the United States. Since the mid-1990s when NAFTA was first instituted, organized criminal smugglers of narcotics, people, and guns, in particular, have increasingly constructed the Arizona-Sonora borderlands as a battleground of rival criminal networks, gangs, warring drug cartels, and execution squads. The U.S. government's crackdown on the Arizona border to curb unauthorized migration has fueled rivalry between traffickers to such an extent that, as of this writing in July 2007, criminal violence in the borderlands of Sonora and Arizona has reached epidemic proportions (Rotstein 2007). Now pervasive in the state of Sonora are a host of increasingly violence-prone border criminals: (1) border bandits who rob migrants, (2) gangs of thieves known as *bajadores* who hijack other smugglers' cargos, (3) paramilitary hit squads performing execution-style murders for drug cartels, (4) border extortionists imposing fees on migrant transporters, (5) violent former cops-turned-hit men for drug gangs, (6) corrupt police and other local officials who collaborate with organized criminal smugglers, and (7) ever-more diversified criminal syndicates merging the smuggling of drugs, people, and guns (Rodríguez 2007). The roots of this organized criminal violence stem from rival smugglers' greed over the high profits from human and drug smuggling. Competition for profits is generating intense intergang warfare over control of smuggling routes and rivalry to control turf, local police, and town officials. All of this intergang competition and vying for profits, routes, and influence is fueled by the border crackdown orchestrated by the U.S. government. Increasing numbers of Border Patrol agents and National Guard soldiers at the Arizona border have made it more difficult for smugglers to get people and drugs across, thus raising smuggling risks and costs. Increased costs and risks for criminal smugglers provoke higher levels of armaments, firepower, and overall violence associated with gangs' protection of cargo, routes, and operatives (UPI 2007, April 24).

The rise of organized crime in the Arizona-Sonora borderlands has its roots in NAFTA's failures to diminish the gap in income between the United States and Canada, on one hand, and Mexico on the other. In effect, many Mexicans were excluded from increasing income and other wealth-generating benefits of NAFTA. The Council on Foreign Relations summarizes NAFTA's economic integration failures as follows:

> NAFTA has transformed Mexico, but it has also deepened . . . the divisions that exist in the country. . . . [T]he northern part of Mexico . . . has grown faster than the center and the south. . . . [Moreover,] officials hoped that Mexico would grow much faster than its more

industrialized partners and begin to narrow the income gap among the three countries. However, investment has been modest. . . . The gap in wages has led many Mexicans to travel north in search of higher incomes. (Council on Foreign Relations 2005)

In other words, the architects of NAFTA failed to design North American economic integration in such a way as to generate sufficient investment flows, wage improvements, or fairer trade provisions to protect Mexicans' basic human rights to a living wage. As many Mexicans could not earn a living wage within their own communities, they began to migrate in the mid-1990s and after in ever larger numbers to Mexico's northern border and then, without authorization, to the United States. The U.S. government's response, which was further aggravated by the attacks of September 11, 2001, has been to militarize the border rather than legalize the new workers already in high demand by U.S. employers. A failure by the formal economy to deliver more jobs and increasing wages within Mexico has driven many Mexicans into the underground economies of the region as well as across the U.S.–Mexico border. The upsurge in organized crime—previously present but lower keyed—is linked to NAFTA's failures to deliver a living wage to ordinary Mexicans. Organized crime mushroomed along the Arizona-Sonora border in the 2000s in the wake of U.S. government crackdowns that made smuggling of anything more difficult, dangerous, costly, and, consequently, more lucrative. In the end, Mexicans' lack of living wages, the waves of emigrants leaving Mexico in search of higher wages, U.S. militarization of the border, and the concomitant expansion of organized crime at the border have significantly undermined human security in the Arizona-Mexico borderlands (Murphy Erfani 2007).

Rampant organized crime along the border is essentially undermining a key rationale for regional integration itself: that is, the promise that economic integration will improve the standard of living and well-being of all residents in the region. Instead of stabilizing the border economy and society, the explosion in organized crime and violence along the Arizona-Sonora border has seriously eroded basic human rights to personal safety and security. Virtually everyone in northern Sonora is exposed to dangers associated with organized criminal violence, particularly now, in mid-2007, as the Sinaloa and Gulf drug cartels have transformed Sonora into a battleground over smuggling routes, profits, and control over local officials (Corchado 2007). This drug cartel war engulfed an entire town in mid-May 2007 when a commando-style assault force of about fifty enforcers associated with the Gulf cartel drove into the northern Sonora town of Cananea to attack the local police (Nevárez 2007). Twenty-three people were killed as a result of the revenge attack on local police (Nevárez 2007). These Gulf cartel commandos are highly trained, elite military deserters who call themselves the Zetas and act in increasingly autonomous fashion from their old cartel handlers (Corchado 2007). In the assault on the town, the Zetas were reportedly retaliating against Cananea police for breaking deals to permit Gulf cartel traffickers to operate in exchange for bribes (Corchado 2007; Iliff 2007). Fifteen police in Cananea resigned in the wake of the Zeta hit on the town (Nevárez 2007). In fact, Mexico's attorney general told Mexican legislators that the Zetas now control several regions of the country and have been taking control of police forces: "They are taking our police away" (Corchado 2007).

At the same time, the fact that the Zetas are also engaged in an inter-gang war over control of key border entry points with a rival gang called La Gente Nueva ("The New People") further threatens the personal safety of residents throughout the state of Sonora (Corchado 2007). La Gente Nueva group receives funds from the rival Sinaloa cartel and is comprised of former police officers. The group reportedly formed to counter Zeta influence and to avenge the lives of hundreds of police officers murdered by the Zetas (Corchado 2007). La Gente Nueva tactics are brutal, gruesome, and designed to terrorize Mexico's security forces: execution-style murders, decapitations, and torture of victims are common "narco-messages" designed to threaten rivals and government officials (Hanson 2007). La Gente Nueva has even displayed its acts of violence in videos and on web sites (Hanson 2007; Birns and Sánchez 2007).

Through sheer violence and the terror of "narco-messages," bribes, and infiltration, organized criminals threaten to cripple Mexican police at the border, increasingly undermining the rule of law via intimidation, brutal violence, vast financial resources, and advanced weaponry (Birns and Sánchez 2007). The February 26, 2007, murder of the police chief of Agua Prieta, Sonora, exemplifies the assault on border police forces so evident again 2½ months later in the Zeta attack on the police station and town of Cananea. In the border town of Agua Prieta, Police Chief

Ramon Tacho Verdugo was gunned down in a drive-by shooting carried out in broad daylight by hit men in two Jeep SUVs using assault rifles. The hit men targeted the chief as he walked out of the police station (APSLW 2007, Feb. 28). Like the commando raid on Cananea, investigators have linked the assault rifles employed in the Agua Prieta hit to the underground economy of illicit guns trafficked out of Arizona into Sonora (Associated Press Worldstream 2007). Mexican criminal organizations send "straw purchasers"—people with clean records—to Arizona to buy weapons from licensed gun dealers. The guns are then smuggled south across the border using the same infrastructure employed to smuggle drugs and people to the United States (Associated Press Worldstream 2007).

Assault weapons, such as AK-47s, increasingly turned up in Sonora after the U.S. Assault Weapons Ban expired in 2004 (UPI 2007, Jan. 17). When the ban expired, Arizona had no laws prohibiting the purchase of unlimited numbers of semiautomatic rifles all at once without paperwork (APSLW 2007, May 25). In addition, legitimate vendors at U.S. gun shows sell devices that effectively convert semi-automatic guns to automatic fire (UPI 2007, Jan. 17). Finally, private individuals sometimes exploit loopholes in Arizona gun laws that allow private sellers at gun shows to sell guns without doing a background check on buyers (UPI 2007, Jan. 17). In sum, the *Arizona Republic* reported in late May 2007 that "cartel operatives flood Arizona to buy semiautomatic assault rifles, grenades, plastic explosives and rocket launchers in bulk . . . " (APSLW 2007, May 25). Mirroring this flood of illicit weapons, from approximately 2004 to 2007, at least twelve police chiefs were gunned down by hit men in Mexican cities, including in the border cities of Tijuana and Nuevo Laredo (APSLW 2007, Feb. 28). Given the targeting of officials, police chief resignations at the U.S.–Mexico border have soared: the Arizona-Sonora border town of Naco, Sonora, has had twelve different police chiefs in the past three years alone (APSLW 2007, Feb. 28).

Beyond intimidating and crippling border police, drug gangs and execution squads have been attempting to silence portions of the Mexican press by targeting journalists and threatening newspaper owners in Sonora and other Mexican states. In fact, the international press group Reporters Without Borders designated Mexico as the second most dangerous place in the world for journalists to work in 2006, with Mexico following only Iraq as the country of highest risk (Reporters Without

Borders 2007). Organized criminal violence, including violence against the press, escalated along the Arizona-Sonora border in the first half of 2007 (UPI 2007, April 24; Braine 2007). For instance, in Sonora in mid-April 2007, Saul Martínez Ortega, a reporter for a small newspaper in Agua Prieta, was abducted after being forced out of his Suburban by gunman armed with assault-style weapons. Kidnapped in front of a police station, the reporter had been investigating an earlier kidnapping incident, according to his brother. The Sonoran attorney general's office suggested that the victim was involved with drug trafficking, but no clear evidence of that was apparent (APSLW 2007, April 18). Associated Press writer Ioan Grillo claims that many journalists in Mexico refrain from reporting on drug gangs altogether for fear of retaliation (Grillo 2007). That fear is not without foundation, and cartel threats extend to newspaper owners as well. The *Cambio Sonora* newspaper in Hermosillo closed in late May 2007 after assailants from a passing car threw a hand grenade at the paper's offices (UPI 2007, June 8). Overall, in 2006 alone, nine journalists were killed in Mexico, according to Reporters Without Borders.

Beyond organized criminals' intimidation of the press and the police, by far the greatest violence and human rights abuses at the Arizona-Sonora border are suffered by migrants and the ordinary people who transport migrants. As the U.S. government seals off regular smuggling routes with technology and more agents, drug gangs increasingly use migrants as human decoys to clear new smuggling routes for drug shipments. In the process, drug smugglers extract "protection" fees from migrants and obtain the added bonus of using the migrants to test the waters to see if a smuggling route is safe enough for a subsequent drug shipment (O. Rodríguez 2007). In other words, drug gangs at the Arizona-Sonora border are diversifying into criminal syndicates that combine drug and human smuggling for the dual purpose of extorting "protection money" from migrants and safeguarding drug shipments from the border patrol (O. Rodríguez 2007). This practice of extortion by drug gangs became evident in spring 2007 in and near the border town of Sasabe, Sonora, a key staging area for border crossing. Migrants and local officials in Sasabe told the Associated Press that armed extortionists were stopping vans headed north and filled with migrants at a gas station in Altar, a town ninety minutes driving from the Arizona state line and on the route to the border at Sasabe. At the gas station, the drug-trafficking operatives charged each migrant ninety dollars and dictated exactly where and when the vans could cross the border (O. Rodríguez 2007). These extortion practices also target people who transport migrants through Sonora to the border. In fact, at the end of April 2007, Mexican police found two bullet-riddled bodies of men who had been gagged and executed. One victim's wife reported that her husband had resented armed men demanding money in exchange for allowing him to drive migrants to the border (O. Rodríguez 2007). These execution-style slayings send a clear message: if migrants and their transporters do not comply by paying protection fees and following border-crossing directives, the drug traffickers will respond with deadly force.

As drug-trafficking extortionists deny Mexicans their basic constitutional rights to move freely through the Sonoran borderlands, *bajadores*, border bandits, and other organized criminals roaming northern Sonora and southern Arizona have increasingly victimized migrants and their transporters and smugglers. Respect for migrants' basic human right to life has sunk to new lows in the first half of 2007: reports of numerous shootings of migrants reflect the escalating violence and the extent to which migrants have become expendable pawns in the smuggling corridor of Arizona and Sonora. On January 27, 2007, four heavily armed assailants opened fire on a van of twelve migrants near Eloy, Arizona, killing the driver and wounding a passenger (Rotstein 2007). On February 8, 2007, a gunman forced a pickup with about twenty migrants to stop along a desolate road in Ironwood National Monument near Tucson, killing three people and wounding two others (Rotstein 2007). On March 30, 2007, two armed men from Sinaloa with high-powered weapons ambushed a pickup truck transporting twenty-three migrants near Green Valley in southern Arizona. Two migrants were killed and another wounded in what the assailants alleged was a bungled attempt to interdict drugs, not migrants (Rotstein 2007).

According to federal officials, Arizona leads all other southern border states in the United States in the number of "rip-offs" (kidnappings) of migrants held by one group of armed smugglers and stolen by another group of armed traffickers called *bajadores* (Billeaud 2007). Rip-offs tend to be lucrative for smugglers since ransoms often range from twelve hundred to twenty-five hundred dollars per migrant, and there are less overhead costs for employees and no need to recruit migrant crossers or guides ("Smuggling could be behind Arizona killings," 2007). Migrants have been "ripped off" from other *coyotes* within a few feet of the border itself. Migrants have also been kidnapped through raids by rival human traffickers who invade the drop-houses of other smugglers in the Phoenix metropolitan area ("Smuggling could be behind Arizona killings," 2007). As a result of such escalating intergang rivalry and violence, migrants often now report that they fear border criminals as much or more than U.S. border patrol agents. One migrant in Altar, Sonora, told a reporter in February 2007, "I'm a lot more afraid of the *narcos* (drug smugglers) than *la migra* (border patrol)" (Donohue 2007). Migrant fears of being killed, kidnapped, or extorted by gangs and bandits have scared many potential crossers such that they now avoid the regular staging town of Altar (Donohue 2007; O. Rodríguez 2007). Although the U.S. government claims that its thirteen thousand agents at the U.S.–Mexico border as of May 2007 are "helping deter illegal immigration" (White House 2007), one U.S. official (off the record) and Mexican officials on the ground at the Arizona-Sonora border insist that would-be migrants are being scared away from the border by organized criminals and the violence of narco-traffickers and gangs rather than deterred by the Border Patrol (Donohue 2007; O. Rodríguez 2007). A recent AP survey showed that, of migrants crossing through one of three principal Arizona corridors, the percentage relying on a smuggler to cross the border had increased steadily: 18 percent hired a smuggler in 2000, 28 percent in 2003, and 55 percent in 2005 (Spagat 2006). From these data and the analysis of escalating violence just presented, it appears that organized criminal smugglers have prospered much more from NAFTA than ordinary residents of the region. And, organized criminals and bandits and criminal violence may now be functioning as a greater deterrent to unauthorized migration in Arizona-Sonora corridors than the U.S. Border Patrol.

Black Markets in the EU–Africa Borderlands: Spain's Costa del Sol as Organized Crime's Portal to Europe

With smuggling and organized crime on the rise in parts of the U.S.–Mexico borderlands, Spain since joining the EU has also become a hub for organized crime and black market operations, and the Costa del Sol in southern Spain has become the "money laundering capital of Europe." Beginning in 2001, the year leading up to the introduction of the euro on January 1, 2002, washing dirty money in Spain through real estate transactions has converted Spain into a money-laundering magnet for organized crime (Burgen 2006). Compared with Mexico, where migrant remittances from the United States account for most informal capital flows, most black market monies flowing into Spain derive from illicit trafficking in arms, narcotics, and humans and from prostitution. After joining the European Economic Community (EEC) in 1986, the Spanish economy benefited from considerable EEC aid and investment flows from EEC member states (Arango and Martin 2003). As a result, an economic boom occurred in the second half of the 1980s and an immigration boom followed, shifting the source of immigrants into Spain away from EU-Europe to Morocco, Latin America, and the Philippines (Arango and Martin 2003, 3). By 2001, many people were rushing to get rid of European currencies that were about to become worthless, by converting such monies into durable real estate assets (Burgen 2006, 1–3). In effect, this pre-euro property construction and investment spree taught organized criminals that Spain had great potential as a site for money laundering (Burgen 2006, 2). From that point forward, Spain's construction industry attracted money launderers from around the world. Spanish real estate transaction law actually facilitates money laundering as a result of a stamp tax of about 10 percent. To avoid some of the tax, virtually every real estate transaction in the country includes some black market money whereby buyer and seller agree to set an artificially lower, taxable price for the property only to then finalize the rest of the deal in cash (Burgen 2006, 1–2).

Since 2001, Spain's lax property transaction law and practices, the introduction of the euro, and increasing corruption among public officials opened the floodgates to organized crime, a phenomenon that had been virtually absent in Spain before the mid-1990s (Burgen 2006, 1). Organized criminal syndicates are involved in laundering money earned illegally outside Spain as well as domestically within the country. For instance, Chinese criminal syndicates act throughout Spain as gangs to dominate pirate trade in music CD-Rs, movie DVD-Rs, and optical disk software (IIPA 2006). In effect, the Chinese syndicates function as gangs controlling teams of street vendors who sell pirated optical disk products; the gangs employ street vendors who are predominantly undocumented immigrants (IIPA 2006). These gangs operate burning labs and distribution centers across Spain, including in Madrid, Barcelona, Grenada, Girona, Tarragona, and Alicante (IIPA 2006, 488).

Undocumented immigrants are the predominant workers in Spain's underground economy (Fuentes 2005, 8)—a very important component of the economy in certain regions of Spain and for certain economic sectors, such as domestic service, construction, and labor-intensive agriculture (Fuentes 2005, 15–16). In fact, the Spanish government has often been very lax in sanctioning employers who hire unauthorized workers. This has been particularly true of employers operating in the southeast in Almería and Murcia, where the government has catered to farmers that hire low-paid, undocumented labor to keep labor-intensive farms competitive in European agricultural markets (Fuentes 2005, 16; Arango and Martin 2003, 1–3). Organized criminal gangs within Spain employ undocumented immigrants, particularly women from Eastern Europe and Latin America, in the prostitution industry (Burgen 2006, 4–5). Eastern European gangs composed of organized criminals from Russia, Romania, Kosovo, and the former Czech Republic, for instance, often specialize in the prostitution of women from the former Communist bloc (Jones 2004, 36). The most vulnerable women are those from East Europe who speak no Spanish and are controlled by small mafias of pimps who exploit six to seven trafficked women. The women are held as indentured servants, and sold from one pimp to another such that the debts that they owe can never be paid off. The pimps threaten such trafficked women if they attempt to leave (Burgen 2006, 5). Because Spanish law formally prohibits people from living off the gains from prostitution, which is otherwise legal, all revenues from the underground economy of prostitution must be laundered. Figure 4.2 displays two estimates of the size of Spain's underground economy from 1978, before accession to the EEC, through 1998, four years before the introduction of the euro. It is clear that, according to monetary estimates, the underground economy in Spain has generally been increasing as a proportion of the Spanish economy since 1978. This ongoing increase in black market activity was particularly evident after Spain's accession to the EEC in and after 1986.

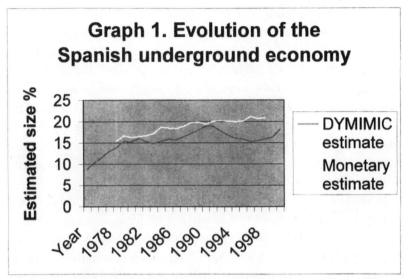

FIGURE 4.2. The evolution of the Spanish underground economy. The upper line is a monetary estimate, and the lower line is a dynamic multiple-indicators and multiple-causes (DYMIMIC) estimate. (From Alañón Pardo and Gómez Antonio 2004, cited in Fuentes 2006)

Spain's Costa del Sol, often dubbed the "Costa del Crime" by the British tabloid press, is now a favorite location for money laundering as well as organized criminal operations within the European Union. Organized crime is so pervasive on the Costa del Sol that in May 2006, four EU countries (the "E4")—Spain, the United Kingdom, France, and the Netherlands—sent a squad of officers to the Costa del Sol to set up headquarters there to fight organized crime and international narcotics trafficking (*Agence France Presse* 2006). The range of underground commerce and organized criminal activity is wide: Eastern European gangs operating on the Costa del Sol have even been reported to engage in armed robberies involving rocket-propelled grenade launchers (Jones 2004). In a sting operation in 2005, Spanish police investigating in the Málaga area found Chinese and Romanians engaged in sexual exploitation and human trafficking; French gangs involved in fraud; British criminals engaged in narcotics and vehicle trafficking and money laundering; Colombians engaged in cocaine, heroin, and arms trafficking; and Moroccan gangs trafficking in narcotics, document forging, and promotion of illegal immigration (*Agence France Presse* 2005). Much of the black market money from such crime is laundered via real estate transactions: that is, purchases of land and construction and sales of hotels, vacation apartments, second homes, department stores, and other leisure industry real estate (Tarvainen 2006). So much money laundering via real estate development has occurred in and around Málaga and Marbella that the countryside in Andalucía is quickly disappearing. On the road from Málaga to Marbella, newly built vacation communities dominate the coastline. The Costa del Sol is now, in fact, more than 50 percent built up (Burgen 2006, 3).

This continuing, runaway building boom in real estate development reflects the economic clout of nearly five hundred international organized criminal rings laundering money through real estate purchases and development (Tarvainen 2006). Spain's seemingly unstoppable construction boom also reflects massive corruption among local government officials in charge of regulating real estate development. In the high-brow coastal resort city of Marbella, for instance, two recent former mayors have been indicted for involvement in corruption networks linked to real estate development. Spanish police arrested the mayor of Marbella and several town councilors in March 2006 in a multi-billion-euro corruption scheme involving development permits and money laundering. As a result, Spanish national authorities dissolved Marbella's municipal government entirely and appointed a caretaker government from the region (Ausseill 2006). Consistent with the Marbella scandal, the most common form of official corruption involves local public officials and city councilors accepting bribes and kickbacks in exchange for issuing building permits and for changing the status of land otherwise protected against building development for environmental or other reasons. These local real estate corruption networks sometimes include banks, judges, and local police in combination with local municipal officials (Ausseill 2006). Political parties across the board are reportedly implicated in the corrupt municipal practice of selling building permits. In fact, these permit sales are rumored to be a principal way in which all Spanish political parties fund themselves (Burgen 2006, 4).

In sum, four primary facts about the EU's underground economy in Spain stand out. First, the EU-era Spanish economy depends heavily on the vitality of the construction industry. Secondly, the construction sector is fueled primarily by organized crime rings, those rings' underground commercial activities, and such criminals' need to launder massive quantities of dirty money. Third, organized criminal commerce as well as "legitimate" agricultural and other labor-intensive industries in Spain rely heavily upon the low-paid labor of undocumented immigrants. Fourth, the continued influx of increasing numbers of undocumented workers into Spain, where unemployment is the highest of any EU member country, can be explained, in part, by the exceptionally high demand for low-wage labor to bolster the competitiveness of Spanish businesses. Finally, the availability of so much low-cost immigrant labor is a product of persisting, massive income disparities and reduced job chances afflicting the world outside the advanced industrial West.

Conclusions

The underground economies of people smuggling, product counterfeiting, illicit real estate construction, money laundering, and official corruption in EU-era Spain are extensive. Black marketers often profit from the labor of unauthorized migrants and exploit the human rights of such laborers. Moreover, organized criminal syndicates dominate black market operations in Spain. However, those criminal syndicates' level of violence and threats to civil society and public security are much less than in the U.S.–Mexico borderlands of Arizona and Sonora.

NAFTA's underground economies of pirated music, movies, software, and other nonmedicinal consumer goods tend to subsidize consumption levels of Mexicans whose low wage levels would otherwise not allow them access to music, movies, and other consumer products. Underground piracy practices in Mexico improve, in some respects, ordinary Mexicans' socioeconomic security. However, NAFTA's persistent failures to increase foreign investment and deliver living wage jobs to Mexicans in Mexico has set the stage for a massive escalation in human, drug, and gun trafficking at the Arizona-Sonora border. Moreover, as U.S. government crackdowns have made smuggling risks and costs higher, organized drug gangs have taken over human smuggling and smuggling routes and are engaged in increasing intergang rivalry over high profits, turf, and influence. As a result, organized criminal violence has increased dramatically in 2007, and the personal security of migrants and many borderlands residents has been gravely compromised. Organized criminal violence at the Arizona-Mexico border is much greater than at the EU's border in southern Spain.

Notes

1. See AskOxford on the definition of "piracy": "the unauthorized use or reproduction of another's work." http://www.askoxford.com.

2. U.S. Money Control Act of 1984, Section Laundering 18 U.S.C. § 1956.

5

In the Footsteps of Spirits

MIGRANT WOMEN'S TESTIMONIOS IN A TIME OF
HEIGHTENED BORDER ENFORCEMENT

Anna Ochoa O'Leary

IT WAS EARLY SPRING when I interviewed a group of four
migrant women who found refuge at the Nogales, Sonora, migrant
shelter, Albergue San Juan Bosco. The weather outside had yet to shed
the harshness of winter but inside the shelter the women radiated warm
support for each other after their border-crossing ordeal. The objective
of my research, "Women at the Intersection: Immigration Enforcement
and Transnational Migration on the U.S.–Mexico Border," had been
inspired by my scholarly interest in death on the border, and in the spring
of 2006, I began to systematically collect the *testimonios* of repatriated
migrant women on their border-crossing experiences.[1] The interviews
with migrant women focused on their encounter with U.S. immigration enforcement agents, and these experiences were couched within
broader social and economic contexts that informed their decisions to
migrate. My conversation with four of the women on this cold March
evening began like many others. Their stories by then had become all
too familiar: descriptions of the arduous trek through an inhospitable
desert; the almost inevitable attack by border bandits ("bajadores"), who
robbed them of their meager possessions; and, ultimately, apprehension
by the U.S. Border Patrol and eventual repatriation to Mexico. This particular evening, however, the dialogue turned towards reflection on the
women's vulnerabilities and fears. They described the familiar pattern of
being led in groups across the border by their *guías* (guides), and the
practice of short rest periods after hours of fast-paced walking. One of
the women, Rosario, gave her account: "Ya después de muchas horas
corriendo, subiendo y bajando terrazería, !pura terrazería! descansamos,
pero yo no pude descanzar." (And after running for many hours, up and
down hills, almost all hills! we rested, but I could not rest.)

The other women nodded in agreement. Another of the women, Catalina, added: "Yo no se cómo, pero los hombres sí, así como iban cayendo así, ¡a dormir! ¡Hasta roncando!" (I don't know how, but the men could, just as they fell to the ground, go to sleep! Even snoring!). At this the women again nodded and laughed. Then Rosario grew intro-spective and solemn, saying:

> Yo—yo no pude descansar; ¡tenía mucho miedo, mucho miedo! Como se oían ruidos. Se oían como pasos, cómo si caminara algo sobre el suelo, y me daba miedo . . . creo que eran los pasos de los que habían ya caminado por allí, de sus almas que todavía caminaban por el desierto. [As for myself—I could not rest, I was too scared, very scared! It was like I could hear noises. I could hear like footsteps, as if something was walking over the ground, and I became fright-ened. . . . I think they were the footsteps of those who already walked through there, of their spirits that still walked the desert.]

Interviews with women at the Albergue San Juan Bosco highlight an intersection as a place where opposite processes converge, not only theoretically but in concrete terms as well. In part, being caught in the intersection can be understood by the fact that for decades, the United States' need for labor and the desire for family reunification have been his-torically central to decisions to migrate. Research on gendered migration patterns, for example, shows that the movement of unaccompanied men is generally followed by that of their wives and family members (Cerrutti and Massey 2001; Donato 1994). In the current study, almost all of the migrant women interviewed had children but considered themselves single mothers by the abandonment of their partners. Counter to this tendency towards family reunification is the hardening of border security measures that, in effect, contribute to family separation (O'Leary, forthcoming). Thus, it is not surprising that the most pressing issue that emerged from this study was that as more and more women migrate, more are likely to encounter conditions that may turn fatal. Their situations can be summa-rized as having been developed by the following patterns:

- A general increase in the time needed to cross the desert and, accordingly, an increase in the time all migrants are exposed to the elements.

- A general increase in the distance of the trek in order to stay out of reach of the Border Patrol and, concomitantly, greater physical stress of carrying water and food over greater distances is placed on all migrants.
- Encounters with unfamiliar terrain and, compared with more traversed migration routes, more treacherous topographies predispose migrants to greater risk of physical trauma, such as broken or sprained limbs.
- Because of the above, many of the women interviewed stated that they had given up in the middle of their trek through the desert.
- Due to any of the circumstances above, or combination of circumstances, many women were ultimately abandoned in the desert by their guides.

The case studies highlighted below further illustrate these troublesome patterns and indicate how women may be at higher risk than men when crossing into the United States without authorization.

Women at the Intersection of Border Security and Transnational Migration

There is little doubt that the migration of women from Latin America has been steadily increasing since the 1980s. By some estimates, female migrants represent about half of all migration from Latin America (Zlotnik 2003). In the Sonora-Arizona region, estimates range from 37.1 percent (Castro Luque, Olea Miranda, and Zepeda Bracamonte 2006) to 48 percent (Monteverde and García 2004). However, perhaps what is most important is the dramatic rise in female migration since 1994, as illustrated in table 5.1.

In spite of this dramatic rise, little is known about women's border crossing experiences. We know very little about the effects on women of intensified efforts to secure the border from unauthorized entry into the United States or about their encounters with immigration enforcement officials. Since the Southwest Border Strategy[2] and other measures to seal the border were implemented beginning in 1993, Nogales, like other Arizona-Sonora border cities, has experienced exponential growth in migration-related activities due to the "rechannelling" or "funneling"

TABLE 5.1. Migrants by Gender, Nogales, 1993–1999

	1993–94	1994–95	1996–97	1998–99
Men	92.4	95.1	84.3	62.9
Women	7.6	4.9	15.7	37.1
Total	100.0	100.0	100.0	100.0

Source: Castro Luque et al. 2006.

of migration traffic through Sonora (Cornelius 2001; Rubio-Goldsmith, et al. 2006, 7). Up until now, many undocumented migrants who were apprehended in Arizona were "voluntarily" removed[3] from the United States at the Nogales, Arizona, port of entry. According to a Department of Homeland Security web site,[4] the Tucson Border Patrol sector, which includes Nogales, led all other sectors with 439,090 apprehensions in 2005. Unfortunately, these statistics are not disaggregated by gender categories, obfuscating information that would shed light on gender and migration.

The research on the brutal murders of women in Juárez, Chihuahua, Mexico (Camacho 2004; Urquijo-Ruiz 2004) has been important for bringing to the public's attention the unprecedented level of violence against women who migrate in the post-NAFTA period (Greenlees and Saenz 1999; Hirsch 2002; Márquez and Padilla 2003). Little is known about women once they cross into the United States. We can assume that they face the same numerous risks as their male counterparts: exposure to unscrupulous human smugglers and border bandits, drowning, pedestrian and automobile accidents, and risk of injury and even death as they scale fences and hike through inhospitable desert terrain in an effort to avoid detection (Eschbach, et al. 1999). However, how risks vary by gender is still underresearched. Newspaper accounts have been instrumental in making public several cases of border patrol agents' sexual assault of migrant women (Cieslak 2000; Falcon 2001; Steller 2001; Urquijo-Ruiz 2004). Yet, these cases have only raised more questions than answers about how common these occurrences are. The five-year research on the sharp rise in migrant deaths on the U.S.–Mexico border since 1993 by Eschbach and his colleagues considered gender as one of several variables but was inconclusive in terms of a gendered distribution of migrant mortality due to intensified border enforcement (1999). In this study, women accounted for only 15 percent of approximately sixteen hundred migrant fatalities on the U.S.–Mexico border between 1993 and 1997. It was speculated that women were more likely than men to avoid the dangerous journey over rough terrain by using false documents to enter through official ports of entry and thus contributed significantly less to the total migrant mortality rate. However, more recent information strongly indicates that women may indeed shoulder a disproportionate risk of death with stepped-up efforts to secure the U.S. border with Mexico. Research on the number of bodies recovered in the U.S. Border Patrol Tucson Sector since 1991 by the Binational Migration Institute at the University of Arizona[5] confirms that deaths of presumed migrants due to exposure to the elements increased dramatically since 1994 when harsher measures to enforce the border between the United States and Mexico were implemented. In addition, of the bodies of presumed undocumented border crossers recovered in the desert from 2000 to 2007, it was found that after controlling for age (younger than 18 years of age), women were 2.70 times more likely to die of exposure than all other causes of death when compared with men (Rubio-Goldsmith, et al. 2006). Moreover, with the rising costs of migration correlated with increased border surveillance and enforcement, women may be less able to procure false documents (*papeles chuecos*) at three thousand dollars per person that would enable them to cross by car and in this way avoid the more perilous route through the desert on foot (O'Leary 2009).

After summaries of the political and historical bases for this research and the task itself, I will discuss some of the findings by way of three narratives. Through these, a prominent feature of the intersection will be fleshed out, which consists of the potential for encountering death. Both the goal of crossing into the United States undetected and the failure to do so can be seen as opposite sides of the same coin: both the result of poverty and the involuntary migration that may help relieve it. Poverty thus lies at the heart of women's encounters with the physical and psychological migration trauma that may prove fatal. Moreover, the ways in which women are subjected to harsh and punishing realities lie at the heart of border enforcement practices. At the international border, boundaries that delimit nation and nationhood reflect sociopolitical practices created by established power relations that designate who belongs and who does not. The intersection can be seen as the "space" in which the politics of "otherness" and marginalization is carried out. However, as more and more women enter and exit the intersection of oppositional forces, the outcome in terms of risk calls into question the established disciplinary mechanisms by which exclusion is enforced. The intersection thus reveals the extratextual insight necessary for assessing underlying social currents upon which immigration enforcement policies are premised and for raising concerns about the clash between economic and political realities. These testimonies also recount women's brushes with death in attempting to cross into the United States through the inhospitable Sonoran desert. Their experiences have been contextualized within broader economic and social environments in an effort to render as complete a portrait as possible of migrant women who were temporarily suspended in the "intersection" of diametrically opposed border processes: immigration enforcement and transnational movement.

Immigration Enforcement in the Age of Heightened Border (In)Security

The increased policing of the U.S.–Mexico border area began long before the terrorist attacks on the World Trade Center on September 11, 2001 (Dunn 1996). While a concern for national security justifies to a large degree military intrusion into civilian life, it also invites the escalation of the use and abuse of armed enforcement by policing authorities[6] and civilians alike,[7] leading to a less secure environment. The extent to which undocumented migrant women are made vulnerable by the increased policing along the border is still underresearched. Critics have long argued that in the interest of border security and the rapid hiring of agents, standards for screening, training, and supervising agents may have been relaxed, which led to the rash of high profile cases involving sexual misconduct by Border Patrol agents between 1993 and 2000 (Steller 2001). More recently, the intensification of anti-immigrant rhetoric during the 2006 elections has worked to aggravate a climate of fear and distrust, and greater insecurity for residents of border communities. The existing political climate is important for understanding how information about noncitizens' rights is obscured. Under U.S. law, migrants are entitled to protections regardless of their legal status (Hull 1983). Racist attitudes and hate messages, however, threaten the rights of noncitizens

(Johnson 2004) and have been known to justify, condone, and encourage the use of harsher mechanisms of control of racialized groups, including legal residents and citizens. Furthermore, the harsh treatment of racialized groups may go unreported because offenses often take place outside public purview or lie outside the legal definitions of misconduct (Milovanovic and Russell 2001). Offenses against racialized groups also may go unreported because those victimized are members of social groups already marginalized based on other social divisions, such as gender and ethnicity. In the case of undocumented migrants, violations of their rights remain undisclosed by the simple fact that victims are repatriated or deported and they have little or no opportunity or incentive to denounce their offenders.

The Research

The present research was conducted at a migrant shelter, Albergue San Juan Bosco, in Nogales, Sonora, Mexico. Nogales, Sonora, a Mexican border city fifty-five miles south of Tucson, Arizona, lies within the funnel, or channel, created by the Southwest Border Strategy. Like many other cities along the Arizona-Sonora border, Nogales is experiencing rapid growth due to the high influx of migrants, of which up to 48 percent are estimated to be women (Monteverde García 2004).[8] Many studies suggest that gendered migration patterns, those in which the movement of unaccompanied men is followed by that of wives and other family members, are undergoing change (Cerrutti and Massey 2001; Donato 1993). These studies suggest that the migration patterns of women increasingly resemble those of their unaccompanied male counterparts. For example, the growing research on domestic workers, one of the fastest growing labor sectors and one that undocumented women are most likely to engage in, shows that more Latina women are leaving their own children behind to take care of the families of others in the United States (Hondagneu-Sotelo 2002; Ibarra 2003). In addition, similar to their male counterparts, once women begin migrating, they are virtually trapped in a migrating cycle (Donato 1994). The increase in the migration of women without spouses and family and the cyclical nature of migration also raises the chance that they will experience multiple detentions and also the chances that they will become the victims of violence (Monteverde García 2004). Without systematic documentation of what occurs at the intersection of two powerful but contrary processes, border enforcement and mobility, such policies may very well be institutionalizing and normalizing death and extreme suffering.

The research began in the spring of 2006 with six weeks of piloting the logistics and the semi-structured questionnaire at the migrant shelter that was the site chosen for the study, Albergue San Juan Bosco. Like other migrant shelters that have sprouted along the U.S.–Mexico line, Albergue San Juan Bosco is dedicated to the aid of repatriated migrants who, upon their release from the custody of U.S. immigration enforcement authorities, find themselves without shelter or a support system in the area. Unlike the other two shelters in Nogales, Albergue San Juan Bosco is a nongovernmental organization and depends almost entirely on local volunteers. It accommodates both male and female migrants.[9] Guests at the shelter typically stay only one to two days at Albergue San Juan Bosco before either attempting to re-enter the United States or returning to their communities of origin. On account of this fast-paced population turnover, a Rapid Appraisal (RA) method was chosen for this research. RA emerged initially from development research (Carruthers and Chambers 1981) but it has increasingly been used in the development and assessment of public health interventions.[10] Consistent with RA methods, a topic guide was used to interview migrant women who arrived at the shelter and to get at the heart of migrant woman's experiences. The topic guide was designed to investigate, among other things, what women's experiences were while in the custody of immigration enforcement agents in Arizona and how those experiences affected their lives and their decisions to attempt to cross again or to return to their communities of origin.

In September of 2006, I began to visit the shelter every two weeks, with the goal of systematically collecting data. Each "visit" consisted of three consecutive nights from 7:00 p.m. to approximately 10:00 p.m. in which I interviewed women who had been repatriated by U.S. immigration officials. In the ten months of the study (September 2006 through June 2007), my research assistant and I interviewed one hundred women. The number of participants for each interview varied, as the number of women who showed up at the shelter each night was unpredictable. With more visits to the shelter, I fell into the shelter's rhythm, and gained rapport with the managers and volunteers. Being of Mexican heritage and a native speaker of Spanish, while not a guarantee that I would be considered a person to be trusted, was, I believe, also helpful in projecting myself as trustworthy (*de confianza*) among shelter guests. This enabled me to ask and receive their permission to record the interviews.

Although perceived policy needs were built into the research design, the research also adopted a postmodern approach through the use of women's narratives. These small narratives, or testimonies, that explain practices and local events contrast large-scale, dominant explanations of social phenomenon, or grand narratives. Postmodern scholars argue that grand narratives mask the contradictions inherent in existent social orders and view opposition as disorder, deficient or irrational (Lyotard 1984). Discovering oppositional thinking is seen as key to challenging the existing order and to destabilizing the grasp of oppressive systems. The discovery of this individualized knowledge represents an attempt to "deconstruct"—to unmask and make transparent the rationales that support authoritarian structures and systems. Through deconstruction, then, the dominant forces in articulating ideas that maintain harmful constructs may be transformed.

Conceptualizing the Field Site

For this research, I reworked a framework suggested to me by Cunningham and Heyman (2004) who argue that national borders are particularly well suited for empirically examining two salient but diametrically opposed processes: those posed by enclosure and those posed by mobility processes. The process of enclosure is better understood by the challenges that impede its implementation. Conversely, mobility is better understood in the context of the barriers that impede or restrict it. I used this framework to conceptualize a space or field site where these two processes intersect (fig. 5.1). This framework is also consistent with Hannerz's suggestion for organizing transnational research where, instead of the conventional community study of migrants at the end or beginning of their migration journey, migrants are viewed as somewhere in between two points: temporarily suspended in an interstitial space (1998). This space, the "O" in figure 5.1, is thus structured by horizontal systems that

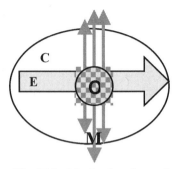

C = Context: The U.S.–Mexico border region
E = Enclosure: The immigration enforcement system
M = Mobility system(s)
O = Outcome is the intersection of competing processses

FIGURE 5.1. A conceptual framework of horizontal and vertical processes.

"enclose" (such as walls, surveillance, patrolling), and vertical mobility systems (such as migration, commerce, smuggling) that facilitate transnational flows. In keeping with the "intersection" concept, migrants at the shelter can be seen as temporarily unable to move forward in their migration journey and unable or unwilling to go back to their communities of origin. Theoretically, such spaces exist wherever oppositional forces come to be situated and compete with each other, which might be true wherever immigrants are found.

In the Footsteps of Spirits: Migrant Women's Testimonios in a Time of Heightened Border Enforcement

What follows are three cases in which migrant women described to me their experiences with being abandoned by their guides in the middle of their journeys through the desert. These three women were chosen in part because they represent different stages of the life cycle. In this way, their stories enrich our understanding of the issue of abandonment with a wider range of worldviews, predicaments, and social contexts.

Gabriela

In September of 2006, I met 24-year-old Gabriela, who had come from the state of Mexico.[11] She had traveled with a group of people on the bus. At first they were strangers, but through the course of the long bus trip to the North, they all became friends. As their friendship grew (perhaps with the tension upon their approximation to the border), Gabriela and her companions bonded. They resolved to make the crossing together and support each other no matter what. Gabriela's story about her ordeal and the migrating group members' commitment to each other is different from most stories of migrant women in that Gabriela was profoundly touched and spiritually inspired by the strength of the group's solidarity. Upon telling me her story, she grew animated and, in spite of her ordeal, seemed to radiate a renewed hope and resolve. She would attempt to cross again into the United States as soon as she could.

Gabriela explained that there were eighteen people traveling together as they commenced their walk through the desert. One group of ten walked ahead, and the rest, those she considered her friends, walked behind the lead group. She felt lucky in that they encouraged and supported each other as they grew tired. By the third day of walking, they had developed into true friends:

> Mi grupo por suerte fue muy bueno. Todos se convirtieron en muy buenos amigos. Un rato uno me iba jalando, otro me arrempujaba allá atrás . . . Éramos ocho personas, seis hombres y dos mujeres . . . El tercer día ya nos hicimos buenos amigos . . . Nos lo demostramos todos. Hicimos un pacto de que nos íbamos a apoyar y lo cumplimos. [It was fortunate that my group was very good. Everyone became fast friends. At once, one would be pulling me, then another would push me from behind . . . There were eight of us, six men and two women . . . On the third day we became friends . . . We proved it to each other. We made a pact that we would support each other and we honored it.]

Gabriela mentioned that the group was already in U.S. territory when they had to stop because the Border Patrol was performing a search, utilizing dogs. She says it was already nighttime so they stayed in that area overnight to avoid the Border Patrol. A day of travel had been "lost."

According to her, after they stopped, she and some of the other women began to feel really tired, because the "*terreno*" (terrain) was difficult to navigate. The last day was the most difficult, but it was when she came to realize she truly had friends. The other woman reassured her that they would not leave her behind.

> Llego un momento en que sí ya me sentí desesperada porque veía que el grupo se iba quedando atrás. Ya en ese momento estábamos dentro de Estados Unidos, nada más teníamos que alejarnos un poco más, para que la migra no nos echara. La migra pasaba cada cinco minutos, y pensé 'no, en realidad estoy poniendo en riesgo la vida de diez y ocho personas, y no se me hizo justo.' [There came a moment in which I felt desperation because I saw our group lag farther and farther behind. We were at that moment inside the United States, and we had but go a bit farther so that the Border Patrol would not toss us out. The Border Patrol passed by every five minutes and I thought, 'No, in reality I am putting at risk the lives of the eighteen others,' and I did not think that was right.]

So after she noticed that her group of eight was falling behind because she could not walk any faster, she decided to tell them that she could not go on, and that it was not fair that she should be holding them back. She sat down on a rock and told them, "Chicos, I cannot go on. (*Están a un paso.*) You are nearly there. Continue onward (*¡síganle!*)." She felt that they had made it this far and she would not risk the chance of the group reaching their destination because she was no longer able to continue. However, her friends chose to stay with her saying, "¡Si te quedas tú, nos quedamos todos!" (If you stay, we all stay!) She sensed a mixture of both courage and sadness: "Sentí tanto valentía como tristeza."

After they talked about it for a while, the group asked her to try again—"¡Échale ganas; ya estamos cerca!"—but she could not walk anymore. She told them she just could not do it, and she told them that she would just walk down so the migra could see her, and they would find her. Again, she expressed her mixed feelings: "Me dio más sentimiento; pero también me dio más fuerza."

She said her female friend was the youngest and the strongest of the group. "Ella estaba extremadamente fuerte, no sé de donde sacó fuerza." The young girl told all the men to go. She told them that she was more familiar with the area and with a powerful voice she told the men to go and that she would stay with her until the migra came: "Con una voz así de mujer dominante les dijo, 'váyanse, yo me bajo con ella hasta que nos encuentre la migra.'" However, no one wanted to leave. So Gabriela turned around and started to walk down the hill. They had no choice but to leave.

Gabriela explained that her young friend had told her from the beginning that she would stay with her, because she herself had experienced being left behind on her first attempt to cross. She had suffered terribly because she did not know the terrain, nor had she a friend in the group to lean on. She had been terrified. Gabriela felt that because of this experience, her friend had the courage to stay with her. She made a promise, and Gabriela became emotional upon remembering this and began to cry. Her voice broke again as she continued with her story:

Y sí, ella . . . ella fue como . . . ella fue mi . . . mi angelito. Ella me llevó del brazo y ella fue mi bastón cuando ya no podía. [And yes, she had become like . . . she became my little angel. She took me by the arm and she was my cane when I could no longer walk.]

Gabriela says that she never imagined in her life that she could ever come across people like those in her group.

Alejandra

In January of 2007, I met Alejandra, a mother of two from San Felipe de Progreso, Toluca. It was a particularly busy night at the shelter with many women arriving. Alejandra walked about stiffly, a characteristic I had begun to recognize in many migrants whose muscles were sore after days of walking in the desert. Experts explain that a buildup of lactic acid in muscle tissue occurs during strenuous exercise, commonly resulting in muscle spasms or cramps and subsequent soreness. With increased conditioning, it takes longer for lactic acid to build up in the muscle tissue. However, most migrants are unprepared for the two- to four-day vigorous walk through the desert, one that is more often than not punctuated by sprints and often up and down hills and gullies. Alejandra thus suffered on this night through the routine of tending to her two children who accompanied her, a 14-year-old girl and a 12-year-old boy. She seemed relieved to have gotten them showered and fed and could now attend to her own needs while I talked to the other women. She untangled her wet hair, attentive to the accounts of others, nodding her head on occasion to agree with common experiences.

Alejandra and her children had also faced a harrowing ordeal, which began after they had been walking through the desert for two days. They had been led by a guide and were among a larger group of about twenty migrants. After two days of walking, Alejandra began to fear that she and her children could not continue. The weather was cold and rainy when she decided she could not go on. Adding to the physical stress was her concern over the safety of her daughter. She suspected that the *pollero* had developed a sexual interest in her daughter, so she was working extra hard to keep a watchful eye on him. The guide would pull her daughter by the arm so that she would walk in front of the others next to him. He scoffed when Alejandra protested, saying that he was only doing it to keep the young girl from getting left behind. Alejandra, who measured around 5'2" and weighed about 160 pounds, was having considerable difficulty in keeping up with them. She finally decided that she had had enough and would return to Mexico. The guide retorted that she and her children were only keeping the group from advancing and left them. Alejandra then made an attempt to retrace her steps but soon the three became disoriented. They wandered for two additional days in the desert trying to find their way back. In that time, it rained and the temperature dipped to near freezing. The small supply of food that they carried was soon gone, and they huddled together at night, covering themselves with the plastic trashcan liners they had taken to protect themselves from the rain. At one point they lit a fire to keep warm and to attract the attention of the Border Patrol, so they could be picked up. At another point, they met with a Border Patrol agent on an all-terrain vehicle, but he did not stop. He simply waved at them as he passed them by. They continued walking until they met with another agent, who did pick them up and took them to the processing center. They were then repatriated. Both children were very polite and attentive to my inquiries. The daughter was slight and timid, but Eric, the son, was engaging. Eric was eager to join in the conversation to explain how they used black plastic garbage bags to cover themselves from the rain and the wind and how they rested under whatever bush they could to protect themselves from the elements.

Marcela

Marcela was one of the oldest women I interviewed. She was a patient and sympathetic listener as some of the other women told their stories on the evening of Thursday, March 22, 2007. She entered the United States on foot through the desert somewhere near Sasabe, Arizona. She was traveling with a group led by a guide. Two of the others were individuals she knew from her home state of Hidalgo. She did not know the guide. In Hidalgo, she had contacted a guide through a *coyote* she did not know personally and who told her to go to Altar. She left Hidalgo in the hopes of finding her nieces in Houston, Texas. She had only three boys, and her nieces regarded her as their mother, calling her "*mámi*," and insisted that she go visit them. However, there was more to this story. Her situation at home was perhaps the most important reason why she journeyed into the unknown. By her description of her husband's behavior, it appeared that her husband was suffering from paranoia. Earlier that evening, we had listened to Guadalupe and her account of domestic abuse by her husband. Marcela added that physical abuse was just one kind of abuse. The other, which she thought might be worse, was psychological abuse, such as she endured. For years, her husband had been accusing her of trying to kill him. He made her taste all of his food before he ate and insisted that she was trying to kill him to keep all of their possessions. "*¿Cuáles?*" she said, since they had nothing. The psychological drain on her was so extreme that at times she felt that she, too, was going insane. She left him for a while, only to find another woman living with him upon her return. Without a place to call home, she decided to take up her nieces' invitation to go to Houston. She was worried about getting a job because of her age. She was afraid to work in a maquiladora after hearing of the deaths of migrant women in Juárez. However, to have remained in Hidalgo with her husband, she said (*"fuera peor"*), would have been a worse fate. There was no one there now to support her. She said that she had read about the risks involved in crossing the desert. As she weighed those risks, she felt that staying on in Hidalgo and being subjected to the type of abuse she had experienced offered equally deadly risks.

Marcela said that her experience crossing the desert paled compared with accounts she had heard. Her journey with a group of migrants began in the late afternoon. She estimated that they had walked for about eight hours and into the night when the accident occurred. Because it was dark and she could not see, she fell several feet off a cliff (*un barranco*). She remembered rolling several feet before she caught hold of a grassy type of plant with her hand, and this saved her from further injury. Her leg was hurt, but not broken. However, she was unable to get up and this clearly posed a serious problem for everyone. What devastated her more, however, was the group's decision to leave her behind. With this decision, her faith in humanity was destroyed. Two members of the group were from Hidalgo, *compatriotas*, no less. On hindsight, she realized that she could not hold them back in their quest for "el famoso sueño" ("the famous dream.") She was even more disillusioned that no one, not even her so-called friends, offered to stay with her. She wondered if she suffered this fate because of her age. Although she was 56, she appeared to be in good health. But the group left her. They set a gallon of water beside her, a pint of "suero" (the electrolyte drink), and some crackers. In severe pain, she drifted in and out of sleep for several hours.

At some point, she woke and evaluated her situation. She drank the water and the suero. She said that she had an awakening and said to herself that this was not the way that she wanted to die: alone with her face in the dirt. No, she said, she would not die here, not like this.

So she pulled herself up and found that she could manage to walk. For three days she walked in the desert trying to find a road so that the migra could pick her up. At night, she was guided by lights that she said she saw in the distance. She made a fire to keep warm and hopefully to attract the migra. She saw the helicopters overhead, but no one came. Towards the end of the third day, she came to a water tank. Cows gathered around the tank, and she became again afraid when she saw some of the steers paw the ground, thinking that they were warning her to keep away. She sat in the shade until finally the cows began to lie down. She then proceeded to walk quietly around the herd so as not to upset them. She decided to follow the trail of cow dung which lead her to a path that she hoped would lead her to somewhere or someone. Indeed, she soon came to a road and followed it to a ranch, "Las Margaritas," with a flag bearing a skull and crossbones. She remembered thinking that perhaps the flag was meant to discourage intruders. Not dissuaded, however, she approached and saw a man, an Anglo rancher. She drew nearer and communicated "migra" to him. He did not seem to know Spanish but appeared to understand because shortly thereafter, a Border Patrol truck came and picked her up. She was taken to the detention center and processed, then returned to Mexico.

Conclusion

With my focus on the notion of "intersection" and on the migrant women who temporarily inhabit it, their near encounters with death illustrate the cost of immigration enforcement measures in terms of their toll on the human condition. For migrant women, the need to negotiate the U.S. system of enclosure reflects the contradiction between U.S. immigration laws, its concurrent need for labor, and the devastation of the Mexican rural economy. Interviews with women at the migrant shelter reflect where they have been and what their next step may be in fleshing out the intersection and allow us to formulate a more humanistic understanding of the border-crossing phenomenon. Migrant women's testimonies in this way not only shed light on physical realities grounded in extreme poverty, but also illustrate how the intersection of conflicting processes contribute to a humanitarian crises in which the likelihood of death is increasingly present.

A common theme that emerged from the interviews with women was their lack of preparation for the increased time that was needed, with the increased surveillance and patrolling, to cross the border. Women complained that instead of the expected two-day walk through the desert, they were being asked to walk for longer periods of time before arriving at their pickup point. Many said they had been assured of only a two-day walk and felt that they had been deceived by those helping them make the journey. The confusion in terms of the time needed to reach their destinations may be related to changes in enforcement policies that began in June 2006. At that time, a border enforcement measure entitled "Operation Jumpstart," designed to support U.S. Customs and Border Protection, was implemented. It consisted of deploying six thousand National Guard members to border states to assist with "executing logistical and administrative support, operating detection systems, providing mobile communications, augmenting border-related intelligence analysis efforts, building and installing border security infrastructure, providing transportation and conducting training." After receiving assistance with these tasks, agents who were currently performing them would be free to resume enforcement and patrolling duties, "arresting aliens illegally entering the country" (U.S. Customs and Border Protection 2007). In part, this may have accounted for the increase in time migrants needed to arrive at their destinations. For example, Gabriela complained that because of increased surveillance, their group spent an extra night hiding to avoid detection and in this way, a day of travel had been "lost."

One implication of this measure is increased exposure to the elements, such as extreme cold or heat. Alejandra and her children were forced to shield themselves from freezing cold and rain after she decided she could not go on. Another implication is the need to plan for additional water and food. And unplanned events, such as Alejandra's concern for her daughter, may lead to additional days in the desert, which could deplete an already small supply of food. Based on the number of complaints, such as having been deceived by their guides, it is very probable that migrants may be experiencing longer periods in which they are deprived of food and water, further increasing their susceptibility to becoming weak and dehydrated, which would lessen their survival rate if they are abandoned.

Guides also appear to be moving farther from the areas that are intensely patrolled, and they may be leading migrants into less-familiar environments. This would expose them to a greater probability of getting lost and the increased risk of physical trauma. Women seem to be particularly vulnerable in this regard and are more likely to give up, and many are ultimately abandoned in the desert. Gabriela complained that she began to feel really tired, as did some of the other women, because the terrain was difficult to navigate, and she decided she could not go on. In a similar way, Alejandra experienced considerable difficulty in keeping up with the guide until she finally decided that she had had enough and would return to Mexico. However, prior information of the trials that are in store is also no guarantee that migrants will be prepared for the arduous journey. For example, Marcela had heard about how difficult it would be, but this did not prepare her for the experience. Perhaps her fatigue, combined with low visibility, had caused her to fall, which predisposed her to possible death if not for her resolve.

The fact that these women survived their ordeals does not diminish the role that the potential of death plays in mediating the process of rejection and expulsion in the context of immigration enforcement policy. As Inda argues, death does not have to be direct but can be indirect in that the risk of death is multiplied and distributed among those who are perceived as less worthy of living (Inda 2007, 138). In providing narratives of women who experience these situations, I hope to provide a counterbalance to the political rhetoric largely based on a "rational" appraisal of what increased border security measures hope to accomplish. If direct death is not a goal, then the multiplication of the risk of death (indirect death) appears to be. In this regard, women's narratives about their near encounters with death may, in a postmodern sense, have the power to influence others to take action and encourage a more productive dialogue about the assumptions upon which current immigration enforcement policies depend.

Notes

1. Support for the initial pilot study for this research was provided by a Social and Behavioral Science Research Institute (SBSRI) Small Grant at the University of Arizona. The research subsequently was made possible by a Fulbright grant awarded for 2006–2007.

2. This strategy involved the intensification of border closures known as Operation Hold the Line (1993), Operation Gatekeeper (1994), and Operation Safeguard (1995).

3. Not all migrants that are apprehended are charged with a crime, but are simply "removed" from the United States. In this way, "removal" is differentiated from "deportation." Many migrants may be apprehended and released several times before being charged with "illegal re-entry after removal." When found guilty of this charge, migrants serve sentences, after which they are deported. The vast majority of the detainees in Arizona, roughly between 75–90 percent, are serving sentences for illegal re-entry after removal.

4. Yearbook of Immigration Statistics. 2005. Data on Enforcement Actions Table 36. http://www.dhs.gov/ximgtn/statistics/ (accessed March 11, 2007).

5. The Binational Migration Institute at the Mexican American Studies and Research Center (MASRC) at the University of Arizona seeks to comprehensively document and analyze the interaction between migrants and immigration enforcement authorities.

6. In 2004 alone there were four incidents of shootings of suspected migrants by Tucson Sector Border Patrol agents.

7. There has also been an increase in civilians assuming policing (vigilante) roles along the border in 2005.

8. This figure is consistent with the percent of female migrants in Latin America and North America (Zlotnik 2003).

9. Albergue Plan Retorno, which was closed in early 2007, sheltered only men, and Albergue Menores Repatriados typically only shelters unaccompanied minors under the age of eighteen, although on occasion, women may also be sheltered there.

10. Robert Chambers may be the scholar most commonly associated with pioneering "rapid rural appraisal" techniques. Beebe (2001) provides a comprehensive history of the adoption of the method in a wide range of disciplines. Often known by different names, RA remains consistent with the early procedures advanced by Chambers and others.

11. The names used for all the migrant women interviewed are pseudonyms.

Toward Action in Civil Society, Policy, and Transnational Policies

Introduction to Part II

The four chapters in Part II continue, in part, to analyze gender-based perspectives on violence, security, and immigration, but they also point toward action and solutions. Action can occur in civil society, through nongovernmental organizations (NGOs), policy change, and transnational NGO and international norm diffusion. Action can occur (or be resisted) from the global to local levels.

Kathleen Staudt unpacks institutions, both nongovernmental and governmental, in her chapter on "Violence against Women at the Border." She begins by addressing femicide in Ciudad Juárez, but moves on to the broader, routine problems of violence against women. NGOs organized dramatically over femicide, but less around domestic violence and the deep intransigence of local and state law enforcement authorities. In "Femicide on the Border and New Forms of Protest," Carol Mueller, Michelle Hansen, and Karen Qualtire also look at femicide, but from the perspective of new social movement activism which uses transnational, traveling caravans for justice. Although gender-based violence provokes the journeys, the critique of global neoliberalism deepens the conceptualization of solutions. Olga Aiken Araluce examines femicide from national and transnational vantage points. In "Transnational Advocacy Networks, International Norms, and Political Change in Mexico," she shows how the international spread of norms about violence against women have impacted the discourse of the federal attorney general's office, and, hopefully, its future behavior in establishing the sort of the "rule of law" that addresses gender-based violence. Finally, David Shirk and Alexandra Webber look at multiple borders through which most women are trafficked for sex work in "Human Trafficking and Protections for Undocumented Victims in the United States." Although national and transnational policies are in place to address human trafficking, solutions aim more toward criminalizing traffickers than protecting victim-survivors or reducing the poverty and violence in home countries that generate profiteers who turn human beings into commodities for sale and resale.

6

Violence against Women at the Border

UNPACKING INSTITUTIONS

Kathleen Staudt

VIOLENCE AT THE BORDER has been conceptualized in militarized terms, from low-intensity conflict (Dunn 1996) to three "border wars" (Payan 2006). Large, complex bureaucratic institutions are dedicated to the control of immigration, drugs, and organized crime, with staff and budgetary attention mainstreamed in government and media reports. In this chapter, I focus on another border conflict, one that involves low-profile gender war between men and women, mostly male-to-female interpersonal violence and murder. That conflict is so common, ordinary, and everyday that it rarely and only recently surfaces in mainstream government and media reports. However, femicide in Ciudad Juárez put violence against women—both victims and survivors—and government institutional impunity on the agenda.

Since 1993, Juárez has acquired fame from the horrors of sexualized killings, mainstreamed in media and popular culture. Young women, raped and mutilated before death, were dumped in the desert periphery of Mexico's fifth largest city or, on occasion, in city streets. In 2001, killers disposed of eight bodies in a cotton field near the Asociación de Maquiladoras, AC, a membership organization for the hundreds of foreign-owned export-processing factories established since the 1960s through Mexico's Border Industrialization Program. Municipal and state police demonstrated little interest in finding the killers, solving the crimes, or preventing future violence. Over a decade, Amnesty International, activists, and other official sources counted 370 murdered women, a third of them fitting what became the femicide formatted profile: in their teens, poor, thin with long hair, and exhibiting grotesque signs of torture before death (Amnesty International 2003; Morfín 2004; Washington Valdez 2005, 2006; Monárrez Fragoso 2002; García 2005).

Mothers of the victims organized to seek justice, followed by human rights and feminist activists from Mexico, the United States, and transnational NGOs like Women in Black and Amnesty International. Documentary films, mostly notably Lourdes Portillo's *Señorita Extraviada*, dramatic performances such as Eve Ensler's *Vagina Monologues*, and musical groups like Los Tigres del Norte mainstreamed femicide as an everyday word in Mexico, the United States, and the world. Slow to respond, government institutional decision makers appointed women as seemingly bureaucratic decorations to lead investigations and research.

Journalists and theorists spun multiple theories about women-killing, many of them linked to the peculiarities of Ciudad Juárez and the border as a pathological place of rapid global industrial production. Theorizing pointed to drug cartels, the sons of rich families, organ harvesters, corrupt police, snuff filmmakers, and foreigners, especially sex offenders (or all of the above). And many Americans have been willing to believe the worst about Mexico and its infamous, demonized city that is ironically named after one of Mexico's most beloved presidents: Benito Juárez.

If one-third of the murdered women fit the femicide profile, what about the other two-thirds? In this article, I focus on general border women-killing, including nonspectacular domestic violence fatalities and the everyday conditions that can lead to murder, including interpersonal and domestic violence. My framework focuses on institutions as they intersect with everyday life. By institutions, I mean organized collective action (or inaction), both in government agencies and NGOs, including social movement groups. I argue that both governmental and nongovernmental institutions belatedly framed general violence against women as a legitimate criminal and human rights offense worthy of organized attention in the region.

To unpack institutions is to dissect, differentiate, and diagnose organizational practices. I focus on governmental institutional resistance, not surprisingly, but a resistance that is not intractable as shown in my chapter's mirror-like comparisons of institutional police practices and their flaws in addressing domestic violence on both sides of the border. Another critique involves the tension among civil society activists over issue framing, connections with government, and fundraising primarily to pay staff salaries.

This chapter is organized into four sections, building on my introduction that has established the clear gruesome femicide at the border. First I conceptualize institutions, both governmental and nongovernmental organizations. Then I contextualize gender power relations at the border, followed by an analysis of women's experiences with and strategies to counter domestic violence. Finally, I compare governmental and nongovernmental institutions, focusing on Mexico's northern border and comparing it with the thirty-year ordeal of slowly changing, but heavily bureaucratized, law enforcement around domestic violence in the United States.

My research strategies and sources for this chapter are multiple. First, I have been an active participant observer in the binational Coalition Against Violence toward Women and Families at the U.S.–Mexico border since its inception in 2001. Second, from 2004 to 2005, with support from the Center for Border Health Research, I collaborated with a large health NGO in Ciudad Juárez to conduct workshops and to generate data from a sample of 615 women, aged 15–39, on the incidence of domestic violence and women's strategies to deal with that violence. (For a full analysis of the research findings, see Staudt 2008b, chap. 3). According to international health organizations, and national academic and official definitions, domestic violence involves harm among household participants that can be physical, sexual, psychological, or verbal. In this study, I focus primarily on physical and sexual violence.

Institutions: Government and NGOs

Social scientists have long focused on institutions and social movements that embody leaders, strategic actions, policies, and follow-up implementation procedures (or lack thereof), all of which are amenable to comparison and evaluation. Feminists add insight to such focus with attention to "masculinist" institutions (Lovenduski 1998) that embed socially constructed privilege from organizational birth thereon.

Analysts have also conceptualized social movement "framing" strategies (McAdam, McCarthy and Zald 1996), political opportunity structures (Tarrow 1998), and "missed opportunities" (Meyer, Whittier, and Robnett 2002, 17). Feminist scholar Sonia Alvarez has warned about the "NGOization" of women's organizations in Latin America (1998).

Many NGOs are increasingly dependent on funding, which reduces their autonomy and independence and thus, potentially, the way they frame their work and pursue their strategies.

Law enforcement agencies, such as the police, are among the most masculinist and militarized of official "domestic" agencies. And nations that call themselves democracies have hardly responded to women's interests and voices or facilitated their entry into formal, representative offices until recently. In Mexico, women only gained the voting franchise nationwide in 1953 (and in the United States in 1920). The percentage of women in elected national legislative branch positions in Mexico is impressive (23 percent) compared with levels in the United States (16 percent) (Intergovernmental Parliamentary Union 2007), but at state and local levels, few women are elected to office in Mexico.

The second wave of the women's movement in the United States, beginning in the late 1960s, resulted in a strong broad-based feminist agenda (Evans 2003). Initially, many leaders from the feminist movement conceptualized government at local, state, and national levels, in this federal system, as part of the problem rather than the solution, especially with regard to response to violence against women: rape, domestic violence, and treatment by the police and courts (Kravetz 2004). After establishing autonomous counseling and crisis centers in the 1970s staffed with volunteers, feminists and other professionals sought to engage with representatives, change laws, and acquire diverse funding, including revenue from the state, to establish NGOs. They set up nonprofit organizations—such as battered women's shelters, rape crisis centers, and entrée—to provide counseling and to change practices among those whom Lipsky (1980) calls "street-level bureaucrats": local police and sheriff officers, judges, and prosecuting attorneys, who operate with considerable discretion on the frontlines of interaction with the public. Activists and professionals made headway, but the struggle continues in a heavily bureaucratized law enforcement system that needs constant civil society oversight (Staudt 2008b, chap. 5).

Many feminist, human rights, and pro-democracy NGOs in Mexico, learning from experience, are wary of and cynical about government rhetoric and co-optation. While federal in form, Mexico's government is quite centralized, a relic of colonialism. In her path-breaking book about gradual decentralization, Victoria Rodríguez warns that state governors

FIGURE 6.1. Antiviolence marchers at a solidarity march across the border at El Paso on December 4, 2005. Some of the mothers of murder victims are holding a sign calling for "Justice for our daughters." (Photograph by Kathleen Staudt)

are the "modern viceroys" of Mexico (1997). While municipal police handle minor crimes, serious crimes (like femicide) are addressed at the state level, with responsibility lodged in the State Judicial Police and public prosecutorial office (Ministerio Público). Legislators in the state of Chihuahua (only 10 percent of whom are women) belatedly passed laws against domestic violence and sought, unsuccessfully, to reduce penalties for rape.

Nongovernmental organizations operate in the partial democracies of the U.S.–Mexico border region (Staudt and Coronado 2002 on weak civic capacity)—conceptualized as "partial" due to the historically muted voices of women and of marginal economic classes who together comprise more than half the population of both sides of the border region. Old and new NGOs focus on violence against women, particularly after the rise in women-killing, ranging from newer informal mothers' groups and antiviolence coalitions to older registered nonprofit organizations, such as the El Paso Center Against Family Violence (CAFV), and *asocia-ciones civiles*, such as the Casa Amiga counseling center NGO in Juárez.

The signature comparative book of public policies and practices to reduce violence against women is Weldon's thirty-six–country study (2002). In careful analysis, she explores explanations for progressive policy practices that include legal reform, funded counseling centers and shelters, training for law enforcement personnel, and preventive public education. Weldon finds that social movement activism explains policy adoption more than ideology, religion, female political representatives, women's bureaucratic machinery in government, or national income. Border analysis shows the need to unpack social movement activism and law enforcement institutions.

At the U.S.–Mexico border, dramatic, sustained social movement activism brought local, regional, national, and international attention to femicide and ultimately and belatedly to the broader issue of violence against women, but activism was not conflict-free. Conflicts emerged over the use of funds raised between women of different economic classes (Gaspar de Alba 2003; Wright 2006; Rojas Blanco 2005) and of different regions with different priorities around femicide versus violence against women (Staudt 2008b, chap. 4) or what Benford calls "framing disputes" (1997, 415). Moreover, differences emerged among NGOs and activists in terms of sustained commitment to the mundane follow-up to dramatic performance activism, both of which are essential to civil society pressure, oversight, and the reform of public practices to address the grim, everydayness of domestic violence. In the body of this chapter, I unpack and analyze these institutional issues with respect to antifemicide activities that gradually broadened to address domestic violence and public insecurity.

Bordering the Context: Gender Power Relations

For much of human history, violence against women has been normalized in many societies and cultures. Only in recent decades have women's movements, globally to locally, put pressure on governments to make laws, or to strengthen law enforcement that would treat physical and sexual assaults in the home comparably to such assaults on the street. Even with comparable treatment, women's testimony has often been treated as suspect, especially in cases of sexual assaults.

Anthropologists and critical religious studies have called attention to "myths of origin" and their legitimization of male domination and privilege. Such myths represent a cultural hegemony connected with gender power relations, constantly contested and constantly changing. Mexico's myths of origin are particularly vivid and widespread, thanks to the prolific writing of the late Octavio Paz. In *Labyrinths of Solitude*, he takes a whole, lengthy chapter to analyze La Malinche, *la chingada o la traidora*—the violated traitor who slept with the conqueror. "The *chingón* is the *macho*, the male; he rips open the *chingada*, the female, who is pure passivity, defenseless against the exterior world" (Paz 1961, 77). Roger Bartra calls Paz's theorizing hegemonic, but also gives extensive space and attention to the constructed feminine, a combination of the Virgin of Guadalupe and La Chingada (1992). A close reading of their interpretations reveals a Freudian-like analysis of gender relations (Staudt 2008b, chap. 2).

Besides myths and hegemonies, an analysis of concrete realities is in order. In the United States, for example, the widespread availability of guns puts intimate partners at risk. Gendered income opportunities or inequalities, both in the United States and Mexico, can enable or cripple violence survivors' ability to exit dangerous relationships. With grim constancy and uniformity, women earn less than men and continue to have access to a narrower set of job opportunities than men. In El Paso, for example, Hispanic (Mexican American) female workers earn 37 percent of what Anglo (White) male workers do (Romero and Yellen 2004, from census data).

With Mexico's Border Industrialization Program of the 1960s, female workers entered industrial production in large numbers, initially comprising 80 percent of the workforce in Juárez. Although *operadoras* in assembly-line production earn meager wages, earned income puts resources and potentially some power into women's hands. Elsewhere, in a Mexico City study of home-based workers, such resources provided women with leverage in negotiating household relations or exiting from them (Bený ería and Roldán 1986).

In Juárez, industrial production grew to enormous levels, employing a female majority but increasingly a more gender-balanced workforce by the 1990s, when it reached a high point of a quarter million workers in

2000. However, Mexico's official minimum wages of US$4–5 daily did not keep pace with the cost of living and inflation, including the higher wage zone at the border that amounts to just a few cents more per day (Staudt and Vera 2006; see also Kopinak 2004). Despite the depressed wages, the size and scope of the female workforce is enormous, giving rise to male backlash.

In her book on the United States, Susan Faludi (1991) used the word "backlash" to mean men's resentment at women's gains in opportunities and earnings. Faludi cites increased rates of rape and domestic violence, although it is impossible to determine whether the incidence of rape and domestic violence actually increased or whether the increased rate was due to more women reporting it, given the de-legitimization of "normalized" violence against women. After pressure from the women's movement, counseling and rape crisis centers opened, first on a voluntary basis and subsequently as nonprofit organizations offering shelters, batterer intervention programs, and public education. State laws and law enforcement changed, and with financial incentives from the federal government, police officers became better trained to attend to victims (perhaps better called survivors) and to collaborate with the nonprofit community. Still, one in four women reports the experience of physically harmful domestic violence (USDOJ 2001).

The backlash argument is applicable to Juárez (developed fully in Staudt 2008b, chap. 2). In her insightful comparisons of gender construction at maquiladoras, Leslie Salzinger analyzes the early 1990s media portrayals of women workers—portrayals that almost invited resentment against women (2003; see also Rojas Blanco 2005).

Not coincidentally, the Juárez–El Paso border in the early 1990s became a major drug gateway, as traffickers sought land routes after the U.S. War on Drugs reduced Colombia–Florida routes. From 1992 onward, sharp increases in murder rates occurred for both men and women in Juárez, though not in El Paso, which is the second or third safest big city in the United States, based on felony crime indicators. Although the absolute number of male homicides surpasses that of females in Juárez, the rate of increase in women-killing was higher than for men (Staudt 2008b, chap. 2). Moreover, sexualized murders, involving rape and torture, became the signature markings for women-killing, what activists increasingly labeled femicide. The term "femicide" demasculinized the

FIGURE 6.2. A reminder of crime and violence in the borderlands: a reward of US $5 million offered for an infamous alleged drug dealer known as "Blue." Such billboards also publicize the human trafficking problem. (Photograph by Tony Payan)

crime category, treating it instead as a hate or misogynistic crime and dramatizing the language.

Mothers of the victims faced neglect, incompetence, and even threats from the municipal and state judicial police, the latter of whom are responsible for investigating serious crimes in Mexico's legal system. Police treated the disappearance of daughters very casually, losing reports or completing them without detail, and once some of the cadavers were discovered, police even misplaced bones. Mothers organized groups, gave public testimony, and became immortalized in Lourdes Portillo's documentary, *Señorita Extraviada*, shown widely in Mexico and the United States in Spanish and in English. Mothers invented public icons and symbols seen everywhere in Juárez: pink and black crosses, painted on telephone poles and walls, especially visible on the main thoroughfares of Juárez.

By the late 1990s, media on both sides of the border treated the murders with more gravity and seriousness. Media view their audiences as hungry for crime stories, which are perhaps even titillating to some viewers and readers. Cross-border, transnational movements and coalitions formed, ultimately bringing widespread visibility to femicide. Coverage of Juárez, Mexico's complex city of 1.5 million people, involved one of two stories: drugs or femicide.

Numeric metaphors are a powerful force for political pressure, according to Deborah Stone (1997). Numbers are also used in resistance strategies. For almost a decade, from 1993 onward, the authorities in Mexico disputed the amount of femicide in Juárez, minimizing the problem and criticizing activists for exaggeration. Depending on which political party was in power, the PRI or the PAN, the number of sexualized murders varied. And one governor dismissed the notion of serial women killers, calling the murders "mere lovers' quarrels" and highlighting high murder rates in U.S. cities (Corchado 2004).

Meanwhile, domestic violence was and is an omnipresent part of everyday life, uncounted and unreported. Until 2003, antiviolence activists focused primarily on the murders, and the authorities continued their ineffective, perhaps complicit routines without accountability to the public, particularly that half of the population in Juárez living below Mexico's poverty line.

Domestic Violence: Muted, but Ever-Present in Daily Life

All the emphasis on femicide muted public attention to "ordinary" domestic violence. In fact, antifemicide activists hardly acknowledged that domestic violence murders also formed part of the total, except for serious and justified critiques of a federal female appointee report that seemed to minimize the serial killings (López-Urbina 2004; analyzed in Staudt 2008b, chap. 5). Dramatic organizing, from informal mothers' groups to NGOs on both sides of the border and transnational NGOs, framed their movements on the sexualized-torture murders, rather than the more "routine" domestic violence murders.

However, Juárez feminist/human rights activist Esther Chávez Cano had addressed murders and domestic violence, founding Casa Amiga in 1999, a counseling center that serves many women and children, survivors of abuse. No battered women's shelter opened in Juárez until 2005, in a city of 1.5 million, twice the size of El Paso with its thirty-one shelters (four of which "specialize" in survivors of violence) until Casa Amiga opened a small shelter serving ten families. NGOs like these require funds, most of them privately generated, amid multiple fund-raising efforts to support activism among occasionally competing groups.

Institutions North of the Border

El Paso's antiviolence NGOs, birthed as volunteer organizations, have grown into strong nonprofit organizations over the last thirty years, sustained with funds from private sources, fees for services (such as the Battering Intervention and Prevention Program [BIPP]), and government sources. Until 2001, NGO leaders collaborated primarily with other providers and law enforcement agencies, each with their own victims' advocates, rather than feminist civil society organizations in El Paso, which had been weak and dormant for some years. This changed when CAFV director Clemencia Prieto, as co-chair of the Coalition against Violence toward Women and Families at the U.S.–Mexico Border, collaborated with civil society human rights organizations and moved toward greater public advocacy in the early years of this organization, from 2001–2003.

El Paso's police department, proud of its second- to third-safest-city designations annually, a designation based on "serious" felony crimes, reported twenty-eight thousand domestic violence calls to 911 emergency dispatch in 2004 (Romero and Yellen 2004). El Paso is not unusual, as many U.S. cities are home to what some victims' advocates call a violence "epidemic." Only a fraction of calls proceed to trial, and first-time offenses without weapons are treated as less serious crimes, i.e., misdemeanors. These domestic violence reports include all types of domestic conflict (father-son, siblings, etc.), but most are husband-wife. Once adjudicated, most perpetrators are men, as are 90 percent of the approximately six hundred people who enroll annually in the 26-week court-ordered BIPP.

Institutions South of the Border

Domestic violence, an underreported crime in many countries, was and is suffered in relative silence. Although Mexico produces national-level studies of domestic violence, broken down to the state level (INMU-JERES 2004), its incidence was unknown at all municipal levels, such as in Juárez until the research for this study was conducted. Police reports did not disaggregate assault crime data by gender. Domestic violence was the screaming silence in an city infamous for femicide.

In 2004–2005, I collaborated with the Federación Mexicana de Asociaciones Privadas, AC, a large health-oriented NGO in Juárez, to learn the incidence of domestic violence and women's strategies to deal with violence (details about design and findings in Staudt 2008b, chap. 3). We generated a large sample of women, aged 15–39, and the NGO organized a set of three, 2-hour workshops with an interactive curriculum, group meetings, and homework. The first 404 women formed the representative sample, from which I will summarize major findings for this chapter. Before the workshops began, women completed questionnaires that tapped their demographic characteristics, sentiments, and experiences with and strategies to deal with violence at home and in the workplace.

Women in the representative sample matched educational characteristics from the 2000 Census. Approximately two-thirds completed less than *primaria* education (6 grades), while the other third achieved some *secundaria* or above (7+). The majority of respondents (64 percent) lived in households with an income of less than one thousand pesos weekly (~US$100), and 55 percent lived in houses with one to two rooms. Most women were migrants, born in other parts of the state of Chihuahua or north-central states in Mexico; native Juarenses comprised only 30 percent of the sample.

To live in Juárez is to live with everyday fear about public safety, crime, and substance abuse. The city is huge and growing; new migrants lack social capital, that is, relationships of trust with kin, friends, and extended family. In queries about security in their *colonias* (neighborhoods), half reported the presence of security, most often in the form of police patrols. With a widespread reputation of police corruption and impunity, this is a mixed blessing. Over half of the women (53 percent) said they felt fearful either "sometimes," "the majority of the time," or "always." I was surprised at the high percentage of women (57 percent) who said that sadness affected their daily activities. No doubt some of this sadness relates to migrants' mourning for lives left behind, in perhaps idealized versions of the countryside. But it also reflects life in a big, fearful city and, given domestic violence rates reported below, in approximately one-fourth of cases, in small, fearful households.

We administered the survey, with a series of questions about violence, prior to workshops, so we could compare before and after results for that question series between workshop participants and the matched sample. Although I do not report on those research results here, the pre-workshop findings were startling and important. Most participants expressed high levels of awareness about violence against women; knowledge about the laws, rape, and official investigation agencies; and cynicism about men and their excuses for violence, such as alcohol, or men's promises to change. Almost all respondents (97 percent) believed it was illegal for a man to punish his wife physically, and 94 percent asserted that forced sexual intercourse was rape. Women did not see violence against them as normal or legitimate, thus reflecting strong senses of their human rights. This was even more pronounced among the younger women in the sample, under age 25.

Once workshops began, women formed smaller groups to diagnose the causes of violence and present solutions to reduce or eradicate violence. The workshops generated posters, from which I analyzed the themes women expressed in words, pictures they pasted from the media, and their own drawings. In the most common theme, for one-fifth of the posters, women identified men's disrespect and devaluation of women. Other posters identified causes like poverty, drugs, government corruption, and child abuse.

While the women's analysis was strong, they were not always able act on their beliefs, given their economic and social circumstances. In responses to queries about physical violence from partners, 27 percent reported experiences and 11 percent reported sexual assault (half of the latter from their husbands or partners) during their lifetimes. These violence survivors exhibited characteristics similar to the overall sample: migration, low income, and limited education. But one factor separated sample survivors from the rest: psychological and verbal abuse (for example, humiliation, threats, and chronic partner anger). Three-fifths of the survivors reported very high rates of such abuse, possibly undermining their wherewithal to exit dangerous relationships.

Women responded to violence with various strategies. Some fought back and told others, but most did not, living in isolation and silence about the abuse. Few survivors called the police (just 19 percent), for there is widespread mistrust of police not only from the sample in Juárez, but also documented elsewhere in Mexico (Staudt 2008b, chap. 5). The reluctance to report is not unique to Juárez or Mexico. Antiviolence advocates and researchers in the U.S. report that survivors, on average, experience abuse multiple times before calling the police.

Physical altercations can be deadly, so much so that "domestic violence homicide" is a criminal justice category in some countries like the United States. Domestic violence merits immediate attention, to protect the safety of the victim, for it can quickly and easily turn into murder.

To the extent one can extrapolate from the physical and sexual violence figures in the representative sample to the city population for that age group, approximately one hundred thousand women are at risk. Numbers like these are striking, just as femicide totals. These women have survived for now, but some could obviously become fatalities. Emergency response is limited in Juárez, and shelter space is practically nonexistent. Institutions offer no BIPP-type experience that would diminish the tendency for serial batterers to move on to the next women when they finish with their earlier targets. Gloria Terry, then director of El Paso's Center Against Family Violence, reports that husbands/partners threaten women from both sides of the border about abandoning them in the desert. In one instance, a man went so far as to warn his partner that if she didn't obey him, he would take her to Juárez and shoot her in the desert (García 2004). The distance between domestic violence and femicide is all too narrow in the terrorism of some women's everyday lives.

Institutional Practices and Responses

Valiant journalists, researchers, and border, national and global NGOs have documented the femicide in Juárez (Monárrez Fragoso 2002; Washington Valdez 2002; Chávez Cano 2002; Amnesty International 2003; García 2005). While most of the bodies identified are Mexican, there have been U.S., Dutch, and Central American victims. Binational problems require binational solutions. Thus far, those binational solutions have been meager, given the complexity of national sovereignty. The United States does not welcome Mexican police action in its sovereign territory, just as Mexico does not welcome U.S. police action in its territory, unless by invitation.

In the late 1990s, Mexico invited U.S. FBI assistance to run suspect profiles through its database, to little avail. Local police departments in El Paso and Juárez have long cooperated over stolen vehicles. Drawing on this precedent, the binational Coalition Against Violence asked publicly at marches and rallies, over and over, for the same cooperation to occur over murdered women. Such cooperation began in 2003 with a public ceremony among officials from both sides of the border, instigating occasional coordinated training and an 800 telephone tip-line.

On occasion, Mexican officials ask for assistance on suspects who may be registered sex offenders in the United States. A match was found in 2006 that aided in the identification of the person who raped and murdered an 8-year-old girl in Juárez. The state of Texas requires nineteen types of sex offenders to register and posts their pictures, names, aliases and addresses on its government web site, an imperfect system for under-reported crimes (Ramshaw 2006). No doubt unregistered sex offenders move freely in the state of Chihuahua, preying on potential victims there as well.

Feminists, mothers, and human rights NGOs in Juárez networked across the border, to cities in both Mexico and the United States, and globally in dramatic activism that peaked in late 2003 with preparations for V-Day 2004, or Día V on February 14, 2004 (see Staudt 2008b, chap. 4, for a full analysis). Mexico City and Hollywood movie stars joined activists from the border and world for the largest solidarity march ever, with five thousand to eight thousand people across the borderline. Some tension emerged between those focused on broad-based violence, covered in the *Vagina Monologues* performances, versus specific femicide in Juárez, with some antifemicide activists at alternate plays calling for boycotts of the cross-border solidarity march. But even the credible special investigator and federal appointee Guadalupe Morfín framed the issues to include the whole problematic city economic and social infrastructure, broader than identifying the serial killers alone, in her report (2004).

In response to NGO high-profile activism, government agencies at the national, state, and local level have responded to a limited extent. Politicians no longer deny or minimize the deaths publicly, blaming the victims. Business and government leaders got very busy, after global activism peaked on V-Day/Día V 2004, trying to change *the image* of the city. Plan Juárez, a high-end NGO with support from the business and U.S. maquila sector, used a complex planning process from Spain to develop a plan for the year 2015, emphasizing the problems of public safety and the need to strengthen law enforcement. Coupled with a non-transparent five-million-dollar grant from the U.S. Agency for International Development to the state attorney general's office in Chihuahua, several changes have taken place that activists hope will be more than cosmetic. For example, video cams have been placed in high-crime zones and maquila enclaves to monitor areas and collect evidence (although cameras pointed toward the sky, not the ground, in the case of one homicide); and efforts to reduce the "culture of violence" include the bizarre program to destroy violent toys in large bonfires. The state and municipal police public relations offices have strengthened their relationships with the press with immediate, specific information about investigations. Activists hope that weak or dirty government institutions will change, not simply the image of the city.

Concluding Reflections

In this chapter, I have highlighted violence against women, a near omnipresent problem globally, with its special dimensions at the border. Domestic violence transcends both sides of the U.S.–Mexico border, but gruesome sexualized rape-murders, known as femicide, made Ciudad Juárez infamous for women-killing. Politicians initially blamed the victims, and law enforcement institutions did little to locate killers and prevent such crimes. Institutions, both governmental and nongovernmental, require unpacking to diagnose the problems and foster actions to eradicate violence against women in national and transnational settings like the border region.

Both activists and government officials used numeric metaphors to make or dismiss their challenge of police impunity or defend inaction for allegedly "normal" crimes, officially excused and tolerated far too long. Activists, beginning with mothers of victims at the local level, networked to binational, national, and international levels to press Mexico for its inaction, for femicide is, as Congresswoman Marcela Lagarde says, *un crimen del estado* (a crime of the state) (in Morfín 2004, 12). The State, at complex federal, state, and municipal levels, is responsible for public safety and law enforcement. Nationwide in Mexico, activists and crime victims criticize law enforcement institutions as ineffective and complicit with criminals.

Femicide totals come from plural perpetrator profiles: probable serial and opportunistic killers and domestic partners. Whatever the perpetrator profile, death for the woman is equally tragic. Domestic violence, affecting at least one-fourth of women on both sides of the border, is a serious problem that can lead to murder, already rampant in Juárez. Surprising silence about domestic violence exists: victim-survivors often delay reports, suffering in silence, and activists focused on the horrifying murders for eager media until recently. When equally gruesome murders occur elsewhere, at rates that surpass Juárez, who will continue the sustained work necessary to change resistant masculinist institutions?

Paradoxically, feminist and human rights activists initially also muted attention to domestic violence as well. In El Paso, activism from decades past produced nonprofit organizations that continue to raise awareness and counsel and shelter survivors. In Juárez, activism began over femicide, and some tension arose over whether to prioritize femicide or violence against women generally, including domestic violence. This tension peaked in 2003–2004, just as organizing peaked in cross-border solidarity efforts. Agenda struggles ultimately resulted in a broader base to pressure institutions to increase public security, and to reduce and prevent violence against women. Mexico's federal government has acknowledged femicide in multiple cities along with widespread domestic violence. Meanwhile, the national women's institute (INMUJERES) and the women's institute in Chihuahua state government (ICHIMU) disseminated creative social marketing to remind people on an everyday basis about domestic violence as crime. I have even seen telephone cards, used by men and women, with pictures of famous women media figures who have black eyes and bruises and the words (translated): "Whoever hits one woman hits all women." Increasingly, multiple activisms press for institutional change both from within and outside government. Femicide was an issue in the 2006 presidential campaign, and feminists engaged in the process, however problematic the state remains.

Feminist and human rights NGOs effectively framed and reframed activism for some governmental and other societal changes. However, these modest changes offer no consolation to mothers still searching for their daughters' killers. If governmental institutional resistance in Mexico takes as long as the three-decade process that transpired in the United States for its still flawed bureaucratized response, many women's lives in Mexico will be lost. Women's responses in the survey demonstrate clearly that they reject violence against them and accept no excuses for abuse. Whether human rights awareness is as high among men, in word or deed, has not yet been addressed in research.

Meanwhile, global activists move on, from one femicide crisis to another. Currently, Guatemala exhibits higher femicide rates than Juárez, and rapes in Darfur garner much media attention, thanks to transnational organizations like Amnesty International and Save Darfur, among many other groups. Women's dead and violated bodies, methodically counted in numeric metaphors, raise awareness of misogyny worldwide. This dramatic activist and media attention is welcome and necessary, but sustained civil society activism must remain in places like Juárez for counseling and shelter and for persistent oversight in consolidating and monitoring law enforcement changes.

Besides social movements, with their flair for dramatic, media-catching attention, nonprofit advocacy NGOs also have a role, for they dedicate ongoing rather than episodic attention to issues year-round. Social movement activism should complement NGOization to sustain pressure for awareness, and legal and policy changes, including the tedious and detailed everyday government institutional enforcement practices among resistant street-level bureaucrats who implement policies. Thus far, the resources to facilitate sustained action, at national and binational border levels, are caught up in drug and oil wars, rather than the everyday gender wars that wreck havoc on women's lives and well being.

Acknowledgments

I am grateful to many people for their help during my six years of research and action but especially to political scientist Irasema Coronado, *colega y amiga*, and Co-Chair of the Coalition Against Violence toward Women and Families at the U.S.–Mexico Border.

7

Femicide on the Border and New Forms of Protest

THE INTERNATIONAL CARAVAN FOR JUSTICE

Carol Mueller, Michelle Hansen, and Karen Qualtire

FEMICIDE IS SPREADING throughout Latin America with frightening speed (Paterson 2006). On the eve of International Women's Day 2006, a delegation of Latin American women traveled to the headquarters of the Inter-American Commission on Human Rights (IACHR) of the Organization of American States in Washington, D.C., to testify to the increasing seriousness of a regional problem. Although there are more femicide victims in post-war countries like Guatemala, the epicenter of the problem has been the unsolved murders of young women in Ciudad Juárez, Mexico. As in Juárez, evidence of torture, mutilation and sexual abuse has become a signature of the killings throughout the region.

Most of the efforts to stem this tide originated and continue within the communities where mothers and families have borne severe personal losses, where local human rights organizations have lent their resources and political influence, and where courageous lawyers and journalists have contributed their professional skills (T. Rodríguez 2007; Washington Valdez 2006). And yet, it has not been enough. The murders continue, and local organizations of parents have reached outside their local and national communities to international nongovernmental organizations (NGOs). Parents have contacted human rights organizations such as Amnesty International (Amnesty), feminist organizations like Violence Against Women International (V-Day International), and NGOs with a specific focus on Latin America such as Mexico Solidarity Network (MSN) and the Washington Office on Latin America (WOLA).

This chapter is one in a series on campaigns that these binational and international NGOs have been able to offer the parents of Ciudad Juárez in bringing this issue to the attention of the international community. Buzzelle and Mueller's earlier work (2005) examined the massive reframing of international norms and organizational mandates that was necessary before a coalition between Amnesty and V-Day International was possible.[1] Their coalition made possible the large-scale, celebrity-infused march from El Paso into Juárez on Valentine's Day of 2004. Along with the Amnesty Report of 2003, the threat of the march and the march itself placed unprecedented international pressure on President Fox to bring federal attention to the failure of law enforcement in Ciudad Juárez and the state of Chihuahua. In the present chapter, we examine the way in which the constraints on mobilization of grievances at an international border influenced the role of a binational NGO, the MSN, and, in particular, their fall 2004 "International Caravan for Justice."[2]

Femicide in Ciudad Juárez

Since 1993 a plague of women's murders has come to characterize Ciudad Juárez as "the best city in the world to kill a woman" (see T. Rodríguez 2007; Washington Valdez 2006; and Amnesty International 2003).[3] The characterization stems from the unabated series of killings of women in this border city of two million. Before 1993, there was an average of three women murdered each year, but in that year, the number reached two per month. The numbers continued to increase, and by 2001 there was approximately one killing of a woman per week, nearly half of whom had been sexually assaulted and tortured before death. The murders including sexual assault have disproportionately targeted younger, slender women with long, dark hair. Although more men are killed in Juárez than women, the ratio of women to men is higher here than any other city on the border or in Mexico as a whole.

There is considerable debate about the actual number of women killed and about the number of those who have been sexually assaulted. The most definitive account remains the report by Amnesty International in the summer of 2003, which estimated a total of 400 with approximately 150 of these fitting the pattern of sexual assault and torture (Amnesty International 2003). Estimates of the number of women who have disappeared and never been found is much higher. Six years after the Amnesty report, the murders, many with horrific "signatures" of torture and mutilation, have not stopped despite the enormous efforts by families of the victims, local activists, and international organizations. Increasingly, it is recognized that these murders should be called what they are, "femicides."

Although the term "femicide" has been in existence for over two hundred years and has always meant "the killing of women" (Russell and Harmes 2001), it is hardly a household word. It has also been equated with the Spanish "feminicidio" or "female genocide." Diana Russell, an activist concerned with violence against women, characterizes it as "killing of females by males because they are females" (2001). This refers to its origins in a hatred of women, with murder implying a sense of superiority and empowerment over women, often including sexual cruelty for the victims and a sense of pleasure and control for the male committing the crime (Russell 2001, 13–14). From dowry deaths in India to the stoning of women under the Taliban in Afghanistan, femicide is a global issue. Yet, in some locations, it becomes particularly acute. The free online encyclopedia, Wikipedia, now uses the murders of women in Ciudad Juárez and Guatemala to illustrate the meaning of "femicide."

While the cause of femicide on a global scale may be the long-standing tradition of patriarchy and the near-universal belief in the inherent inferiority of women, the causes in any particular location are also more locally determined (Parrot and Cummings 2006). Most observers and students of the femicide in Ciudad Juárez and Chihuahua believe that it is the combination of the free trade zone with its maquiladoras that hire young women from the economically threatened interior of Mexico and the influence of the drug cartels on law enforcement that have allowed the situation to achieve such dramatic proportions (Velasco 2005; Washington Valdez 2006). However, our concern in this chapter is not with the causes of the femicide, but with binational efforts to bring it to an end. We will present an overview of these efforts, but the focus is on one of the specific campaigns of a binational organization, the MSN.

Grassroots Efforts by Mothers of the Disappeared

The plight of the mothers and families of the disappeared women of Juárez and Chihuahua bears a striking resemblance to that of the Mothers of the Plaza de Mayo in Argentina during the late 1970s and early 1980s. Facing the generals after a 1976 coup, mothers of disappeared young men and women who had opposed the dictatorship came to recognize and know each other as they attempted to get official help in locating their missing children (Bouvard 1994). On their rounds from one police station to another, these mothers of working class Buenos Aires gradually came to realize that their concerns were not isolated but part of a more general pattern of repression. Soon, they were gathering once each week to march in the Plaza de Mayo wearing white shawls to represent their role as mothers and the diapers that their children had once worn (Bouvard 1994, 74). The Mothers became internationally famous because of their defiance of massive repression and, with the help of a failed Falklands War, helped to bring down the dictatorship (Keck and Sikkink 1998).

The mothers of Juárez have yet to reach this level of fame and success, in part because the source of the murders is so intricately woven into the fabric of this border city's economy and politics. In turn, such border cities are critical to the economy of the country. With a preference for young female workers, the primarily U.S.-owned maquiladoras of the free trade zones attract young women from the distressed agricultural hinterland. They come to a borderland where a condition of impunity has been created by the pervasive influence of the drug cartels (Naím 2005).

Yet, the mothers have also found each other and organized to oppose an equally oppressive political system that has similarly attempted to thwart their efforts. Like the Mothers in Argentina, they conduct their own investigations, post fliers of the missing, and, eventually, keep their own records of the disappeared and murdered. They paint the pink crosses on telephone poles that have become a symbol of the femicide. With the help of friends and family, they search the deserts on the outskirts of the city for bodies of the missing. Five years after the series of murders began, in June of 1998, the first organization of families was formed, Voces sin Eco (MSN 2004). Due to internal divisions encouraged by official interference, the organization accomplished little other than giving a public face to the growing unity of families of the disappeared/murdered women. But they also reached out to unions and human rights and feminist groups in Juárez as well as the rest of Mexico.

On International Women's Day the next year, hundreds gathered for a march in Ciudad Juárez led by the mothers of the victims, and joined by the mayor and several federal deputies. A supporting march was held in Mexico City. By 2000, additional organizations had been formed, with Nuestras Hijas de Regreso a Casa (Bring Our Daughters Home) in Juárez and Justicia Para Nuestras Hijas (Justice for Our Daughters) in Chihuahua City. The head of the major domestic violence shelter for women in the city, Esther Chávez Cano, has been an outspoken critic of law enforcement efforts. On April 16, 2002, mothers occupied the Chihuahua state capital demanding increased funding for law enforcement and benefits for survivors. Meanwhile, the disappearances and the murders continued.

North-South Collaboration and International Intervention

Because local efforts by the mothers and families of the murdered and disappeared women of Juárez were unsuccessful in stopping the femicide, they turned increasingly to the international community for help. In this attempt, they followed much the same strategy as the Mothers of the Plaza de Mayo who also brought international pressure to bear on the military dictatorship to release their disappeared adult children from detention camps, torture and death (Keck and Sikkink 1998). Differences in the help mobilized internationally stem from the facts that the U.S.– Mexico border is the longest in the world where an affluent, powerful democracy borders a poor third world country, and that Ciudad Juárez sits directly across the border from the U.S. city of El Paso, Texas.

Most attempts to exert influence across national borders have involved the mobilization of NGOs in the North that provide information and access to the decision makers of powerful, affluent democracies on behalf of aggrieved groups in the South (Keck and Sikkink 1998). Such was the case in Argentina, except that the generals made the mistake of inviting Amnesty International to visit the country and redeem its reputation from the claims of the Mothers and other human rights activists. Instead, after talks with the Mothers and access to the documentation of the disappearances, Amnesty's report showed that the generals had a policy of systematically eliminating their opposition. The report earned Amnesty the 1977 Nobel Peace Prize. The regime was then denounced by the governments of the United States, France, Italy and Sweden with the U.S. Congress eliminating all military aid to Argentina. Disappearances dropped sharply by 1978.

The indirect approach of this North-South collaboration in which northern NGOs intercede on behalf of southern grievances has stemmed in large part from the considerable geographic and political distances that separate most claimants and global decision makers, as well as the lack of a democratic structure, either locally or internationally, that might bring them together. For the mothers of the disappeared daughters of Ciudad Juárez, however, distance is not the problem. Instead, it is the fact of living on the border with a first world country that is the source of the problem, but it also allows direct access to the NGOs of North America.

Shortly after creating the formal organizations, the mothers of Juárez began to make contacts with these NGOs across the border and in Europe. With the support of other NGOs, the mothers led a march in front of the Organization of American States in Washington, D.C., in the summer of 2002, demanding that the murders of their daughters be considered "crimes against humanity" (MSN 2004, 105). In the fall of 2004, they participated in the MSN's Caravan for Justice (Paterson 2004). Just before International Women's Day 2006, they joined with other women from Latin America to present their case to the Inter-American Commission on Human Rights of the Organization of American States (Paterson 2006).

In the mid to late 1990s, the mothers and families of the Juárez victims appealed to Amnesty International to intervene as the leading international human rights organization (Buzzelle and Mueller 2005). At that time, however, Amnesty's constitutional mandate covered only violence and abuses by states; it left no room for intervention in domestic sources of violence—even when state negligence seemed to perpetuate such abuses. It took the efforts of the international women's movement until the biannual meeting of Amnesty in Dakar, Senegal, in 2001, before it changed its mandate and, not coincidentally, for the first time, elected a woman as executive director. This change was furthered by the reframing of the Inter-American Convention of 1994 and the changes in emphasis at the UN Human Rights Conference in Vienna in 1993 to encompass violence against women (Joachim 1999). Supported by these sources of legitimacy, Amnesty was now empowered to answer the request from the mothers of Ciudad Juárez. Its report on the Juárez murders, "Intolerable Deaths," was published just before its biannual International Council Meeting in Mexico City in August 2003. With representatives of its fifty-eight national sections in attendance, Amnesty organized demonstrations both in Mexico City and Ciudad Juárez; Irene Khan, the new executive director, personally presented the report to Mexican president Vicente Fox. Amnesty's thorough review of the systematic failures of law enforcement in Ciudad Juárez and Chihuahua was a devastating indictment of both local and national governments. The international human rights organization followed up in 2004 with a proposal for human rights reforms to the Mexican Congress in 2004, as did the UN High Commissioner for Human Rights.

In October of 2003, a coalition of NGOs—the MSN, the Latin American Working Group and the WOLA—organized a three-day U.S. congressional delegation led by Hilda Solis (D-CA) to Ciudad Juárez. (MSN 2004, 31). In the next few months, Solis spearheaded House Resolution 466 condemning the murders and calling for supportive action by the U.S. government. An identical resolution was introduced into the Senate by Jeff Bingaman (D-NM), Kay Bailey Hutchison (R-TX), and Mary Landrieu (D-LA). The House resolution first won unanimous support from the Western Hemisphere Subcommittee of the International Relations Committee in the fall of 2005, followed by support of the full Committee. To proceed more quickly, Solis and Bingaman reintroduced the measure as a joint resolution on International Women's Day 2006. By the following year, the resolution had been approved in both houses.

Amnesty's new Campaign Against Violence Against Women (Amnesty International 2003) also meant that it could now lend its support to countless other efforts to bring governments to account for the murders in Juárez. Shortly after presenting its report to President Fox, Amnesty agreed to a joint venture with Eve Ensler's V-Day International, an NGO dedicated to ending worldwide violence against women, funded by the proceeds of the thousands of annual performances of Ensler's *Vagina Monologues* (Ensler 1998; Buzzelle and Mueller 2005). The two international NGOs cosponsored, with the mothers and families of Ciudad Juárez, a march from El Paso into Juárez on Valentine's Day 2004. With the celebrity attraction of Jane Fonda and Sally Field from the United

States, thousands crossed the international bridge from El Paso, Texas, into Ciudad Juárez where they were joined by another three to five thousand led by the mothers and families of the victims to assemble at the central monument to Benito Juárez.

The secretary general of Amnesty, Irene Khan, was back in Ciudad Juárez in August 2005 with a delegation of Amnesty representatives from Mexico, the United States, the Netherlands and Switzerland. Although Khan lauded the creation of a special federal commission and prosecutor and the more respectful attitude by law enforcement to the families of victims, she also expressed disappointment about the limited number of cases investigated, the lack of attention to the murders in Chihuahua City, and the lack of a clear strategy linking federal and local authorities (Amnesty International 2005, 2006). The mothers of the murdered, she noted, were doubtful that justice would ever be accomplished.

International attention spread to Europe in 2005 when Radio Netherlands and Novib held seminars in both the Hague and Mexico City (van der Wel 2006). According to van der Wel, for Oxfam: "Journalists were present, representatives of the Mexican embassy, victims' families, Mexican NGOs (human rights and women's organizations), Amnesty International, the Dutch TUC, Dutch politicians, and members of the European Parliament." The Dutch efforts were followed in April 2006 by two days of hearings denouncing the femicide in Mexico and Guatemala by the European Parliament's Committee on Human Rights and its Committee on Women's Rights and Gender Equality. In concluding its hearings, a final statement called for the governments of both countries to honor the international agreements and treaties they have signed on human rights and violence against women ("Annie" 2006).

In addition to the multiple efforts of international NGOs, there has been an outpouring of support by artists from a variety of media.[4] In addition to the impressive documentary by Lourdes Portillo, *Señiorita Extraviada*, two other documentaries and several motion pictures have been made. The most visible movie was the high-budget *Bordertown* starring Jennifer Lopez and Antonio Banderas, and including Martin Sheen and Edward James Olmos. The film was nominated for the Berlin Film Festival's top Golden Bear Award in February 2007, and Lopez was awarded Amnesty's top award for media work on human rights issues. The movie was released in the United States in August 2007. Released the previous year, *The Virgin of Juarez* stars Minnie Driver, who, like Lopez, plays an investigative reporter. Three films by local filmmakers are also in production, including a love story set against the background of the murders. *Muertas* by Ryan Piers Williams, starring Masiela Lusha, America Ferrera, and Francesco Quinn, was also filmed in El Paso in the summer of 2005. Rock stars Sonidos Latinos played in Ciudad Juárez the same summer to draw attention to the murders. The celebrated Chilean writer, Roberto Bolaño, who died in 2005, set his massive new novel, *2666*, in a Mexican border town where a serial killer preys on female factory workers. Even boxer Marco Antonio Barrera offered the purse from his fight with Robbie Peden (September 2005) to help in ending the murders.

The families of the victims, as well as local activists, have mixed feelings about the media attention. When Mexico's TV Azteca showed a two-week series on the murders in 2004, there was an outcry from the families because of the use of actual names of the victims and the gruesome details of the murders that were shown (T. Rodríguez 2007). The mothers then persuaded the popular band, Los Tigres, to cancel a concert in Ciudad Juárez that was promoting their hit single, "The Women of Juárez," a song denouncing the killings.

The joint efforts by the mothers and families of the victims and their international supporters have had some effect on law enforcement practices (see Washington Valdez 2006 for a summary), and yet the femicide goes on. The international supportive actions continue as well. Our major concern in this chapter is the effort by the MSN to bring attention to the murders and to mobilize opposition within the United States through its "International Caravan for Justice" that crossed the country in the fall of 2004 (Hise [2006]; Paterson 2004). Beginning on the Canadian border, the Caravans followed five different routes across the United States and then joined together in Ciudad Juárez on the Day of the Dead, where participants met with families of the missing women, activists, and city officials (see table 7.1).[5]

Mexico Solidarity Network

The MSN is a "grassroots-based NGO dedicated to fundamental social change" on both sides of the border, offering a basic critique of the

TABLE 7.1. Routes for the International Caravan for Justice by Host Cities, Mexico Solidarity Network, Fall 2004

East route (11 cities)	East Coast route (17 cities)	Midwest route (12 cities)	Southwest route (10 cities)	West Coast route (13 cities)
Buffalo, NY	Amherst, MA	Milwaukee, WI	Ft. Collins, CO	Seattle, WA
Toronto, Canada	Cambridge, MA	Minneapolis, MN	Greeley, CO	Olympia, WA
Brantford, Canada	Hanover, NH	Madison, WI	Laramie, WY	Portland, OR
Rochester, NY	New Haven, CT	Rock Island, IL	Boulder, CO	Corvallis, OR
Columbus, OH	Fair Haven, CT	Moline, IL	Denver, CO	Arcata, CA
Cincinnati, OH	New York, NY	Chicago, IL	Las Vegas, NM	Sacramento, CA
Louisville, KY	Washington, D.C.	St. Louis, MO	Santa Fe, NM	San Francisco, CA
Nashville, TN	Richmond, VA	Columbia, MO	Albuquerque, NM	Santa Barbara, CA
Memphis, TN	Durham, NC	Kansas City, MO	Las Cruces, NM	Los Angeles, CA
Dallas, TX	Greensboro, NC	Tulsa, OK	El Paso, TX	San Diego, CA
El Paso, TX	Asheville, NC	Norman, OK		Phoenix, AZ
	Atlanta, GA	El Paso, TX		Tucson, AZ
	Jackson, MS			El Paso, TX
	Houston, TX			
	Austin, TX			
	San Antonio, TX			
	El Paso, TX			

current economic relationships of the United States and Mexico. The MSN opposes neoliberal economic policies and chooses to challenge those "existing power relationships" by working to promote change. Its major strategies of change include becoming directly involved with affected communities, bringing together activists and elected officials, encouraging high school and college students to be active in political and social issues, and seeking alternatives on a binational basis to accomplish change within the communities and civil society.[6] In anticipation of the summer of 2006, students at campuses as far apart as Dartmouth and Mills College were raising money to spend a summer in Ciudad Juárez to help families of the victims (local papers from each college).

MSN focuses on a number of bilateral issues, such as amnesty for undocumented workers, human rights in Chiapas, ex-Braceros in both the United States and Mexico, fair trade, day laborers, and the Coalition of Immokalee Workers in southern Florida. It also works with many Latin American groups on human rights issues. MSN has organized thirty different delegations to Mexico, speaking tours, educational outreach programs in the United States, and fair trade campaigns, all in an effort to help educate and bring awareness of the results of neoliberalism that confront both sides of the border.

MSN has been in existence for seven years with three locations. The central office is in Washington, D.C., with a national coordinator, a legislative coordinator, and a legislative assistant. MSN shares office space in Washington with the Nicaragua Network, a lobbying group that supports "social and economic justice for Nicaragua." Both MSN and the Nicaragua Network share the address with international A.N.S.W.E.R., a coalition of individuals and organizations formed after 9/11 that seeks to build an "anti-racist, peace and social justice movement." MSN is a member of the A.N.S.W.E.R. steering committee, along with Pastors for Peace, the Nicaragua Network, the Haiti Support Network, the Partnership for Civil Justice–LEDF, and others. Two additional MSN offices, supported largely by student interns, are located in Chicago and, at the time of the Caravan, in San Francisco.

MSN first became aware of the femicide in Ciudad Juárez when they were attempting to organize unions in the maquiladoras on the border.[7] As MSN organizers tried to talk about working conditions, women kept coming back to the pattern of killings that befell young maquiladora workers and the absence of any responsible response from law enforcement. The problem was particularly serious in Ciudad Juárez. As MSN's involvement increased, they began working with other organizations to raise public awareness. Because of their commitment to grassroots mobilization, their first approach was to the parents of the victims. They helped mothers of the victims come to Washington, D.C., to speak to the Inter-American Human Rights Commission and to members of Congress. To reach out to a broader public, MSN organized a national caravan to cross the United States and give the mothers of the victims an opportunity to tell their story.

"Caravans" as Instruments of Social Change

"Caravans for Justice" don't appear among the events that typically characterize the modern protest repertoire (Tarrow 1998; Tilly 1995, 2004). Strikes, demonstrations, rallies, and marches have all served activists for several hundred years when the relatively powerless seek to influence the more powerful in the name of collectively held grievances or claims on the powerful. Some of the more famous marches of the post–World War II period in the United States include the civil rights marches of the 1950s and 1960s: from Selma to Montgomery, Alabama, in 1966; the March on Washington in 1963 and Martin Luther King's "I have a dream" speech; and the 1968 Poor People's March on Washington. In Mexico, more recently, the 2001 March for Indigenous Dignity by the Zapatistas galvanized the country. Internationally, hundreds of marches and demonstrations across the globe in February 2003 comprised the largest popular protest in world history against an impending war.

Although the modern repertoire of collective action is extensive, these march/demonstration/rallies are considered the most typical—serving as the archetype of modern protest forms that are studied by countless scholars in the many versions of event analysis (Rucht, Koopmans, and Neidhardt 1998). Effective marches/demonstrations have several typical features: (1) they are usually directed toward an important center of decision making where claims can be targeted and binding commitments made by the target of claims; (2) a premium is placed on the number of marchers or demonstrators where size reflects either direct or indirect political influence as well as a latent threat to law and order; and, finally, (3) the addition of elements that Tilly argues exist for all forms of social movements or "WUNC"—worthiness, unity, numbers, and commitment (1995, 2004). Although we are not claiming that the efforts to bring justice to the families of the victims of Juárez is yet a social movement, we nevertheless see the International Caravan for Justice that works on their behalf as one of a class of innovations in protest form that attempt to deal with the constraints of cross-border mobilizations.

When all four elements (WUNC) are successfully orchestrated, organizers can expect to influence the targets of their claims both directly and indirectly through the mass media coverage of the event. In democracies, it is the anticipated effect of such disciplined masses on the electorate that is thought to create influence on behalf of claims (Tilly 1983). What then of caravans? If caravans are not the same as marches or demonstrations, how are they different and what is the source of their potential influence, if any? Does the MSN "International Caravan for Justice" have this potential on behalf of the women of Ciudad Juárez?

In the contemporary transnational protest environment, caravans have assumed an importance that can hardly be ignored. The original "caravans," associated with the trade routes of the Middle East and Africa, consisted of groups of merchants, pilgrims, or travelers who journeyed together in deserts or other hostile regions, usually for mutual protection. Muslim pilgrims on the journey to Mecca employed as many as ten thousand camels. These caravans for mutual protection lasted well into the nineteenth century. Caravans on the medieval Silk Road protected a vital trade route from Europe to China, while other caravans carried human cargo of slaves across Africa to ports on the Atlantic coast. Only in the last few years have trucks replaced the camel caravans that carried salt across the Sahara to the fabled city of Timbuktu since the twelfth century (Rainier 2003).

Modern "caravans for justice" still support a long journey of a group of people with a beginning and/or a destination of some significance. But, trade has been replaced by the goal of justice and protection and by the need to create solidarity among activists and to raise awareness among bystanders either directly or through mediated messages. Most "caravans for justice" follow a route in which some stops represent sites of significant injustice, sacrifice or victory. In the twenty-first century alone, dozens of caravans seeking justice have embarked on virtually every continent. These caravans incorporate more familiar forms of protest including mass rallies, demonstrations, marches, and more innovative forms of collective claims making.[8]

Within the United States, 2004 saw a caravan supporting the freedom of Leonard Peltier in Tacoma, Washington; a caravan of buses recreating the Freedom Summer Ride from New York City through the center of the civil rights struggle in the South, seeking to reopen the murder case of Chaney, Goodman and Schwerner, who were killed in Mississippi in 1964; in Los Angeles, the "Caravan for Justice" culminating in a protest at Governor Schwarzenegger's office and a rally in Koreatown calling for legalization of immigrant workers; and the "Marriage Equality Caravan" taking buses from California to Washington, D.C., to rally support before the November elections demanding repeal of antigay measures like the Defense of Marriage Act. In 2005, the "Journey for Justice Bus Caravan" traveled the spine of the sanctuary movement to Fort Benning, Georgia, to protest the reopening of the School of the Americas relabeled as the new Western Hemisphere Institute for Security Cooperation—in the same location and in the same buildings. Also in 2005, Cindy Sheehan took her caravan of three buses of antiwar protesters on different routes across the country to converge in Washington. And early in 2007, a caravan for justice left San Diego for Washington, D.C., seeking a humane solution to the immigration issue.

The caravan is also uniquely suited for extended mobilization within and across international borders. In Chile, the "Caravan for Life and Justice," consisting of families of the disappeared, culminated at the National Stadium in Santiago in October 2001. This caravan commemorated the twenty-eighth anniversary of the 1973 military operation known as the "Caravan of Death" when agents of the Pinochet regime traveled to detention centers executing political prisoners. Nobel Peace Laureate Rigoberto Menchú and Argentine rock star Charly García were to appear at the Stadium where the Caravan hoped to reopen the trial of Pinochet and other army officers. The next year, in Australia, "Hope Caravan" traveled to the Woomera detention center to join the actions in the Festival of Freedom at Easter, translating a spiritual occasion into one of political action.

Other caravans have operated across international borders. In July 2005, 120 supporters of the "Caravan for Justice in Palestine" were forcefully deported by soldiers and sent back to Jordan after they crossed the Israeli border. Caravaners from eighteen different countries had been on the road for over two weeks on their way from Strasbourg, France, to their destination in Jerusalem, where they had expected to demand that Israel comply with an International Court of Justice decision the previous summer declaring the Apartheid Wall unlawful.

In October 2005, twelve countries in Asia launched the "People's Caravan for Justice and Sovereignty" from India with the goal of reaching the World Trade Organization ministerial meetings in Hong Kong by December. The caravan passed through sites where events associated with the struggle against neoliberalism have taken place. Organizers noted that the Caravan process would "voice the unheard demands of the poor, dalets, tribals, women and men, forest dwellers, people living or affected by HIV/AIDS"—all of those affected by neoliberalism. The Caravan arrived in Hong Kong in three double-decker buses, participants having traveled by bullock carts, bicycles, elephants, camels, horses and trucks. En route, the caravans in each country sparked a wide range of supportive actions—from protests against the Trade Related Intellectual Property Rights treaty in Cambodia to a "Month of the Poor" in Vietnam. In each country, anti-neoliberal organizations supported the Caravan at its different stops.

We seem to be witnessing the birth of a new form of protest in the global spread of "caravans for justice" that characterize the new century and, sometimes, extend across political borders, such as the twelve-country Asian People's Caravan for Justice and Sovereignty and the Caravan for Justice in Palestine that traveled from France to Israel with participants from eighteen countries. The major difference between marches and caravans seems to lie in the importance of the journey for building solidarity among participants, the events along the way as a means of raising consciousness, and, frequently, the importance of a symbolically important destination.

Whereas the purpose of a march is influence as a political outcome, the purpose of the caravan includes personal and collective witnessing while expanding the breadth of support. In other words, though strategic concerns are a central focus of the caravan, personal witnessing by victims of injustice, building solidarity through shared experiences in small groups, and promoting a broader agenda are essential to the caravan's ethos.

The latter goals come through very clearly in the type of media reporting that caravans receive. Rather than mass media attention to numbers and the potential or reality of violence (McCarthy, McPhail, and Smith 1996; Mueller 1997), it is primarily the alternative media that cover caravans through the web sites of sponsoring organizations or the Independent Media Center (Indymedia) coverage of participant-journalists (Meikle 2002; Kidd 2003). The progress of the caravan is reported through the personal experiences of these journalists or of other participants in terms of their worthiness and commitment. Although reports that are so personal, like those of Indymedia, create a sense of vicarious participation, it is more difficult to maintain the illusion of unity if an individualized report gets off message. Numbers as a source of political influence are also more difficult to attain. Instead, the caravan approaches policy influence by building a dispersed support base that is more diffuse and personal. In most cases, it eliminates the threat of potential violence; at the same time, it provides a more intensive tutelage than marches or demonstrations in understanding grievances and/or claims from the perspective of its own framework. Though marches are clearly not irrelevant for cross-border protests (for example, the Amnesty–V-Day Valentine's Day March of 2004 from El Paso into Ciudad Juárez), the Asian People's Caravan and the European Caravan for Justice in Palestine demonstrate the unique potential of caravans for bringing together a diverse group of participants for a cross-border journey in which the stops along the route or the destination may have symbolic importance.

The International Caravan for Justice

In the case of the Mexico Solidarity Network, the framework for understanding the femicide in Ciudad Juárez is anti-neoliberalism. That is, MSN sees social injustices, like femicide, as a result of a neoliberal economic system (see MSN 2004). Interviewees organizing for MSN described the purpose of the caravan very similarly, principally as an attempt to raise awareness to femicide within the context of neoliberal globalization. The variance in the message revolved around how femicide and globalization were described. First and foremost, the caravan was described as an attempt to raise awareness to the issue of femicide as an outgrowth of a poor country's creation of export-free zones with maquiladoras that disproportionately hired young women and, thus, created a magnet at the border cities for potential victims. Young women from the hinterland of Mexico for whom subsistence farming no longer offered a viable way of life filled these roles.

The second theme emphasized the inordinate number of attacks and homicides against girls and women of lower socioeconomic status, namely, the poor women of a poor country who have few resources for protecting themselves. From the unlighted neighborhoods in which they live to late-night shifts, the lack of transportation or legal representation, their lack of resources marks these young women as potential victims. And third, the MSN Caravan issued a demand for justice for the slain victims of Juárez and a call to end the atrocities. Thus, the femicides as well as the corruption of law enforcement (or impunity) that permit them in border cities were seen as a byproduct of corporate America's globalization strategies. Thus, from MSN's point of view, ending women's victimization is contingent upon changing the economic relationships between rich and poor countries.

With three different themes, it was possible for sponsoring organizations in the caravan cities to share at least one emphasis, such as that on social justice, but not necessarily embrace MSN's commitment to an antiliberal economic critique. The three somewhat separate themes in MSN's framing laid the foundation for coalitions along the route with a diverse assortment of sponsoring organizations to help make local events a success. Nevertheless, the organizations that supported the MSN caravan and formed a coalition with it in each city did not have to share this entire framing of the issue. As indicated in table 7.2, where types of organization are given for each of the five routes, most of them share a social justice perspective, if not one of anti-neoliberalism.

Coalition building was the underlying theme in planning the caravan's routes. The MSN is a network of members, most of whom actively participate in other organizations as well. Routes were organized by MSN interns, with the exception of the West Coast route, which was organized by a formal MSN staff person. The necessary criteria for selecting cities and sponsoring organizations were given by the Washington director of MSN to the organizers: lodging, a meeting place, media, and access to one or more public officials. With these guidelines and the understanding that sponsoring organizations would share at least part of MSN's

TABLE 7.2. Routes for the International Caravan for Justice by Type of Organizational Sponsors, Mexico Solidarity Network, Fall 2004

Type of organization/No.	East route	East Coast route	Midwest route	Southwest route	West Coast route
	Number (Percent) Example	Number (Percent) Example	Number (Percent) Example	Number (Percent) Example	Number (Percent) Example
University department, program, or club/74	8 (20.5) McMaster University Labor Studies/ Canada	33 (57.9) Univ. of Texas at S.A., Women Studies	9 (50.0) Univ. of Missouri Latin American Studies	14 (40.0) Univ. of Wyoming Stop Violence Project	10 (28.6) Portland State Univ. Students for Unity
Latin American school or interest group/23	6 (15.4) Latino Cultural Center	6 (10.5) Mississippi Hispanic Association	4 (22.2) MEChA at Univ. of Wisconsin	4 (11.4) El Centro Amistad	3 (8.6) Casa de La Raza
Local amnesty group/17	3 (7.7) AI Vanderbilt	2 (3.5) AI Club/ Asheville	3 (16.7) AI in St. Louis	2 (5.7) AI in Laramie, Wyoming	7 (20.0) AI Chapter 48
Feminist/16	5 (12.8) Nashville NOW	7 (12.3) Amherst Feminist Alliance	0	3 (8.6) Women in Black	1 (2.9) Blackwhole Collective

Peace and justice group/14	Mid-South Peace and Justice Center 3 (7.7)	Rhizome Collective 4 (7.0)	0	Rocky Mountain Peace & Justice 2 (5.7)	Portland Central America Solidarity 5 (14.3)
Domestic and/or violence group/13	Sexual Assault Centre of Brant 5 (12.8)	Texas Council on Family Violence 1 (1.8)	0	Moving to End Sexual Assault 5 (14.3)	The Riley Center 2 (5.7)
Religious group/10	Thomas Jefferson Unitarian Church 3 (7.7)	St. Rose of Lima Parish in Fair Haven 1 (1.8)	Epiphany Church 2 (11.1)	Friends Meeting Place/Quaker 3 (8.6)	San Xavier Mission 1 (2.9)
Multicultural/9	Pine Tree Native Centre 3 (7.7)	International Link 2 (3.5)	0	The Breakdown Collective 2 (5.7)	Traditions Fair Trade Café 2 (5.7)
Labor group or union/8	Elementary Teachers Federation of Ontario 3 (7.7)	Fuerza Unida 1 (1.8)	0	0	CWA Local 7901 4 (11.4)
Total/184	39 (100)	57 (100.1)	18 (100)	35 (100)	35 (100.1)

framing and concern about the issue, the organizers began to develop their routes. Planning began with pre-existing contacts; from these, the first cities were selected. Additional cities were then targeted because they provided links between coalition events along the journey to Juárez. Table 7.2 lists the types of sponsoring organizations in each city in order of frequency with examples of each type of organization for each of the five routes. At the national level, a sponsor such as Amnesty International's Stop Violence Against Women campaign circulated information throughout its state chapters. Amnesty representatives also helped plan events in both interview sites, San Francisco and Denver.

State-level planning began by enlisting pre-existing contacts through local organizations and delegating responsibilities. Brainstorming sessions led to identification of groups like Latina/o organizations, immigrant organizations (day labor facilities), followed by university groups like Movimiento Estudiantil Chicano de Aztlán (MEChA) and justice centers. This illustrates the way in which a shared framework for understanding issues by multiple organizations across the country provides a supportive network for launching larger campaigns. NGOs use other grassroots organizations on a local level to spread the word of their issues. The local network then does the legwork. The national organization needs to tap into the labor power available through networks of local activists. This relationship is mutually beneficial in that the local activists gain visibility by association with a current issue of social justice and help to maintain the enthusiasm of their own membership. Recruited participants at the local level have much less responsibility, like promoting the event by distributing flyers or building an altar for gifts and offerings or making and selling sweatshop-free t-shirts.

In selecting sponsoring organizations, organizers first looked for groups with sensitivity to the issue. Only with issue sensitivity would organizations be willing to meet the additional criteria. Corresponding to this criteria is the representation of MEChAs, churches, domestic violence shelters, Latina/o organizations, and human rights activists (see table 7.2). Next was the expectation of meeting the needs of the caravans specified originally by the MSN director. There were four informal requirements for host cities: lodging for participants, media contact, a location for the event, and a meeting with public official(s). These criteria dictated the necessity for supporting organizations and institutions with multiple resources. Colleges or universities with International Studies, Latin American Studies, and Women's Studies departments have stipends and meeting rooms to offer, and people with flexible schedules who can plan and organize. This accounts for the high representation of colleges and universities, which were the most frequent type of sponsoring organization. When a respondent contacted by the MSN organizers agreed to meet the necessary requirements, coalition building could go forward in that city.

Organizers' understanding of the Caravan's purpose emphasized that they sought to influence policy and raise awareness through direct contact with individuals and indirectly through mass media coverage. Grassroots public education at the Caravan stops explained how to take appropriate action for this specific issue, because most of the individuals contacted already had some sympathy for the cause. The use of media to mainstream the issue was an attempt to stimulate broader public involvement. Organizers saw mainstreaming as a way to "pull the heartstrings" and develop a more sympathetic public. When it's available, coverage by the mass media provides public legitimacy and spreads awareness of the issue of femicide on the border as well as the role of the global economy in this issue.

Was the Caravan Successful?

The official position of MSN is that the Caravan was highly successful. In the report summarizing the results of the Caravan, they state the following:

> The International Caravan for Justice in Ciudad Juárez and Chihuahua was the largest and most successful international effort to date drawing attention to the decade of largely unresolved femicides in Chihuahua state. Five mothers and one sister of femicide victims accompanied five routes as the caravan traveled from Canada and the northern US, converging in Ciudad Juárez on November 1, 2004. Fifty-three cities hosted the caravan with public events, press conferences and meetings with public officials. Over 7,000 people participated directly in the caravan and millions learned of the situation in Chihuahua via extensive media coverage. The caravan spent six days in Ciudad Juárez

and Chihuahua, participating in public events, marches, public testimonies, meetings with members of Congress and local and state officials, press conferences, and ceremonies. For the first time ever, mothers of the femicide victims met with the governor of Chihuahua and the president of the state Supreme Court (MSN 2004).

In terms of the broader goals of the Caravan, pressure was directed at the Mexican government and the Fox administration during the inauguration of new government officials in the state of Chihuahua. In the United States, the Caravan promoted increased pressure for passage of Representative Solis' then House Resolution 466 and Senator Bingaman's Resolution SR 392.

In terms of the Caravan's organizers, outcomes were evaluated based on the perceived goals and their responsibilities on different routes. State and local organizers viewed the success at a specific point in time, the point at which the event took place in their city. If the event was successful locally, then the campaign was also viewed as successful. The successful outcomes of individual caravan stops were highly contingent on local organizers and their coalition-building efforts. Similarities in construct along separate routes were not planned or inclusive. Nonetheless, there is an undeniable resemblance in each of the five routes in terms of the type of organizational sponsors and the level of local interest (see table 7.2). This is due to the relationship of organizations and groups that are sensitive to the issue being presented and their ability to meet the required needs. This is particularly true for the Southwest and West Coast routes where interviews were conducted.

State-level planning and participation indicate that the MSN is a small organization with few full-time employees. Based on this reality, organizers felt that the campaign did an outstanding job in promoting awareness and creating political pressure. The Caravan was seen as a very effective way of mobilizing people and raising awareness. However, the Caravan also incurred serious financial costs for the MSN, and a repeat of the same strategy is not anticipated. When the number of aggregate hours that went into the production of the campaign was considered by organizers, there was some disappointment. Since the Caravan ran in October 2004, the interviewees involved in organizing the routes and events along the routes have moved on. Internships have ended, and promotion of different issues is supported, but in each individual, the Caravan, like most activism, left a sense of solidarity that continues to motivate organizers to take action and promote awareness of injustice and exploitation.

Conclusions

Femicide continues in Ciudad Juárez. After a brief reprieve in 2004, in which it looked like local and international efforts had finally had an impact, the number of murders of women almost doubled in 2005. International efforts continue as well. In support of International Women's Day 2006, Congresswoman Hilda Solis and Senator Jeff Bingaman reintroduced bipartisan concurrent resolutions (HR 90 and SR 16). The resolutions had passed both houses of the U.S. Congress by the spring of 2006.

In Mexico, one special prosecutor after another has been named by the federal attorney general. Maria López Urbina, who arrived in early 2004, named 120 current and former Chihuahua state government officials as negligent in the murder investigations. After turning over the names to the Chihuahua State Attorney General's Office for possible legal action, she was removed from her post in 2005. Cases against two of the accused were in the courts last fall; other accused officials have sued López Urbina for defamation. She was succeeded as special prosecutor by Mirelli Rocatti, former head of the National Human Rights Commission, who lasted three months in the post. In February 2006, President Fox replaced the Juárez special prosecutor with a new body called the Special Prosecutor's Office Investigating Crimes Related to Violence against Women in the Country, thus taking the focus off Ciudad Juárez (Paterson 2006). At the same time, the attorney general's office created a new federal special prosecutor for crimes against women, naming women's rights lawyer Alicia Elena Pérez Duarte to the position.

The concluding report of the former special prosecutor's office, restricted to the Juárez murders, has disappointed activists in Ciudad Juárez as well as the international NGOs. While supporting the importance of the report's acknowledgement that there had been systematic failures in investigation and prosecution by law enforcement of the Ciudad Juárez murders, Amnesty International criticized the report's attempt to minimize the extent or severity of the murders (Amnesty International 2006).

And yet, there are small signs of change. The Mexican National Institute of Women in a recent survey estimated that forty-five percent of Mexican women have been victims of some sort of violence during their lifetimes. Eight-four percent of the approximately nine million Mexican women who suffer from domestic violence will never report their victimization to the police. Maria Elena Alvarez, the assistant director of the institute, states that "some believe violence is their destiny." However, there is a women's movement in Mexico, which has worked tirelessly on the issue of domestic violence with the result that Mexico's Supreme Court on November 16, 2005, decided that marital rape is illegal.

Are these efforts at the highest levels of the two governments the result of MSN's International Caravan for Justice in the fall of 2004? Are they the result of the march by Amnesty International and V-Day International on Valentine's Day in the spring of that year? Are they the result of popularizing the issue by singers, authors, and movie stars throughout Mexico and parts of the U.S.? Are they the result of the ceaseless efforts to find justice by the parents of the victims? As Charles Tilly writes, it is impossible to trace cause and effect in evaluating social movement campaigns such as the International Caravan for Justice: "Multiple causal chains lead to a plethora of possible effects in a situation where influences other than social movement activity necessarily contribute to the effects" (1999, 268). In this case, the multiple sources of influence on the situation in Juárez greatly exceed our capacity to enumerate. Yet, the attempts to bring justice continue. At the very least, the campaigns mounted by international NGOs continue to keep the issue alive beyond the borders of Mexico and the state of Chihuahua.

The killings continue, and spread. It also becomes obvious that the murders of women are growing in Chihuahua City, in Guatemala, and throughout Latin America, particularly in countries that have yet to recover from devastating civil wars, structural readjustment, or the encroachment of international crime. Kent Paterson, a frequent contributor to the Interhemispheric Resource Center's Americas Program, writes of a "Transnational Parallel State" in which femicide is no longer a local horror:

The social, economic, and political forces transforming the globe and expelling populations across borders likewise put their stamp on the killing of women. Femicides flourish in areas experiencing social upheavals marked by previous or current armed conflicts, violent rivalries between internationally organized criminal groups, the displacement of old economies in favor of new—often illicit—ones and the corruption and weakening of traditional forms of state power. (2006)

Femicide has a long history and is particularly found during periods of profound social and economic disorder. The "witch-craze" that occurred in England in the seventeenth and eighteenth centuries was a way to control women during a period of instability as the dominant religion shifted from Catholic to Protestant, along with a change in political domination and the move toward a more secular society. Additionally, at that time, there were more women than men and consequently women married later or remained single. Like the women workers in maquiladoras, these women were not dominated by men and were actually in direct competition with them. Men were able to continue their control through the fear induced by the "witch-craze," thus enabling a continuing patriarchal structure (Hester 1992, 28–30, 36). In Ciudad Juárez, "witch hunts" make the young, working women of this border city their targets.

Notes

1. See also Joachim 1999 on the international campaign to reframe violence against women as a human rights violation.

2. Parts of the Caravan journey are presented in a documentary by Steev Hise, "On the Edge: The Femicide in Cuidad Juárez."

3. The Amnesty International web page provides more recent accounts of the situation in Ciudad Juárez under its Campaign on Violence Against Women.

4. See sources in Mueller, Hansen, and Qualtire, 2006.

5. In addition to the authors' participating in the Caravan's Phoenix stop, data regarding the International Caravan for Justice was collected from Internet as well as mass media coverage. Interviews were also conducted with participants, members of MSN and supporting organizations. We conducted these interviews both in person and by telephone. The two major interview sites were San Francisco and Denver. Individual interviewees are not identified in the chapter.

6. Mexico Solidarity Network. http://www.mexicosolidarity.org.

7. Interview with field organizer in Phoenix, Arizona, October 2004.

8. See sources in Mueller, Hansen, and Qualtire, 2006.

Transnational Advocacy Networks, International Norms, and Political Change in Mexico

THE MURDERED WOMEN OF CIUDAD JUÁREZ

Olga Aikin Araluce

Translated by Carlos Meléndez and Beatriz Vera

IN CIUDAD JUÁREZ, located in the northern state of Chihuahua on the border with the United States, problems converge, such as drug trafficking, illegal migration and a dramatic growth in population, fueled in recent decades by the manufacturing companies that have attracted thousands of people from the interior of the country, especially women. All of this has turned Ciudad Juárez into a violent and conflictive city. However, since 1993, the number of murders of women and girls has increased astonishingly, at rates higher than men (although the absolute number of men murdered is higher). A considerable number of victims have been young women, aged 15 to 28, who were often brutally beaten, raped and tortured for days before being murdered. Many of the corpses appeared days, weeks or months later, abandoned in empty lots or on the outer limits of the city. At the beginning, the police showed little interest and even hostility toward the families of the victims who reported the murders. The motives for the murders were not clarified, most perpetrators were not captured, and some of those in police custody were declared guilty after torture by the police. Impunity, incompetence, and the refusal of justice made this a national and international scandal by 1999. If, at the beginning, this phenomenon was called the "Dead Women of Ciudad Juárez," now it is referred to as "femicide" and sexist violence against women.

There is no agreement on the number of women who have been murdered or have disappeared. According to the Mexican NGOs involved in the case, there were more than 400 murders and 4,000 disappearances (some of the latter voluntary, others forced perhaps resulting in death) between 1993 and 2005; the Femicide Commission of the Mexican Congress cites between 300 and 500 murdered women in the same period; for the Federal Attorney General's Office (Procuraduría General de la República [PGR]), the number is 379 murders and 47 disappearances.

Despite Mexico's adherence to the 1981 Convention on the Elimination of All Forms of Discrimination Against Women and to the 1988 Inter-American Convention to Prevent, Sanction and Eradicate Violence Against Women, as well as to many other international and regional instruments that regulate violence against women, Mexico did not apply these criteria, language or standards to the Ciudad Juárez problem. Nor did the Mexican authorities frame these phenomena within the categories of gender violence or use gender methodologies for analysis and research in the investigation of the murders, until recently. For a long time, the local authorities conceived the problem in other terms, resorting to explanations that were offensive to the victims and their families, as well as to judicial figures that placed these offenses in the field of honor or passion crimes more than the violation of the women's human rights.

Faced with the inefficiency of the local authorities and the lack of involvement of the federal authorities, a protest network began to form, made up of local organizations that appealed for help from more powerful national and international ones. By 2003, a transnational advocacy network (TAN) for the defense of the rights of women in Ciudad Juárez had consolidated, which included Mexican and international NGOs, as well as the support of international organizations and of governments and parliaments inside and outside Mexico.[1] This network pursued very concrete objectives that would move Mexico toward the observance of international norms, language, and legislation on violence against women and the search for justice for the victims' families. It did not take long for TAN pressure to have an effect on Mexican authorities, who implemented considerable institutional and legislative measures as well as changes in discourse in order to deal with the problem.

Nevertheless, violence on the border continues, and in Ciudad Juárez, the average number of murdered women every year is between twenty-eight and thirty. Therefore, the question is whether the changes implemented by the authorities respond to an instrumental logic that seeks to alleviate the pressure, rather than a real will to change the situation. In this scenario, once pressure disappears, everything will revert to its original status. In this chapter I argue that, although the authorities have responded in rhetorical terms and their behavior has changed, these are directed at appeasement rather than real change. Nonetheless, there are consequences to the changing of discourse: the government is involved in a gradual transformation toward international norms. TAN and the Mexican authorities have generated an intense process of dialogue and information exchange, which transforms the perception and categorization of the Ciudad Juárez phenomenon with long-term effects on the government's approach to gender-based violence. I also argue that, although the Ciudad Juárez problem continues and results are meager, the intense pressure Mexico has received from this transnational/international network has unleashed a process of socialization to international norms in regard to conceptualizing and regulating violence against women in Mexico. In this sense, socialization refers to the induction of new members to preferred forms of behavior (Risse and Sikkink 1999). Through a process of socialization, the noncompliant gradually move toward a vision and methodology that adhere to accepted standards in the international society. In the twenty-first century, TANs are vital actors for the expansion of these processes because, besides using a whole range of pressure techniques, they open vast public debates over the struggle for meaning and interpretation.

Transnational advocacy networks have, under certain conditions, the capacity to generate processes of socialization to international norms. Although their power is not economic or military, they have the ability to place human rights problems within international criteria and frameworks, push for their inclusion in political agendas, and convince governments—through lobbying, persuasion, and even coercion—to comply with their international obligations. Strong and sustained transnational pressure, together with government's material and moral vulnerability, are ideal conditions for the success of these networks. In this respect, the Mexican government has been vulnerable to pressure, due to its liberal image and the commitment to human rights that President Vicente Fox has tried to project internationally.

According to the social constructivist approach, the objectives, identities, and behaviors of states are subject to political norms and ideas prevailing at a given moment (Finnemore 1996). Mexico is engrossed in an international social structure where the legislation, institutionalization and monitoring of human rights are important parts of the political agenda. This is a contextual condition from which Mexico cannot easily escape, since it must be logically consistent with the liberal identity it is trying to project. TANs, appealing to this liberal identity, can provoke certain readjustments in the country's preferences and change its behavior.

The concept of socialization used in this chapter includes two apparently incompatible behaviors: the instrumental and rhetorical behavior used by governments to "get by," which is present in the beginning stages of socialization, and the argumentative behavior, where authorities show a greater openness and disposition to readjust their approaches to the problem under debate (Risse 2000a). Even though the instrumental logic predominates in the beginning stages of the socialization process, this is not often the end of the story. When international pressure is strong and sustained over a period of time, a more argumentative behavior emerges within the target authorities, one that challenges their preferences, identities and definition of the problem under discussion. Although the authorities may persist on an instrumental behavior, the more they discuss and argue with their critics, the more they entangle themselves in discourses and promises from which they cannot easily escape in the future. This is the process of self-entrapment that occurs through different stages, as described by Risse and Sikkink in their model of socialization of human rights norms (1999).

In this chapter, I describe the principal nodes within the advocacy network created for the Ciudad Juárez case, and I analyze the impact that transnational pressure has had on a specific Mexican authority, the Federal Attorney General's Office (PGR). In order to do this, I monitored how the discourse and conceptualization of the problem developed locally and federally and how these changes rendered concrete measures and actions closer to the fulfillment of international norms and laws.

TAN: For the Defense of the Rights of Women in Ciudad Juárez

This story, like many others in the human rights field, begins in the local sphere, specifically in Ciudad Juárez. In 1994, due to the increase of disappearances and murders of women, several local NGOs began to state publicly the lack of interest the local authorities showed to this problem. The fact that petitions by small groups of mothers of the victims were systematically ignored, together with an openly offensive discourse towards the victims, fostered national indignation. By 1998, the movement had the support of many national NGOs dedicated to human rights and women's issues, the National Human Rights Commission, as well as an important group of federal congresswomen. Although by 1999 the international media began mentioning the topic, the local authorities did not respond to society's demands and the federal authorities kept silent or denied that problems existed.

Lacking internal responses from authorities, international appeals were the only way to gain pressure for change. Since the visit by Asma Jahangir, the United Nations Special Rapporteur on Extrajudicial, Summary and Arbitrary Executions and the publication of her critical report, which defines the events in Ciudad Juárez as "a typical example of a sexist crime aided by impunity" (Jahangir 1999), the intervention of foreign organizations in support of the local and national groups has not ceased (see table 8.1).

Since then, the case opened in the United Nations Human Rights Commission and its many Special Rapporteurs. The case has also been addressed by the Convention on the Elimination of Discrimination Against Women (CEDAW), the United Nations Office on Drugs and Crime, and the Inter-American Commission on Human Rights.

The heart of a TAN is usually located at the local or domestic level, where firsthand information is generated, pressure from within is created, and international aid petitioned. This generates the characteristic "boomerang effect" through which, in the presence of a blockage in negotiations between national groups and the government, the former bypasses the latter and finds international allies that can pressure from abroad (Risse 2000a). Accordingly, visible local organizations were formed: Justice for Our Daughters, Our Daughters Returned Home, and Casa Amiga are three groups started by mothers of victims. The Mexican NGO Commission for the Defense and Promotion of Human Rights supported these organizations by providing judicial council and trying to elevate their demands to international organizations. Also, other key actors intervened with more international prominence and

TABLE 8.1. Chronological List of the Most Important Visits and
Reports on the Murders and Disappearances of Women in Ciudad Juárez

1998	The National Human Rights Commission emits Recommendation number 44/98: The murdered women in Ciudad Juárez and the lack of collaboration of the authorities of the Federal Attorney General's Office of the State of Chihuahua.
1999	Report by the Rapporteur Asma Jahangir, in relation to extrajudicial, summary and arbitrary executions (November).
2001	Visit by the Special Rapporteur on the Independence of Judges and Lawyers (May).
2002	Report by the Special Rapporteur on the Independence of Judges (January).
2003	Report by the Rapporteur on Women's Human Rights of the Inter-American Commission on Human Rights, Marta Altoaguirre: Women's rights' situation in Ciudad Juárez, Mexico: The right not to be an object of violence and discrimination (March).
	Report by Amnesty International: Intolerable Deaths. Ten years of disappearances and murders of women in Ciudad Juárez, Chihuahua (March).
	Visit to Ciudad Juárez by a delegation from the Congress of the United States lead by Congresswoman Hilda Solis (October).
	Report by the National Human Rights Commission on the murders and disappearances of women in Ciudad Juárez, Chihuahua (November).
	Report by the International Experts Commission of the United Nations Office on Drugs and Crime on its mission to Ciudad Juárez (November).
	Diagnostic on Human Rights in Mexico presented by the Office of the High Commissioner of the United Nations in Mexico (December).
2004	Visit by the Rapporteur of the European Parliamentary Assembly of the European Council to Mexico (February). Her report was finalized, and two resolutions on Ciudad Juárez passed.
2005	Report on Mexico by the Committee for the Elimination of Discrimination against Women (CEDAW) under article 8 of the Facultative Protocol of the Convention and the Mexican Government answer to it (January).
	Visit to Mexico by the United Nations Special Rapporteur on Violence against Women, Yakin Ertük (February).
2006	U.S. Congress and Senate Resolutions (90 and 16) on the Murders of Women in Ciudad Juárez (May).

moral authority, such as Amnesty International, feminist organizations like Violence Against Women International (V-Day International), and U.S. NGOs specialized in Latin America, such as the Mexico Solidarity Network (MSN) and the Washington Office for Latin America (WOLA). These organizations helped the case to become known internationally and to put very specific pressure on the Mexican authorities, producing a shaming effect. This domestic and international pressure did not fall on barren soil, and it can be said that 2003 was the year of international denunciations and the year that international accusations gained world-wide visibility. It is since that year that we see a response from the Mexican authorities that, although to this date is still unsatisfactory, shows certain political will to resolve the situation.

The most important recommendations made to the Mexican authorities by the Ciudad Juárez TAN are the following:

- To acknowledge that the murders and disappearances of women in Ciudad Juárez is a national problem, not just a local one, recognizing the responsibility of the Mexican government as a whole and thus favoring federal intervention.
- To adopt a gender perspective in the investigation of the crimes, the prevention of further violence, as well as in the creation and implementation of public policies designed to stop violence against women, according to international standards.
- To hold accountable the state of Chihuahua public officials whose negligence, abuse and possible complicity have allowed the killings to go unpunished.
- To promote the participation of authorities from all three levels of government (federal, state and local) and ideally allow the federal government to investigate all crimes.
- To adopt the necessary measures to protect the life of human rights advocates.
- To make authorities and public officers aware of human rights and gender perspectives.
- To promote dialogue and cooperation with Mexican civil society and the victims' families in order to find a solution to the problem.

Although the Mexican authorities were bothered by the deluge of criticisms and suggestions, they have tried to incorporate these recommendations into their policies and programs, but often more in their rhetoric than in their practices.

The Socialization Process in the PGR

In this section, I analyze the effects that pressure and scrutiny have had on one of the most important federal authorities in the Juárez case. The PGR has the authority to review the investigations into the Juárez women's murders to establish if the federal authorities can claim jurisdiction over any of the cases and to determine if justice officials from the state of Chihuahua committed administrative or criminal offenses in their handling of the investigations. (Murder is a state crime but federal authorities can intervene if the murder relates to a federal crime.) I argue that the PGR has responded to the previously mentioned transnational pressure and that it has recently begun to use the language and methodologies on violence against women that are internationally accepted. In addition, some incipient socialization has taken place within this authority: a process of discursive, converging rapprochement between the TAN and the PGR around the perception, conceptualization, and ways to solve the Juárez problem. In order to illustrate this process of convergence, I have applied to the case the socialization model of international human rights norms proposed by Risse and Sikkink (1999). Accordingly I have divided this incipient process of socialization into three stages. Each one of them is analyzed below.

First stage (1993–2001): Denial by the State Authorities

During this first stage, the federal authorities were not involved and the local authorities denied the existence of a human rights problem in Ciudad Juárez. The problem was seen as a phenomenon of a violent and conflictive border and a matter of local concern, a series of state crimes whose jurisdiction corresponded exclusively to the local authorities. The murders were catalogued as "crimes of passion," their numbers were considered "normal," and it was even said that the victims "provoked" them. "They are women of doubtful conduct. They are responsible for what happens to them because of the life they lead. They lead a double life and therefore they are exposing themselves to be killed," declared the

PAN governor of the state of Chihuahua, Francisco Barrio Terrazas, to the *El Norte* newspaper in 1998.

Although Governor Barrio ignored the complaints and petitions presented by local organizations, by 1998 and because of pressure by the Commission on Equality and Gender of the Mexican Senate and the National Human Rights Commission, he finally agreed to a petition made years before by local organizations: the creation of a Special Public Prosecutor's Office to Investigate Women's Murders. Its first director was Sully Ponce. Even though a concession on the authority's part, by 1999 Ms. Ponce declared, as part of the new PRI state government led by Governor Patricio Martínez, that her office would only investigate murders that happened after 1998. The past was buried and files were abandoned, incomplete, or even destroyed, and again, justice was denied. The new administration blamed the previous one, politicized the matter, and insisted on dividing the crimes into periods of government and between political parties in power. The new governor stated:

> I tell the people of Chihuahua; how they can ask us to solve the crimes when all we received from the previous administration was 21 bags of bones? We don't know the circumstances under which these crimes occurred. The files are poorly integrated [a technical meaning, for credible prosecution]. How can we investigate these murders? (Acuña Herrera 1999).

Another important characteristic in this stage of denial is that both administrations, PAN and PRI, did not initially accept the scrutiny of any type of organization, from inside or outside Mexico. Thus, in 1998, they rejected the recommendation made by the National Human Rights Commission, which exposed the "negligence, sexism and discrimination of the state attorney general's office in charge of investigating the more than 200 murders of women since 1993" (Comisión Nacional de Derechos Humanos 1998).

When the Special Rapporteur on Extrajudicial, Summary and Arbitrary Executions, Asma Jahangir, visited Chihuahua and talked to the authorities and to the head of the special public prosecutor's office, she declared that what was happening there was a clear sign of gender violence and impunity on the part of the authorities. Director Sully Ponce of the special public prosecutor's office declared that the rapporteur's vision was "distorted and exaggerated" and that the crimes were close to being solved (Cimacnoticias 1999).

If the local authorities showed intolerance towards national or international criticism, towards local criticism they were relentless. During this first stage and even years later, domestic and international organizations accused the state authorities of Chihuahua of harassing and discrediting the victims' families and human rights activists. This generalized pattern of denial propitiated the "boomerang effect," an appeal to foreign organizations that are able to generate from abroad greater pressure on the Mexican authorities.

Second Stage (2001–2003): Instrumental Adaptation and Strategic Bargaining

In this second stage, we see a progressive involvement of the PGR in the Ciudad Juárez problem, even if it is still labeled as a local matter. During this period the domestic network becomes transnational and, by 2003, all the weight of international pressure is felt by the Mexican authorities.

During this period the PGR opened up to foreign and national scrutiny and adopted measures that claimed to respond to the recommendations of the international institutions and NGOs involved in the matter. It created inter-institutional security programs involving state and federal agencies and participated in the investigations of Juárez together with the Justice Department of the state of Chihuahua, thus creating the Joint Investigation Agency for Homicides of Women in Ciudad Juárez. For the first time, timidly and with great hesitation, the debate over bringing the entire load of cases under federal authority emerged, that is, in the face of incompetence shown by local authorities. At the same time, the Ciudad Juárez phenomenon is seen as a problem of "National Security" and a matter of utmost priority in Mexico, also emphasizing the need to allow the participation of Mexican civil society in the solutions to justice, whether for public safety or national security.

Even though there were advances and political will at this stage, compared to the previous one, it seems that the authorities moved more in the field of rhetorical discourse than in the real fulfillment of international recommendations, perhaps with the intention of gaining time by waiting for international accusations to die down and alleviating the pressure through the appearance of "adequate" discourse. In the reports and public decla-rations, the attorney general of the PGR and his working team still did not see gender discrimination, as the TAN for Juárez had proposed, as one of the fundamental causes of violence against women in Ciudad Juárez. The PGR still argued that reasons underlying violence against women relate mainly to issues such as the context of a violent border, underdevelop-ment and decay of the social fabric of Ciudad Juárez. The term "crimes of passion" was still used in public statements and reports to refer to these murders, a term that the IAHRC suggests is in itself a violation of women's human rights due to an implicit discriminatory justification based on sexist ideas of the acceptable behavior of women. Lastly, dur-ing this phase the gender perspective did not permeate the investigative methodologies used by the police and public officials, which, in turn, did not permit them to comply correctly with international recommenda-tions because the real motives for the crimes were being ignored.

Third Stage (2004–2006): Tentative Engagement with International Norms about Violence Against Women

During this third stage, in the heart of the "boomerang" effect that the avalanche of international reports, public accusations and discredit cam-paigns supported, the PGR showed an argumentative behavior in the communication with its critics. Although instrumental and rhetorical behavior still persisted, this agency showed a new understanding of the Ciudad Juárez problem.

The Ciudad Juárez phenomenon, far from being just a simple local problem of local jurisdiction, was announced as a case of massive viola-tions of women's human rights with serious international consequences. For the first time, in March 2004, the attorney general of PGR used the term "gender violence" to refer to the phenomenon. This happened during the presentation of the National Campaign for the Equality and Safety of Women that same year, when he said that the campaign was based on a "gender perspective" (PGR 2004a).

As a show of good will, the PGR created in January 2004 a Special Prosecutor's Office to deal with the murders and disappearances in Ciu-dad Juárez. This special prosecutor's office took some of the murders under its jurisdiction (the ones that seemed to have federal implications) and reviewed all the files on the Ciudad Juárez murders. It also investigated and documented the cases that presented negligence or inefficiency on the part of the public servants of the state of Chihuahua. In its final report in January 2006, this office explained the Ciudad Juárez phenomenon retrospectively and tried to formulate an integrated explanation. However, this report was not consistent with the domestic and international recommendations to which it supposedly responded. It could be interpreted as a document whose final objective consisted in going through the motions and allowing the Fox administration to exit with a minimum of decorum, although with doubtful respectability in the eyes of the international community. Several arguments validate this vision:

- The report did not adopt the criteria established by international norms since it did not consider violence against women as a manifestation of gender discrimination. In fact, it neither recognized nor used the terms of gender violence or of femicide.
- Lacking a gender perspective approach, the crimes were not classified or conceptualized correctly. For example, the PGR concluded that only the crimes involving sexual violence constituted gender violence and that family-based violence or other forms of violence did not belong in this category.
- The report did not open new investigations to include new evidence or cross-examination of witnesses. It was only based on poorly integrated investigations made by local authorities.
- Even if the report showed that 177 state officials were possibly responsible for negligence, abuse, or omissions in the investigations, none of them were held accountable by the state authorities due to the statute of limitations working in their favor.

This report provoked, once again, a deluge of criticisms and accusations from the advocacy network. However, in February 2006, this special prosecutor's office was closed and replaced with one that had wider, national jurisdiction. This new agency is called the Prosecutor's Office for the Attention of Crimes related to Acts of Violence against Women in the Country. As I will later argue, there are important changes in the creation of this new office.

Although the special prosecutor's office did not fulfill the expectations of many, during this third stage of socialization we can see certain changes in the PGR's discourse and behavior which could be interpreted as socialization to the international language and standards concerning violence against women. Three specific issues support this idea. I will analyze each of them in the following paragraphs.

The Federal Human Rights Clause: The Proposal for Constitutional Reform

In April 2004, President Fox sent a constitutional reform proposal prepared by the PGR to the Senate. This document proposed a reform of Article 73, Part XXI, of the Mexican Federal Constitution. Once passed, the so-called Federal Human Rights Clause would permit federal authorities to obtain complete information on crimes related to violations of human rights when these, due to their magnitude, transcend the jurisdiction of the states. This proposed reform arose as a consequence of the lessons learned in the Ciudad Juárez case and responded to the need to further adapt the Mexican federal structure to international obligations contracted by Mexico, thus giving priority to compliance with international human rights standards beyond the existing Mexican federal structure. If passed, this proposal would mean a partial modification of Mexican sovereignty, specifically the federal pact. Although the Federal Human Rights Clause could be interpreted as a government strategy to project a good international image at the end of the Fox administration, if approved, it would obligate Mexico in the future by creating tighter accountability in the context of international norms.

PGR's Progressive Acceptance of Two Key Concepts: Femicide and Gender Discrimination

During the three phases described above, a fundamental struggle between the Mexican authorities and the advocacy network occurred: the struggle for meaning in the way in which the Juárez problem has been conceptualized and, therefore, the way it is dealt with. While the local authorities and the PGR keep using terms such as "serial sexual crimes," "social violence," or "crimes of passion" to define the problem, the TAN insists that it constitutes gender violence.

According to international legislation, violence against women is understood to be "any action or conduct, based on gender, which causes death, harm or physical, sexual, or psychological suffering to women" (Article 1 of the Inter-American Convention on the Elimination of All Forms of Discrimination Against Women). The CEDAW has also recognized, in its Recommendation 19, the close relationship that exists between sexual violence and sexist discrimination. Therefore, in its 2005 report, it recommended that the Mexican authorities incorporate a gender perspective in their investigations and policies for the prevention of violence against women. In Mexico there has been an interesting adaptation of these concepts to the Juárez case. The term "feminicidio" has been created and has been consistently used by the national press as well as most of the TAN since 2001. Monárrez Fragoso, the Mexican academic who adapted the term from English, defines it as "the misogynous murder of women committed by men from a perceived superiority of gender" and as "continuous and systematic violence that ends in a woman's death" (2003). Thus conceptualized, she explains, femicide describes conditions of inequality between the genders:

> The Ciudad Juárez murders also respond to structural changes in society, to the high level of violence and the presence of drug trafficking, the industrialization and migration processes. Nevertheless what has happened in this border will never be clarified, if gender is not taken into consideration as an essential element of social relationships based on the differences that distinguish the sexes and a primary form of significant power relationships (Monárrez Fragoso 2002).

Even if, during the first two stages, the resistance of the PGR to accept the terms "gender discrimination" and "femicide" can be observed, during the last phase a public debate began that discussed the resistance as well as the confusion and rhetoric that the authorities fall into when interpreting these terms.

Marcela Lagarde, president of the Commission on Femicide (created in 2004 in the Mexican House of Representatives to investigate and act on the femicide problem in Mexico), has emphasized repeatedly how important it is that the PGR adopts new ways of analyzing and categorizing the problem:

> We are not talking of just crimes against women. Talking about femicide is not feminizing the word homicide. We are talking about a serious problem of gender violence against women and we have noticed that for those concerned with the problem, there is no gender perspective (PGR 2004b).

In answer to the multiple explanations that authorities used (lovers' quarrels, drug traffickers, etc.), Lagarde considered that gender-based violence and femicide produced a paradigm shift in the conception of the phenomenon. She also said that family violence is also part of this category, not because there may have been sexual violence, but because there was violence caused by discrimination based on gender differences (PGR 2004b). To acknowledge that femicide exists in Mexico is "painful," in Lagarde's words, and implies facing the phenomenon not only in the state of Chihuahua but also in the rest of the country through an integral and inter-institutional policy. This implies tasks such as investigating its causes, creating gender-disaggregated statistics, modifying sociocultural patterns among the population and public servants, permeating public policies with a gender perspective, eliminating legislative discrimination against women, and categorizing femicide in the law.

Even though, during 2004, the PGR only occasionally and distortedly used the terms femicide and gender-based violence in its public statement, by 2006 there was further progress. The attorney general, Daniel Cabeza de Vaca, frequently used both terms during a presentation at the Senate before the Commission for Equity and Gender and the Commission on Femicide. On that occasion, he stressed that his office and working team would adopt such terms in their working programs and that the newly created Public Prosecutor's Office for the Attention of Crimes Related to Violence Against Women would adopt a gender perspective as a key goal.

Some guarantees exist for moving these public comments beyond rhetoric. The new Public Prosecutor's Office was created as a result of a petition issued to the PGR by the Commission for Equity and Gender and the Commission on Femicide, both of which were deeply involved in its conception, establishment, and agenda. The head of this office is

Alicia Elena Pérez Duarte, a well-recognized feminist with ample experience in the field of human rights who formerly worked on the Juárez problem within the above-mentioned commissions.

The Creation of the Public Prosecutor's Office for the Attention to Crimes Related to Violence Against Women in the Country

This office—in Spanish, Fiscalía Especial para la Atención de Delitos Relacionados con Actos de Violencia contra las Mujeres en el País (or FEVIM)—is the first permanent organization within the PGR and in Mexico created for the attention to crimes related to violence against women. One of the demands posed by the Commission on Femicide and the Commission on Equity and Gender was that this office be headed by a person whose professionalism guaranteed the observance of gender perspectives and methodologies. In this respect Alicia Elena Pérez Duarte is the first recognized feminist to become part of PGR's structure.

FEVIM's official web site explicitly states—following international standards—that violence against women is a result of gender discrimination, and thus incorporated the gender perspective as a fundamental working tool of the agency. FEVIM has competence over crimes occurring in different states of the country in cases of "serious and systematic violations of women or girls' human rights, or when these crimes affect several states of the Republic, are of high social impact, or organized crime is involved, or national security is placed at risk, or when the National Human Rights Commission recommends it."[2]

This advance is substantial because it will permit the PGR to take on cases of women's human rights violations, such as in Ciudad Juárez, where there are systematic and massive violations. This exception to the Mexican Federal Pact could favor compliance with international legislation on women's human rights.

Conclusion

To accept that violence against women is based on gender discrimination and on the historical unequal relations between women and men, and to use the term "femicide" to describe the extreme violence occurring in Ciudad Juárez and in the rest of the country, has definite political and legal consequences. This progressive acceptance (present in some government offices but still resisted by others, especially local ones) has made the Mexican authorities recognize their responsibility for the problem and act on that response by creating institutions specialized in violence against women, as well as new legislation. By January 2007, the Mexican Federal Congress passed the Law on Women's Access to a Life Free of Violence, which typified, among other forms of gender violence, femicide.[3] This illustrates that changes in discourse often have unexpected consequences for governments, obligating them to enter a spiral of changes also pushed by the monitoring processes implemented by transnational advocacy networks. This progressive acceptance, by the Mexican government, of the language proposed by the network, additionally submerging Mexico in political reform processes, made it possible to go from a phase of instrumental rationality to an argumentative one, which additionally implies not only "acceptance" but also "practicing" even as it begins in an incipient way. As such, this is the final phase of socialization, that of institutionalization and habituation.

According to the socialization model of international norms proposed by Risse and Sikkink, after advancing through the stages of denial, instrumental adaptation and argumentation, the offending governments, given the necessary conditions, usually enter the last stage, institutionalization and adaptation. In this stage, international human rights norms are incorporated into internal law and respected; that is, they are socialized into national practices (1999, 2000). However, in the Juárez case, Mexico seems still to be far from reaching this last stage in day-to-day practices. Justice, now and in the near future, seems just a mirage. For institutionalization to occur, deep reform is necessary in the country's justice system, still permeated by impunity and corruption. The road is long, as are the centuries of inefficient law enforcement, devoid of respect for human rights.

Nevertheless, Ciudad Juárez represents a paradigmatic case not only in Mexico but also in all of Latin America. The Juárez case jumped to the world stage and brought to light the existence of this phenomenon, which had been invisible, not only in Mexico but also in other parts of the continent. Femicide is now in the public agenda and denounces not only cases where there is extreme sexual violence but also those in which there is family violence, which is much more frequent and socially accepted.

Femicide, as a concept, has been a novel contribution made by the Mexican network. Not only is it being socialized by the Mexican civil society and authorities, but also at an international level, specifically in the Inter-American system. Not only are there present proposals for its legislation in Mexico, but also in the International Criminal Court for its standardization as a crime against humanity. This is an example of how TANs can modify government's behavior regarding human rights issues, but also an example of how, under certain circumstances, they can influence the creation of new international legislation and standards.

On March 6, 2006, several NGOs from Mexico, Guatemala, Peru, Bolivia and Paraguay presented a report titled "Femicide in Latin America: A Regional Problem" to the Inter-American Human Rights Defense Commission. The purpose of the report was to position the problem of femicide in Latin America. In this document, concern for the increase of violence against women in the region was expressed. It recognizes that this type of violence is being ignored and underestimated by society and the authorities, and urges governments to respond efficiently and firmly to the systematic violation of women's human rights. As well, it calls for national organizations to work together on this problem and to divulge the true situation in Latin America. Femicide is no longer a Mexican border problem. The Ciudad Juárez network has noticeably widened its agenda. This phenomenon, if it remains in the political agenda and if it is legislated at different levels, will elevate the cost of impunity, the cost for justice officers guilty of omission or negligence, the cost for the criminals who commit these crimes, and the political cost, the loss of prestige, for the country that decides not to take matters in hand.

Notes

1. This chapter uses the concept of TAN created by Kathryn Sikkink and Margeret Keck, which they define as "a series of actors who work internationally in the defense of a given cause and who share common values and discourses as well as dense exchanges of information and services" (1998, 1).

2. http://www.pgr.gob.mx/fevim/home (accessed September 2006).

3. This law defines femicide as "the extreme form of gender violence against women, a product of the violation of their human rights, in public and private places, in line with a series of misogynous behaviors which can entail social and official impunity and can end up in murder and other forms of violent death to women" (Foreign Affairs Ministry 2007).

9

Human Trafficking and Protections for Undocumented Victims in the United States

David A. Shirk and Alexandra T. Webber

THE U.S. STATE DEPARTMENT has calculated that since 2004 approximately six to eight hundred thousand people cross international borders as victims of human trafficking each year around the world (USDOS 2004, 2005). Distinct from the smuggling of willing migrants from one country to another, human trafficking refers to the use of coercion for the purpose of labor, sexual, or other exploitation. The phenomenon is commonly described as a modern form of slavery, though the legal definition incorporates a wide variety of exploitive activities, including indentured servitude, child sexual exploitation, and forced prostitution.

The perpetrators of human trafficking often lure their victims into a compromised situation in which they are compelled to accept undesirable terms of service. In the most problematic cases, victims are socialized to become active and willing participants, making it difficult to determine if a person has been coerced or otherwise "exploited." Migrants, especially undocumented persons, are believed to be particularly vulnerable to these forms of exploitation because they often lack the means or legal recourse to challenge their exploiters. By virtue of their immigration status, for example, undocumented persons can be easily intimidated to accept illicit working conditions, work without pay, and other abuses by employers that, under specific conditions, can be classified as "human trafficking."

Yet, it is not clear what portion of the estimated 12 million unauthorized persons living in the United States fall victim to human trafficking. Government estimates of human trafficking have varied widely in the last decade, with recent figures far lower than earlier estimates. In 2000, the U.S. government estimated that 45,000 to 50,000 women and children alone were trafficked into the country annually. After 2004, however, government figures dropped to between 14,500 and 17,500 (Richard 2000). The government attributes the large difference between the 2000 and 2004 estimates to improvement in its methodology for calculating the flow of trafficking victims and not to an actual reduction in the rate of victimization, although the methodology for these estimates is not explained (USDOS 2004). As we discuss later, the number of cases of human trafficking detected and prosecuted is minuscule in comparison to government estimates of the problem.

This said, there are significant concrete instances of exploitation that legally constitute human trafficking in the United States. In June 2002, for example, the *New York Times* reported the case of forty farm laborers forced into indentured servitude in Albion, New York. This followed the infamous case of dozens of deaf Mexicans trafficked and exploited as panhandlers in New York City in 1997 (USDOS 2004, 2005). Also troubling are instances of migrant laborers forced to pay smuggler's fees through indentured servitude, or kidnapped to work for rival gangs of smugglers along the border.

Yet such cases of labor exploitation receive far less government attention in efforts to combat domestic human trafficking than instances of forced prostitution and other forms of commercial sexual exploitation. This is partly due to the fact that human trafficking is more commonly associated with "sexual slavery," particularly in the international arena. The U.S. State Department estimates that between 70 and 80 percent of human trafficking victims worldwide are female, with 70 percent of these women and girls experiencing forced commercial sexual exploitation (USDOS 2004, 23).[1] While comparable official data is unavailable regarding the nature of domestic victimization, recent research suggests that sexual exploitation may not account for such a large share of trafficking cases in the United States. A survey of 131 reported incidents of human trafficking in the United States between 1998 and 2003 revealed that 46 percent involved forced sexual exploitation, while the remaining 54 percent involved forced labor exploitation ("Free the Slaves" 2004). More research is arguably needed to properly document distinct forms of human trafficking to test the government's assumption that sexual exploitation is the predominant type of trafficking in the United States.

In the meantime, it is clear that in recent years the Department of Justice has devoted far greater resources to the investigation of sex trafficking

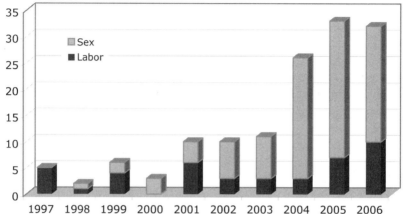

FIGURE 9.1. Trafficking prosecution cases filed by the U.S. Department of Justice, FY 1997–2006. (USDOJ 2005)

cases than to labor trafficking cases (Tenorio 2005). The proportion of forced sexual exploitation cases among all trafficking prosecution cases filed by the Department of Justice grew from 40 percent in fiscal year (FY) 2001 to nearly 90 percent in FY 2004 (see fig. 9.1) (USDOJ 2005). Government efforts to address labor trafficking cases improved in 2005 and 2006, but the overwhelming majority of human trafficking cases prosecuted remained focused on sexual exploitation. One explanation may be that addressing severe forms of domestic labor exploitation would place the government in the politically uncomfortable position of defending the rights of undocumented workers.

Human Trafficking as an Immigration Problem

While the full dimensions of human trafficking remain unknown, it is clear that within the United States trafficking is a crime primarily perpetrated against undocumented migrants. Human traffickers usually target individuals desperate to migrate to improve their economic situation, who often do not realize that they are being victimized. Traffickers often use promises of safe passage to and employment in the United States as a carrot to gain control of their victims, and later exploit them for commercial sex or forced labor (U.S. Department of Justice 2005, 2).

Hence, although immigrant smuggling and human trafficking are different, the line between the two is often blurred as traffickers exploit immigrant smuggling operations to find new victims. Some smugglers offer migrants the opportunity to pay their smuggling fees after entry to the United States, often charging usurious interest rates and costs for room and board. Smugglers may also extort their clients for additional money—or force them to "work off" new debt—before or after smuggling them into the country. Scenarios such as these amount to forms of debt bondage. In addition, once in the United States, smugglers or employers can easily threaten undocumented migrants with exposure to law enforcement and deportation, making them vulnerable to a variety of forms of exploitation. Reports of human trafficking cases provide ample supporting evidence of such abuses (USDOJ 2005).

Recent trends in both immigration to the United States and in U.S. border enforcement suggest that a growing number of undocumented immigrants are at risk of becoming trafficking victims. Women and children, who are particularly vulnerable to trafficking, comprise a greater proportion of undocumented immigrants to the United States than in the past. Moreover, despite high U.S. labor demand, many would-be migrants from less-developed countries do not qualify for legal admittance into the United States due to limited country quotas and the prioritization of family reunification over employment-based immigration. Lured by U.S. employers who face little interior enforcement by immigration authorities, and confronted over the past decade with heightened security measures at U.S. ports of entry, undocumented immigrants increasingly rely on smugglers, who are uniquely positioned to engage in both labor and sexual exploitation (Shirk and Webber 2004).

Above all, human trafficking appears to be yet another unfortunate outgrowth of the current wave of global migration and the inability of U.S. policy makers to respond effectively to it. Comprehensive immigration reform in the United States would go a long way toward reducing the problem of human trafficking. If granted a means to legal immigration status, millions of people who are currently susceptible to dangerous and exploitative labor situations would have access to the same legal protections as citizens and other foreign residents. Without such provisions, Congress has resorted to a series of half-measures and baffling expedients intended to protect victims of human trafficking, with little measurable impact. Below we consider the nature of the government's response to this problem in more detail, with special consideration of the Victims of Trafficking and Violence Protection Act of 2000 and the various protections available to victims of trafficking in the United States (USDOS 2000).

The Trafficking Victims Protection Act of 2000

In 2002, authorities uncovered a prostitution ring that brought hundreds of men to an outdoor brothel to have sex with thirty women and girls at fifteen to twenty dollars per visit. Nearly half of the women were minors and the youngest was estimated to be aged 12. When authorities raided the camp, they found fifteen women and arrested thirty men, mostly undocumented migrants who were later deported. However, federal prosecutors were unable to build a case because only one of the fifteen women (a sixteen-year-old girl) was willing to testify, and the main organizers of the trafficking ring were not captured in the raid. Cases such as this one illustrate the difficulty of combating human trafficking in the United States, since victims often lack legal residency and are reluctant witnesses against their exploiters for fear of retribution.

With the dual intent of providing humanitarian protections to undocumented trafficking victims and enhancing prosecutions of traffickers in precisely such cases, Congress passed the Victims of Trafficking and Violence Protection Act on October 28, 2000 (USDOS 2000). This act became the first law in the United States to categorize human trafficking as a distinct criminal offense with specific penalties. Furthermore, the law represented a significant shift in U.S. immigration law and policy in that it extended temporary nonimmigration status and public benefits to undocumented immigrants who are victims of a "severe" form of human trafficking. Under Division A of the act, which is entitled Trafficking Victims Protection Act of 2000 (TVPA), a severe form of trafficking is defined as "(A) sex trafficking in which a commercial sex act is induced by force, fraud, or coercion, or in which the person induced to perform such act has not attained 18 years of age; or (B) the recruitment, harboring, transportation, provision, or obtaining of a person for labor or services, through the use of force, fraud, or coercion for the purpose of subjection to involuntary servitude, peonage, debt bondage, or slavery" (USDOS 2000, Div. A, Sec. 103 [8]).

Prior to passage of the TVPA, trafficking victims were generally subject to incarceration and removal from the United States based on their unlawful presence in the country. As a result, they were deprived of the opportunity to receive critical aid typically available to crime victims or to assist in the prosecution of their traffickers. Under the TVPA, temporary nonimmigration status is available to qualifying victims either through "continued presence" or a "T-visa." Additionally, even before obtaining continued presence or a T-visa, victims may be eligible for public benefits. We discuss these provisions below.

T-Visa

In recognition of the dangers that trafficking victims may face if returned to their country of origin and the need for victims to testify against traffickers, the T-visa provides a three-year safe haven to remain in the United States. The TVPA permits a maximum of five thousand T-visas each year for victims of severe forms of human trafficking, as well as opportunities for the victim's immediate family to apply for derivative T-visas. Moreover, the TVPA allows the possibility for qualifying T-visa recipients to adjust from temporary nonimmigrant status to legal permanent resident status (USDOS 2000, Div. A, Sec. 107).

To be eligible for a T-visa, undocumented victims of human trafficking must meet each of five mandatory conditions:

1. *Severe Forms of Trafficking*: Victims must prove they suffered a severe form of human trafficking. As explained by the T-visa regulations, "[e]xcept in instances of sex trafficking involving minors, severe forms of trafficking in persons must involve both a particular means (force, fraud, or coercion) and a particular end (sex trafficking, involuntary servitude, peonage, debt bondage, or slavery)" (USDOJ INS 2002, 7).

2. *Physical Presence*: Victims must prove they are "physically present in the United States, American Samoa, or the Commonwealth of the Northern Mariana Islands, or at a port-of-entry thereto, on account of such trafficking" (USDOJ INS 2002, 5). T-visa regulations explain that noncitizen victims who entered the United States either legally or illegally may be considered physically present (USDOS 2000, Div. A, Sec. 107).

3. *Extreme Hardship*: Victims must prove that, if removed from the United States, they will suffer "extreme hardship involving unusual and severe harm." This extreme-hardship standard is applied according to the specific circumstances of each case and focuses on the hardship to be suffered by the victim-applicant, but has not yet been challenged in a court of law (USDOJ INS 2002, 4–8). Consequently, the TVPA and T-visa regulations are the only guides to understanding the legal definition of extreme hardship (Wetmore 2003). It is clear however, that the extreme hardship required of T-visa applicants sets a higher bar than extreme-hardship standards required for other forms of immigration relief.

4. *Reasonable Requests for Assistance*: Victims must prove that they have complied with reasonable requests for assistance in the investigation or prosecution of a human-trafficking crime. At a minimum, to meet this statutory requirement the victim must either report the crime or respond to inquiries made by investigators or prosecutors (USDOJ INS 2002, 10). Minors under the age of 18 are not required to comply with reasonable requests for assistance.[2]

5. *Admissibility*: Victims must either be admissible to the United States or obtain a waiver of inadmissibility from U.S. Citizenship and Immigration Services (USCIS). Victims who are present in the United States without having been admitted or paroled are inadmissible, and accordingly have to obtain a waiver of inadmissibility in order to be eligible for nonimmigrant status.

Public Benefits through Certification

Trafficking victims who receive certification from the Department of Health and Human Services' Office of Refugee Resettlement (ORR) are eligible for public benefits to the same extent as refugees (USDOJ INS 2002, 13). Certified victims may apply for Temporary Assistance for Needy Families—food stamps, the State Children's Health Insurance Program Medicaid, and public housing, among other benefits (U.S. Department of Health and Human Services 2004). ORR automatically certifies a victim of a severe form of human trafficking who has: 1) received continued presence, 2) received a T-visa, or 3) made a *bona fide* application for a T-visa that has not yet been denied (Wagner 2005). Victims under the age of 18 are not required to obtain certification (USDOJ INS 2002, 13).

Access to Legal Services

The TVPA extends to trafficking victims the right to access legal aid from the Legal Services Corporation (LSC) (USDOS 2005, 242). LSC is able to offer legal services to victims of human trafficking as soon as they are identified, with no verification of victimization required (Reyes-Rubi 2005). Identified victims are screened by LSC staff to determine what (if any) immigration relief is available to them (political asylum, a T-visa, a U-visa for crime victims, etc.). LSC can assist victims in filing the I-914 application for a T-visa or derivative applications for family members, requesting employment authorization, and obtaining letters of certification from ORR. Since the LSC is otherwise unable to assist unauthorized migrants, access to its services reflects another significant change in immigration law and policy created by the TVPA.

Despite the extensive list of protections provided under the TVPA, the success of this initiative in protecting victims has been questionable. Unfortunately, there are major discrepancies between the number of estimated victims and the number offered TVPA protections. This raises questions about government efforts to properly identify victims, and especially to consider labor exploitation as a serious component of human trafficking. Moreover, because of the requirement that victims participate as witnesses for the prosecution, this presents a significant impediment for many who might otherwise benefit from TVPA protections. We discuss these problems in greater detail below.

Estimates Are Too High, Too Few Are Protected

Again, government estimates suggest that many thousands of victims are trafficked into the United States each year. Yet, in the four-year period analyzed for this study, from March 2001 to mid-May 2005, ORR certified a total of only 752 trafficking victims and only 491 received T-visas—the most critical protection provided under the TVPA.[3] Rates of ORR victim certification have averaged about 150 per year, with the overwhelming majority of certified victims (94 percent) being adults (see table 9.1). (Minors are eligible for benefits without the requirement of certification.) Roughly a thousand T-visas were approved from 2000 to 2006. The rate of T-visa approval averaged about 45 percent for all principle

TABLE 9.1. ORR Certifications of Severe Victims of Human Trafficking, Adults and Minors, 2001–2005

	2001	2002	2003	2004	2005*	Total
Adults	198	80	145	144	141	708
Minors	0	19	6	19	0	44
Total	198	99	151	163	141	752

Source: Office of Refugee Resettlement, Administration for Children and Families, U.S. Department of Health and Human Services.
*The most recent data are inclusive up to May 2005.

T-visa applications, though approval rates were much higher for derivative applications filed by family members of the victim (see fig. 9.2.).[4]

The large discrepancy between the number of trafficking victims estimated to be present in the United States and the total number of victims receiving protection under the TVPA is the result of several factors: (1) the imperfect nature of trafficking estimates; (2) misidentification of victims by law enforcement; (3) the conditional nature of victim protections; and (4) overly restrictive eligibility requirements for the T-visa.

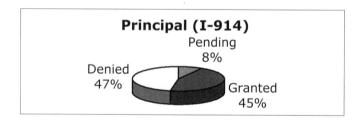

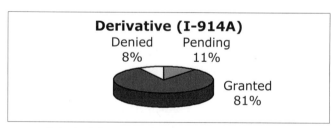

FIGURE 9.2. Principal (I-914) and derivative (I-914A) T-visa applications granted, denied, and pending, March 2001–May 2005. (Office of Communication, U.S. Citizenship and Immigration Services, Department of Homeland Security, electronic correspondence with Dan Kane, August 16, 2005)

Trafficking Estimates Are Highly Speculative

One obvious explanation for the gap between government estimates of trafficking victims and the number of T-visas granted is that the government's estimates are imperfect. Human trafficking is an underground, illicit phenomenon that cannot easily be documented. Therefore, it is likely that government figures on the number of victims present in the United States are inaccurate. More research is required to improve the data on trafficking. For instance, surveys could be conducted within undocumented immigrant communities in the United States to learn more about the rate at which various forms of human trafficking occur and to gauge awareness of the phenomenon.

A second, related problem is that victims who are in fact eligible for T-visas may be only a small fraction of the total number of trafficking victims. That is, the TVPA provides protections only for victims of "severe" forms of trafficking, while government estimates include all forms of human trafficking (including a presumably far greater number of "lesser" forms of trafficking for which there are no special protections under the TVPA). Thus, even if government estimates of the total number of trafficking victims is relatively accurate, these estimates are misleading in that they suggest a far greater number of trafficking victims than those actually targeted by the TVPA. Hence, government estimates must be refined to distinguish the number of victims of severe forms of trafficking (i.e., those who are eligible for T-visas). Moreover, the government should publicly release information on the age, sex, and type of exploitation suffered by victims who have received T-visas and ORR certifications so that these programs can be more effectively evaluated.

Third, it may be that—while very real—the magnitude of human trafficking is greatly exaggerated. Because of the serious impact and extreme nature of some forms of human trafficking—particularly sexual exploitation cases—the problem receives a great deal of attention from well-intentioned advocates, the media, and well-funded government anti-trafficking programs. Yet the magnitude of the problem may be much smaller than it is perceived to be. Moreover, since government estimates of the problem are often based at least partly on the observations and reports of nongovernmental organizations advocating against trafficking, there is a serious endogeneity problem. Advocacy agencies and media organizations rightly have an interest in publicizing and drawing attention to the terrible abuses associated with human trafficking. Yet in part because of the sensationalism with which such cases are often treated, such advocacy efforts may also contribute to the perception that the problem is more widespread than it really is. The fact that human trafficking tends to be conflated with other kinds of established crimes that are also highly exploitative—"regular" prostitution, labor rights violations, child pornography, child sexual molestation, etc.—makes it all the more difficult to define and measure its real magnitude.

Not All Victims Are Identified by Law Enforcement Agencies

Government and victim service agencies attribute the small number of T-visas issued partly to the misidentification of victims by law enforcement authorities. According to Steve Wagner, coordinator of the ORR Trafficking in Persons Program, "the problem is that we're not finding victims at an acceptable rate . . . For the most part, local law enforcement is clearly not aware of the phenomenon [of human trafficking] and the fact that it is a federal crime" (International Rescue Committee 2004, 1). Because human trafficking is a federal crime, federal agencies were the first to be trained to identify victims. State and local law enforcement agencies have only recently begun to receive such training, thanks in part to federal funding (Sheila Neville 2005). However, there is a lack of uniformity in the training provided (Kirana 2005). One U.S. prosecutor interviewed for this study noted that differences in regional concerns and the large number of federal agencies involved in the detection and investigation of human trafficking have presented major challenges for efforts by the Justice Department's Trafficking in Persons and Worker Exploitation Task Force to provide uniform training (Tenorio 2005).

Meanwhile, some NGOs, such as the Vital Voices Global Partnership, report that law enforcement officers continue to ignore victims and instead process them as undocumented migrants (Vital Voices Global Partnership 2005). From the perspective of law enforcement, the failure to identify victims may be less attributable to "a lack of will" on their part than to the fact that victims themselves are often unwilling to cooperate with law enforcement officials. In addition, since many prosecutors are inundated by more cases than can be prosecuted, the government must decide how to expend precious resources—prosecuting a criminal caught red-handed or working to convince victims to cooperate (Tenorio 2005). While the government attempts to do both, this is not always possible. It is therefore advisable to promote more training and coordination among law enforcement and victim-assistance professionals as a means of promoting both increased access to TVPA protections and greater victim cooperation in investigations and prosecutions. Additionally, more funding is needed so that the training expertise that NGOs have developed over the past few years will not be lost (Neville 2005).

Victim Protections Are Conditional

The protection afforded by the T-visa is conditioned on a quid pro quo exchange that requires adult trafficking victims to perform as witnesses in trafficking investigations or prosecutions. At a minimum, victims must report the crime and submit secondary evidence to establish their victimization by traffickers. However, victims may not cooperate with U.S. law enforcement officials because of a lack of trust or fear of retribution. On the one hand, police from a victim's home country sometimes are corrupt and even complicit with human traffickers, and traffickers may even intimidate victims by depicting U.S. law enforcement officers as corrupt, callous, and dedicated to summarily deporting undocumented immigrants. On the other hand, victims may also refuse to cooperate because they fear retribution by their traffickers in the United States or in their home country, against themselves or their families. Lastly, due to the extreme human rights abuses suffered, victims of severe forms of trafficking cannot always compose themselves to serve as effective witnesses.

As a result of these barriers, incentives for victims to cooperate with the government may not be sufficient. Consequently, victims may choose voluntary repatriation rather than cooperate with an investigation or prosecution, even if it means foregoing access to the protections provided under the TVPA. The result is that the victim does not receive critical protection and the government does not have a witness to assist in an investigation or prosecution. It is therefore important for the government to assess, on a case-by-case basis, why victims choose voluntary repatriation. Moreover, reducing the extent to which victim protections are contingent upon cooperation with government investigations and prosecutions may increase the number of victims eligible for temporary immigration status and other protections. In the long run, this could in turn enhance the extent to which victims are able and willing to assist as witnesses.

Restrictive T-Visa Eligibility Criteria

The low number of T-visa certifications relative to government estimates of victimization may also be attributable to excessively restrictive criteria in the qualifications listed above. Naturally, the government must avoid opening the floodgates to fraudulent applications for continued presence by unauthorized residents. However, easing the requirements for demonstrating extreme hardship, expanding authorization for official identification of victims, and relaxing requirements for assistance to law enforcement would likely increase the number of victims eligible and willing to receive T-visa protections without unduly rewarding undocumented immigrants.

Several bills, including the Violence Against Women Act Reauthorization Act (VAWRA) and the Trafficking Victims Protection Reauthorization Act (TVPRA), were introduced in Congress in 2005. The VAWRA and the TVPRA were passed into law in January 2006, reauthorizing previous legal provisions (originally approved in 2000) for another five years. The new legislation provided additional funding for combating a variety of forms of criminal activity, such as date rape, and expanded funding for the U.S.–Mexico Border Violence Taskforce. For example, VAWRA expanded the ability of state and local law enforcement agencies, rather than exclusively federal law enforcement officers, to petition for the continued presence of a victim (Violence Against Women Act Reauthorization, Section 801[a][2]). The new law allows victims whose state of mind is too fragile to withstand working with investigators and prosecutors to nevertheless remain eligible for a T-visa (allowing them the possibility of recovering to cooperate later in an investigation or prosecution) and does not require applicants for derivative T-visas to prove that extreme hardship would result if the visa were denied.

Conclusion

The TVPA clearly represents landmark legislation. The United States was one of the first countries in the world to develop a comprehensive legal framework to combat human trafficking by *prosecuting* human trafficking as a crime; *protecting* victims of severe forms of human trafficking with temporary immigration status, public benefits, and the opportunity to adjust to legal permanent residency; and committing to extensive global efforts to *prevent* human trafficking.[5] Overall, the T-visa reflects the U.S. government's interest in providing humanitarian aid to undocumented victims of severe forms of human trafficking and enhancing the success of government investigations and prosecutions of human-trafficking cases. That is, the TVPA represents an important shift in immigration law because it provides protections that previously were unavailable to undocumented victims of trafficking, who were often misidentified as criminals and deported based on their unlawful presence in the United States. Deportation increased the odds of re-victimization in the victim's home country and, without a victim to serve as a witness, reduced the likelihood of a successful prosecution against the trafficker. The TVPA therefore reflects a new public policy that seeks to end the criminalization of undocumented victims of human trafficking, provide humanitarian protections for them, and promote the prosecution of traffickers.

However, domestic protections for undocumented human-trafficking victims are still limited. Despite large estimates of victimization in the United States, fewer than one thousand victims have received temporary immigration status under either the T-visa or continued presence. Yet, providing more resources to combat an ill-defined problem is not the answer. First and foremost, government assessments of human trafficking into the United States need to be seriously re-evaluated, both in terms of the numerical estimates and the type of human trafficking cases (either labor or sex) occurring on U.S. soil.

Once there is a clearer understanding of the dimensions of the problem, it will be easier to determine how best to ensure that victims meet eligibility requirements to receive certification for the T-visa and other TVPA protections. Notably, the government may need to reconsider the terms under which protections are provided. By expanding access to government protection for undocumented human-trafficking victims—such as reducing the strict criteria for demonstrating extreme hardship—the number of successful investigations and prosecutions is likely to increase in the long run.

Acknowledgments

The research presented in this chapter was first delivered at the October 2004 International Studies Association meeting in Las Vegas, Nevada, and portions of the research were subsequently published by the Immigration Policy Center in a report titled "Hidden Victims: Evaluating Protections for Undocumented Victims of Human Trafficking," in *Immigration Policy in Focus* 4 (8) (December 2005). The authors wish to acknowledge the research assistance of Sara Lockwood and Marco Carrasco, as well as valuable input from Elena Azaola and Chris Tenorio. The authors take full responsibility for any errors or omissions.

Notes

1. More recent data are available, but they do not break down certifications in the categories we work with here.

2. The Trafficking Victims Protection Reauthorization Act of 2003 (TVPRA) raised the age of a minor for the purposes of this law from 15 to 18 (USDOS 2003).

3. The number of I-914 and I-914A T-visa applications pending (92 I-914/68 I-914A), granted (491 I-914/506 I-914A) or denied (519 I-914/ 53 I-914A) did not equal the total number of T-visa applications received (1,084 I-914/601 I-914A.) There are 18 fewer I-914 visas and 26 fewer I-914A visas granted than accounted for across the categories of applied, pending, and denied. The authors questioned USCIS about the discrepancy and were informed that the office was attempting to reconcile these figures.

4. At the time that these data were gathered, reliable information on ORR Certifications and T-Visa approvals was somewhat difficult to obtain, and those data that were available were often contradictory.

5. On October 19, 2005, President Bush signed into law the Senate's ratifications of the United Nations' Convention Against Transnational Organized Crime and its supplementary Protocol to Prevent, Suppress and Punish Trafficking in Persons, Especially Women and Children.

Closing Perspectives

10

Closing Reflections

BORDERING HUMAN RIGHTS, SOCIAL
DEMOCRATIC FEMINISM, AND BROAD-BASED
SECURITY

Kathleen Staudt, Tony Payan, and
Timothy J. Dunn

WE BEGIN THE YEAR 2008 with hopes and anxieties about the next decade in awe of all the contradictions of the U.S.–Mexico borderlands region. It is a prosperous region plagued by enormous inequalities. It is a region of "safest" cities living alongside some of the "unsafest" cities. It is a region that attracts thousands of migrants in spite of colossal violence. It is a region of increasing economic, linguistic, and ethnic integration, facing the construction of hundreds of miles of border walls. These contradictions shine through with greater brightness when we consider that on February 25, 2008, across the Atlantic Ocean, nearly all borders disappeared within the twenty-seven countries, each with their own distinctive nationality, that comprise the European Union and then compare the crumbling of those borders with border policies in North America, particularly in the United States. Even as the Europeans are shedding the old nation-state framework, at the U.S.–Mexico border, hegemonic masculinity (the male privilege that pervades everyday gender relations) meets hypermasculinity in the form of control and militarization strategies (recall chapter 1), without attention to the inequalities that propel migration and backlash, particularly male backlash against females, illuminated in this volume with social democratic feminist perspectives.

Border Contradictions: Toward
Militarization, Toward Democracy or Both?

In 2008, U.S. presidential hopefuls put the borderlands and their mainly Latino voters on the political primaries map in their grassroots campaign organizations and cultivation of established Democratic politicians, many of whom are Latino/a. Will that attention level the political playing field in "third-tiered pluralism" (see Hero 1992 on "two-tiered pluralism" augmented in the introductory chapter) for an historically colonized border region, a system that privileged first-tier white men at the center core but depressed power at the second tier for most women, Latinos, and African Americans, especially at the lower, distant spatial tier of the borderlands? Unfortunately, that may not be the case, at least in the short term through 2010. The enthusiasm of the national elections, particularly in the Democratic Party, and all the constituency-building efforts will likely wear off once power is consolidated, political appointments are made, and the bureaucracy gets back to its work, much of it reinforcing the border. Very likely, the blunt tools of criminalization and militarization in dealing with the border will remain, and yet make little dent in the everyday gender-based violence, illegal drug-related violence, poverty, or the violence perpetrated on immigrants who risk life and limb for a better life. In spite of the rhetoric and the many reports produced by government and academia, the concerns of human and community rights of borderlanders are hardly addressed in national formal law, procedure, and crime reports.

Narrow Border Public Policies Continue, with Hints of Change

From the end of the twentieth century and into the early twenty-first century, the U.S. federal bureaucracy has pursued a narrow approach to border security, focusing on militarization and criminalization strategies, even as it blithely ignores gender-based violence, the demand side of illegal drugs, poverty, and a dearth of public safety in the everyday life of borderlanders. Armed officers in masculinist agencies have increased surveillance with Border Patrol and National Guard troops along with physical barriers: real and virtual technology in the form of walls or fences, lights, webcams, and heat sensors. Those who build walls and produce such machinery enjoy new opportunities for government contracts. With defense contractors in the ascendancy, some wonder if former president Eisenhower's warnings of a military-industrial complex need to be issued again, this time focused on the U.S.–Mexico Border—a "border security industrial complex," so to speak.

FIGURE 10.1. Students walked out of high schools over Representative James Sensenbrenner's bill, HR 4437, at the César Chávez March in El Paso on March 31, 2006. They gathered in the downtown area prior to marching to the border with a sign saying, "These Hands Are *All* American." (Photograph by Kathleen Staudt)

FIGURE 10.2. Students at the walkout in El Paso on March 31, 2006. Their sign draws a parallel between the border fence and the Berlin Wall, and Mexican and U.S. flags serve as binational symbols. (Photograph by Kathleen Staudt)

Border poverty and gender-based violence barely reach the public agenda, at least to mainstream political forces in both the United States and Mexico. And the one item that does, the drug war, serves only to give the border the image of a violent drug-trafficking zone. The millions of law-abiding, honest citizens who live on the border pay a high price for that image in the form of an increasingly militarized or securitized border that tears through cross-border intimacy between and within families that straddle the border. Once elected president in 2006, Felipe Calderón's signature policy change was to follow in the United States' footsteps and deploy soldiers and the federal police to guard public thoroughfares in Tijuana, Matamoros, Reynosa, Nuevo Laredo, and Ciudad Juárez, a form of border militarization, Mexico-style. The Mexican Congress has passed sweeping new measures to reform law enforcement practices, though in a federal system of government, state legislatures and governors (Victoria Rodríguez calls the latter the "modern viceroys of Mexico [1997]), will shape the ongoing change. Perhaps *congresistas* and Calderón will ultimately establish rule of law and control over organized crime and drug cartels, but in the process, the struggle between the state and the transnational criminal organizations is likely to produce even more violence, as is visible already along the border: murders, execution style, of both criminals and law enforcement officials; and mass graves, like the thirty-six skeletal remains found in a back yard in Ciudad Juárez in March 2008. Such increase in violence when criminal organizations challenge the power of the state are not rare: witness the hike in violence in Nuevo Laredo in the summer of 2005. But even if this is "understandable," the numbers are a scary prospect onto themselves. In Ciudad Juárez, for instance, there were over sixteen hundred murders in 2008, symbolizing a very grim year in the Mexico border drug war.

On the U.S. immigration reform front, under third-tiered pluralism, President Calderón visited Mexican-heritage people on a multi-state tour in the United States to renew conversations about the stalled immigration reform. In the process of lobbying for immigration reform, however, he not only said little about gender-based violence, he also dismantled some of the federal investigative and prosecutorial machinery in Ciudad Juárez, machinery that former Mexican president Vicente Fox put in place in the face of increasing national and international activist pressure. Symbolizing President Calderón's choice is the fact that local officials in Ciudad Juárez bulldozed the eight crosses where female bodies were found in 2001, galvanizing transnational feminist activism (Staudt 2008b).

And the paradoxes of life on the border continue. During the 2008 primary elections, U.S. presidential hopefuls sent signals about the willingness to renegotiate parts of the North American Free Trade Agreement (NAFTA), something that would deeply affect labor and labor migration patterns. The debate caused enthusiasm in some groups and uneasiness in others. And yet, things on the border are never that simple. A policy change in NAFTA would present risks and opportunities for different people: Would changes in NAFTA represent nationalist protectionism that stops the U.S. external flow of jobs? How would that affect formal employment in Mexico? Would protectionism for small-scale farmers in Mexico slow the flow of migrant labor northward? Unfortunately, for people on the border, the debate is more about workers in the interior

FIGURE 10.3. An elaborate dune buggy on display at the fourth annual Border Security Conference at the University of Texas at El Paso in August 2007. (Photograph by Kathleen Staudt)

of the United States or Mexico than about how change would affect the border region.

As the Bush administration came to a close in the United States, and his political appointees prepared to leave the Department of Homeland Security, frantic actions were in motion: wall-building, recruitment of Border Patrol officers, and privatizing prisons that house immigrants (who were increasingly punished with prison terms or swift deportation). These actions deepened the militarization of the border and the punitive approach to immigration overall. Such actions nonetheless reveal strains in the United States' own democratic federalism. On the one hand, there is a hypercentralization of decision making in the hands of the federal government, a system that once prized local control to tax, spend, and privilege policies designed at the local level. This is evident in Arizona's and Colorado's recent efforts to create their own guest-worker programs, above and beyond federal jurisdiction, and in the face of agricultural worker shortages.

FIGURE 10.4. U.S. border security policy in practice: mobile observation technology in place between Nogales and Douglas in Arizona. (Photograph by Tony Payan)

Border People React and Survive

As an historically colonized region, the border is accustomed to imposition from above. Still, recently, border resistance to federal actions has been unusually high in some places, evoking acute tensions about place,

space, and freedom in face of centralizing control among a formerly qui-
escent population now realizing their growing political muscle. Ranchers,
environmentalists and locally elected officials filed lawsuits against wall-
building that violates constitutional principles and other laws. President
Juliet García, of the University of Texas at Brownsville, publicly criticized the federal government's efforts to build a wall through campus,
and grassroots alliances emerged across South Texas over "No Wall."
Blossoming networks of NGOs with a border community base have
built amazing alliances between human rights groups and locally elected
officials at multiple parts of the border region, networked with activists
on the East Coast. Perhaps these NGO-local government alliances will
be positioned to establish community-based guidelines about localizing
border policy enforcement, as Heyman once proposed (1998). Without
additional resources or cooperation from the federal government, however, customized local policy operations will be difficult to achieve and
even more difficult to enforce. Federal government agencies are accountable to Washington, D.C., rather than to border people, putting border
democracy on hold. In effect, the border has a gaping democratic deficit.
Few congressional districts are genuinely border districts like Texas #16,
which comprises most of El Paso County, and perhaps a handful of others in southwestern states that stretch northward over the traditionally
defined border zone of sixty-two miles (one hundred kilometers). But a
handful among hundreds of congressional districts gerrymandered into
the mainstream is never a majority.

Paradox on the border is a hydra-like beast. While some have gathered
the courage to oppose the federal government, other border people and
institutions welcome federal and state incentives and subsidies to promote research on border security and techno-fixes to identify crossers,
build prisons and test the limits of local law enforcement officials' resistance to enforce federal laws. As such, they become part of the Border
Security Industrial Complex (in twenty-first-century Ike-like terms) or
BSIC. As El Paso's former police chief Richard Wiles stated publicly, what
will they want us to do next: knock on doors to collect delinquent IRS
tax returns?[1] Arizona legislators passed a punitive law against employers,
threatening business with the loss of their licenses if they hire undocumented workers—even as they grapple with the shortage of agricultural
workers. Near-vacant parts of the border regions, pristine in their stark

FIGURE 10.5. A Día de los Muertos *ofrenda* (altar) remembrance for those who died crossing the border, prepared by the Border Network for Human Rights and displayed at El Paso's Café Mayapan in November 2007. (Photograph by Kathleen Staudt)

beauty, can also be magnets for crime and public safety problems. Murder and kidnapping at Mexico's northern border, in both urban and rural areas, continue unabated, with fear and fright extending to survivors. Much of this violence is associated with the decades-old illegal drug trade, illustrating how prohibition policies such as the "War on Drugs" spill over to supplier networks amid ongoing, dreary drug addiction and malaise in U.S. society. Desert-crossing deaths mount, surpassing forty-six hundred (Dunn 2009), exceeding the total number of U.S. troops killed in the Iraq War, with no evidence that strategies deter those migrants aiming to cross (Cornelius and Lewis 2007). And gender-based crimes also drag on. Few bother to put these pieces together into a single analysis of the border *problematique* and to design comprehensive solutions for what ails the borderland. Over and over, chapters in this collection illustrate how sexual assault, domestic violence, and femicide operate at the periphery of policy attention but at the center of women's daily experiences.

Border enforcement is not the same as comprehensive immigration reform, even if politicians prefer to conflate all border issues. Still, no reasonable immigration reforms stand a chance of passing the U.S. Congress. And yet, wedged between those who apply nuanced thinking to border issues and politicians or policy makers who would rather conflate all issues, a vacuum prevails as immigrants, many employers, and human rights advocates seek a legal way for people to work in the United States, given the economic demand, insufficient visas for Mexico (despite its special relationship with the United States), and a huge bureaucratic backlog in the processing of those seeking naturalization—regardless of the rising costs of becoming a citizen. Children are often caught in the middle, suffering the "sins of their fathers and mothers" and potential deportation, or living in legal limbo as unaccompanied minor immigrant children, without enjoying the legal protections afforded to U.S.-born children. Such are the paradoxes buried at the core of U.S. border policy.

Centering Gender–Based Violence at Borders

On the northern Mexico border, citizens live in fear, lacking both public and private household safety. It has become commonplace knowledge

FIGURE 10.6. A border crossing in Tijuana, with conflicting images of new cars, a woman with her children, and radio DJs advertised on a billboard in the background. (Photograph by Tony Payan)

that law enforcement institutions along the border are profoundly flawed and often deeply corrupt. Nearly all law enforcement institutions on the border are penetrated by well-organized crime cartels (Payan 2006). Amid clashes between law enforcement institutions and criminal organizations, gruesome deaths result—people kidnapped, tortured and dumped around alleys and dusty lots—and other issues are ignored. Gender-based violence, for example, is brushed aside, and yet it stains the border and border crossing: a quarter of women experience physical domestic violence and hundreds of femicide victims died over a decade. Immigrant women are particularly vulnerable, lacking protection as citizens or nationals in a border context where the provisions and bureaucratic complexities of international human rights treaties or national laws and their bulky procedures hardly trickle down to street-level bureaucrats. Masculinist policies toward the border are only likely to further victimize women, even as more women cross borders in hostile desert terrain. Likely, women will face even more routine sexual assaults or worse yet, death, as women's numbers begin to swell the proportions of those who die crossing the border. The border has become indeed a place where "*la vida no vale nada*" (life's not worth anything). And in the process, there is a hierarchy of vulnerability, with many women and children ranking near the bottom.

An internationalist social democratic feminist approach lays bare the hierarchy, highlights new vantage points and questions, and makes visible women's agency in surviving, resisting misogyny, and organizing for change. Chapter contributors center analysis on gender-based violence, security and human rights, and action toward deeper democracy that envelops broad-based security, poverty reduction, and everyday public safety.

In this final, closing chapter of the volume, we summarize chapter contributions in light of the conceptual and practical issues raised in the introduction. In particular, we offer a broad-based and long-term perspective on violence, and human and community security in the U.S.–Mexico borderlands—one that builds on the insights available through focusing on the gender-based perspectives of people's everyday experiences. Such insights draw on feminist theory and democracy, particularly the sort of democracy that engages, networks, and organizes the voices and interests of those concerned with public security, humane policies, poverty reduction, and the empowerment of formerly marginalized people, including many women. Several chapter contributors raise questions about the viability of reforms given the neoliberal global economy that values low-cost labor and cheap commodities over human rights principles. Such values can be tempered with democratic governance and public policies that address the obscene levels of inequality that pervade within and across the borderlands.

Overview of Chapters

Conceptualized in an internationalist social democratic feminist perspective, using a "third-tier" critique of pluralism, the introductory chapter provides an overview of narrow versus broad-based border security, defining their problems and their implied solutions. Using everyday human rights, safety and community security as the standard, narrow approaches are deemed incomplete and ineffective. The narrow border security agenda declares a "war" on drugs and addresses elusive global terrorism rather than reducing crime or enhancing individual and community public safety. Little progress has been made in helping women achieve freedom from everyday violence, whether domestic violence or the infamous femicides in Mexico. U.S. policy is associated with the deaths of thousands of immigrants, most of them from Mexico and Central America. Based on official and academic counts, desert-crossing deaths from 1994 through 2007 add up to the striking figure of forty-six hundred (Dunn 2009).

Part I in the collection sets the stage for a more nuanced understanding of everyday violence in the experiences of people on the move for a better life. In chapter 1, Olivia Ruiz Marrujo examines the experiences of women in risky journeys near and across borders, risks fraught with sexual assault. "Along the U.S.–Mexico and Mexico-Guatemala borders," she writes, "sexual violence has become a fact of life for migrant women." Bandits, gang members, and sometimes officials are part of the savagery. United Nations sources indicate that worldwide, women constitute half of migrants, and rape is increasingly the price paid for gender transgressions, such as unauthorized crossing. Focusing on the Tijuana–San Diego area in the north and Chiapas in the south, Ruiz Marrujo analyzes why migrant women are vulnerable. Among compelling explanations, she includes legacies of male domination and sexual conquest, women's limited judicial rights, and the way "foreigners" are eroticized as less-than-human nationals.

In "Human Rights Violations: Central American Immigrants at the Northeastern Mexico Border," Alberto Martín Alvarez and Ana Fernández Zubieta examine immigrants' pathways across treacherous space through Mexico. Displaced by conflict and civil war, Central American immigrants experience routine undermining of their human rights by civilians and public officials. Through analyzing a relatively large sample of migrants in shelters, the authors find that rights violations occur through punitive laws and ideologies that objectify immigrants as impoverished. Immigrants increase their vulnerability by crossing through remote areas. Although a small part of the sample, women report (and possibly underreport, according to authors) sexual assaults in their journeys. Migrants generally face extortion and robbery, but rarely report crimes to official sources. This chapter shows harsh conditions for immigrants in Mexico, often on their way to the United States. One might think that neither the United States nor Mexico support international human rights principles and treaties, given their punitive practices.

Julie Murphy Erfani describes the everyday production and consumption practices that make up both the formal and the informal markets in the North American and European comparative regional contexts of neoliberal economies in "Crime and Violence in the Arizona-Sonora Borderlands: NAFTA's Underground Economy as a Source of In/Security, with Comparisons to the EU." She argues that regional integration into global markets leads to increased smuggling, money laundering, corruption, trafficking, crime and reliance on migrant workers. Black markets undermine legal commerce and even public safety, yet many consumers profit from underground economies when they buy goods and services prepared through low-cost unauthorized labor, from houses to slaughterhouses, or from restaurants to pirated music or diluted prescription drugs. In that sense, we are all complicit in the "immigration problem." Erfani's solution is for North America and Europe to "focus on decreasing intraregional disparities in wealth rather than on scapegoating unauthorized migrant workers as 'criminals.'" The U.S.–Mexico border is not unique, as her comparison with the European Union border of Spain shows.

Anna Ochoa O'Leary's chapter, titled "In the Footsteps of Spirits: Migrant Women's Testimonios in a Time of Heightened Border Enforcement," addresses women migrants, "caught" and sheltered in Nogales, Sonora, after near-death experiences, robberies, and other physical threats to themselves and their daughters in one of the most dangerous desert crossing zones—the Arizona border. Female migration is on the rise, as is the rate of death for female migrants in this hostile climatic region. In an ethnographic approach, Ochoa O'Leary uses in-depth interviews with three women in different age groups from a sample of one hundred women to illustrate the conditions that push women from poverty-stricken and violent homes into the perilous journey northward.

In "Violence against Women at the Border: Unpacking Institutions," Kathleen Staudt sets the urban scene for femicide in the global economic context of Ciudad Juárez, where over four hundred women were murdered from 1993 to 2006. She extends the problem to include widespread domestic violence and sexual assault, some of which also result in death.

Staudt unpacks institutions, both NGOs and law enforcement agencies, on both sides of the border. Thus far, most NGOs have relied on dramatic performance activism focused on femicide, rather than approaches that address the broader problem of all violence against women. This strategy peaked in 2003/2004, when many transnational activists moved on to other dramatic locales, such as femicide in Guatemala. The border offers a mirror-like image of the problematic law enforcement institutions on both sides of the border: one side, with police and prosecutors who devote little professional attention to femicide and domestic violence, and the other side, with a thirty-year reform process still muddied in fragmented, bureaucratic procedures.

In "Femicide on the Border and New Forms of Protest: The International Caravan for Justice," Carol Mueller, Michelle Hansen, and Karen Qualtire analyze transnational activism across borders around femicide in Ciudad Juárez. Using social movement perspectives, the analysts evaluate Mexico Solidarity Network's traveling caravan approach to increasing awareness of violence against women in the context of harsh neoliberal global economic inequalities. Such movements sustain the pressure for political and economic transformation.

Olga Aiken Araluce utilizes theoretical insights on the diffusion of international norms to analyze the changing discourse of Mexico's federal attorney general's office in "Transnational Advocacy Networks, International Norms, and Political Change in Mexico: The Murdered Women of Ciudad Juárez." Aiken Araluce shows how hard the international NGOs have worked to apply principles and pressure on the government to recognize gender-based approaches to human rights. After extensive resistance, but faced with additional pressure from feminists in Mexico's Congress, the federal government finally began to incorporate discourse on gender-based violence. Such discourse has tentatively affected some legal practices at the national level, but hardly made a dent in state and local municipal practices, where enforcement is grounded in this federal system of government.

David Shirk and Alexandra Webber examine "Human Trafficking and Protections for Undocumented Victims in the United States," broadening the discussion to multiple borders. Shirk and Webber cite the changing official figures about the number of human trafficking victims, the majority of whom are women in sex trafficking operations. They question the figures and challenge the complex legal remedies that focus more on criminalizing the traffickers and less on helping the victims. Few special visas, known as T-visas, have been issued for trafficked human beings.

Toward Broader Security Solutions

With gender-based violence as the centerpiece of our discussion of border security in this volume, we have shown the shortcomings of narrow militaristic approaches and documented the need for comprehensive, poverty-reducing, pro-democratic, gender-based solutions that make freedom from violence and hunger primary goals. The umbrella framework for broad-based solutions is global, or at least regional, encompassing all of North America, including Mexico and migrants from Central American countries. As Douglas Massey and others have argued, solutions require multilateral cooperation rather than the unilateral imposition of U.S.-oriented approaches; moreover, Mexico is a "special case," with a special historical and contemporary relationship with the United States (2002, 155, 157). Solutions derive from human rights principles that must mesh better with national, state, and local laws and their enforcement.

Poor people need a legal way to work, such as renewable temporary work visas. The U.S. Southwest was once part of northern Mexico. Both countries are booming trading partners, friendly neighbors rather than enemies at war. Border cities and towns depend on cross-border shoppers for economic health and well-being. Legal immigrant visa limits are set far too low. The annual quotas are "absurdly low," according to Massey et al. (2002, 159), and equivalent to other tiny countries without a special relationship with the United States. U.S. bureaucracies create complex excessive delays and are increasingly trained to view migrants as threats, rather than workers building prosperity and future social security in North America.

In his analysis of border blockades, which push migrants to deadly vacant and hostile desert crossing zones, and the militarized aftermath of blockade policies, Timothy Dunn calls the problem a "humanitarian crisis" (2009). He contrasts two rights-oriented paradigms: one that takes a citizenship-nationalist view versus one that advances human dignity, respect, and equality. Chapter contributors in this volume affirm that the key to solving this humanitarian crisis is the latter, human-rights approach, one that connects norms with applications in the real and everyday experiences of women and men. The approach is consistent with internationalist social democratic feminism that seeks to reduce inequalities, including gender inequalities, and to promote living wages and freedom from violence within and across man-made borders.

For too long, U.S. xenophobes have demonized Mexico and Mexicans with language so common and familiar that it has become mainstreamed in policy discourse about border security and immigration. Such language, followed by punitive policies, will come to haunt the United States in the future both for practical and principled reasons. Practically, the United States is dependent on trade relations with Mexico and on young labor to replenish the social security system funds. Among practical political consequences, anti-Mexican xenophobes will likely produce voter backlash over the long term, as has happened repeatedly in U.S. history, when the children of vilified immigrant groups (Irish, Italian, Jewish, and Polish, among others) remembered the treatment their families received and voted in ethnic blocks against those who persecuted them. Already in the 2008 presidential elections, Latinos in the southwestern United States have become a critical mass of voters with the potential to swing elections. Their voting power will grow.

In principled terms, many in the United States affirm higher forms of "law," whether human rights or faith-based. Many are also obsessed with peculiarly U.S. definitions and approaches to crime that criminalize larger pools of people as each year passes. Without addressing the impoverishment and violence that push people to migrate, the criminalization approaches lead problems to fester even more. We agree with Peter Andreas and Ethan Nadelmann in their book, *Policing the Globe*, who conclude that "criminalization and international crime control have too often substituted and distracted attention away from the need for more fundamental political, social, and economic reforms" (2006, 251).

Producers and consumers in the U.S.—and increasingly in Mexico—blithely depend on labor in foreign-owned industry labor enclaves known as maquiladoras and their shockingly low wages or on immigrants for their price-sensitive marketplace decisions. With tools like border fences and internment camps, punitive policies criminalize workers and families for crossing the border to escape poverty, although these laws and crime definitions constantly shift with political mood and demagoguery. And what have those who acquiesced to unjust laws become in the process: the barbarians we seek to protect ourselves from, as Coetzee's allegorical novel suggests? We can't have it both ways or all ways. International human rights principles provide a quality standard toward which North Americans can aspire.

To use practical political parlance, "What should be done?" The North American public should move beyond criminalization and militarization strategies to deal with the border and its gender-based violence. Militarization strategies ignore and thus aggravate everyday structural violence that emanates from excessive levels of global neoliberal economic inequalities. The public should also reconnect with human rights principles that are lauded internationally but lost in the practice of national bureaucracies. And the public should end the long-standing ideologies that authorize men to control, dominate, and exercise power over women; masculinist ideologies still embedded in institutions and daily practices. Existing laws are inadequate to deal with everyday misery and violence. The public remains oblivious to lingering misogyny, so institutionalized in law and society. Solutions must focus on gender and gender-based violence. It behooves us not only to document and analyze these realities, but also to make democracy more effective as we transform ugly gender and socioeconomic power inequalities in both governmental and nongovernmental institutions.

Notes

1. "Building a New Vision of the Border: A Conference on Border Policy." Convened by the Border Human Rights Collaborative and the U.S.–Mexico Border and Immigration Task Force, El Paso, TX, November 29–30, 2007.

References

Abramsky, Sasha. 2004. "Incarceration, Inc." *Nation* 279 (3): 22–25.

Ackleson, Jason. 2005. "Border Security Technologies: Local and Regional Implications." *Review of Policy Research* 22 (2): 137–155.

Acuña, Rodolfo. 1972. *Occupied America, The Chicano's Struggle Toward Liberation.* San Francisco: Canfield Press.

Acuña Herrera, Leoncio. 1999. "Me dejaron 21 bolsas con huesos: gobernador." *Norte de Ciudad Juárez* June 20, 10b.

Adital (Agencia de Informacao, Frei Tito para a América Latina). 2002. "Niñas traficadas detenidas como si ellas fueran criminales." November 19.

AFSC. *See* American Friends Services Committee.

Agathangelou, Anna M., and L.H.M. Ling. 2004. "Power, Borders, Security, Wealth: Lessons of Violence and Desire from September 11." *International Studies Quarterly* 48:517–538.

Agence France Presse. 2005. "Wave of Arrests as Spanish Police Target 'Costa del Crime.'" September 15.

———. 2006. "European Anti-drugs Squad Seizes Seven in Spain." May 6.

Alañón Pardo, A., and M. Gómez de Antonio. 2004. *Estimación del tamaño de la economía sumergida en España.: un modelo estructural de variables latentes.* FUNCAS, Documento de trabajo 184/2004.

Albuquerque, Pedro. 2007. "Shared Legacies, Disparate Outcomes: Why American South Border Cities Turned the Tables on Crime and Their Mexican Sisters Did Not." *Crime, Law and Social Change* 47 (2): 69–88.

Alvarado, Jeanette E. 2004. *The Federal Consequences of Criminal Convictions: Illegal Reentry after Removal.* Unpublished manuscript prepared for the State Bar of Arizona.

Alvarez, Sonia E. 1998. "Latin American Feminisms 'Go Global': Trends of the 1990s and Challenges for the New Millennium." In *Cultures of Politics, Politics of Cultures*, ed. Sonia E. Alvarez, Evelina Dagnino, and Arturo Escobar, 293–324. Boulder, CO: Westview Press.

American Friends Service Committee (AFSC). 1999. "Raping Women: Under the Scope of Employment?" August 17.

Amnesty International. 2000. *Israel: Human Rights Abuses of Women Trafficked from Countries of the Former Society Union into Israel's Sex Industry.* AI Index: MDE 15/17/00.

Amnesty International. 2003. *Intolerable Killings: Ten Years of Abductions and Murders in Ciudad Juárez and Chihuahua.* http://www.amnestyusa.org/countries/mexico/document (accessed April 2, 2007).

———. 2005. "Mexico: Truth and Justice for the Murdered and Abducted Women of Ciudad Juárez and Chihuahua." Press Release. AMR 41/033/2005, August 9.

———. 2006. "International Women's Day: Opinion Piece by Irene Khan." Press release. ACT 77/005/2006. March 8.

———. 2006. "Mexico: Killings and Abductions of Women in Ciudad Juárez and the City of Chihuahua—The Struggle for Justice Goes On." AI Index: AMR 41/012/2006 (Public). February 20.

Andreas, Peter. 2000. *Border Games, Policing the U.S.–Mexico Divide.* Ithaca, NY: Cornell University Press.

Andreas, Peter, and Ethan Nadelmann. 2006. *Policing the Globe: Criminalization and Crime Control in International Relations.* New York: Oxford University Press.

"Annie. An American on the West End." 2006. http://theatre smarts.blogspot.com (accessed August 8, 2006).

Anzaldúa, Gloria. 1987. *Borderlands/La Frontera: The New Mestiza.* San Francisco: Spinsters/Aunt Lute Press.

APSLW. *See* Associated Press State and Local Wire.

Arango, Joachin, and Philip Martin. 2003. "Best Practices to Manage Migration: Morocco-Spain," Spain-Morocco, Research & Seminars, June 24. http://migration.ucdavis.edu/ceme/printfriendly.php?id=123_0_6_0.

Associated Press State and Local Wire (APSLW). 2007a. "Feds: Arizona guns finding their way to Mexican drug lords." *Arizona Republic* May 25.

———. 2007b. "Officials say killing of Mexican police chief could be drug hit." *Arizona Republic* February 28.

———. 2007c. "Reporter Abducted in Front of Police Station, Feared Dead." *Arizona Republic* April 18.

Associated Press Worldstream. 2007. "Documents Show How Smugglers Get Guns." *East Valley Tribune/Scottsdale Tribune* March 12.

Association for Women's Rights in Development (AWID). 2002. "A Rights Based Approach to Development." Women's Rights and Economic Change. August 1. http://www.awid.org.

Ausseill, Pierre. 2006. "Spain Targets Urban Corruption as Elections Loom." *Agence France Press* October 26.

AWID. *See* Association for Women's Rights in Development.

Azu, M. 1997. "Violence against Migrant Women." In *Migrant Women's Human Rights in G-7 Countries, Organizing Strategies,* ed. Mallika Dutt, Leni Marin, and Helen Zia. San Francisco: Family Violence Prevention Fund; New Brunswick, NJ: Center for Women's Global Leadership.

Bakare-Yusef, Bibi. 1999. "The Economy of Violence: Black Bodies and the Unspeakable Terror." In *Feminist Theory and the Body: A Reader,* ed. Janet and Margrit Shildrick. New York: Routledge.

Bandura, A. 1975. "Análisis del aprendizaje social de la agresión." In *Modificación de conducta: análisis de la agresión y la delincuencia*, recopiladores Emilio Ribes Iñesta y Albert Bandura. México: Editorial Trillas.

Bartra, Roger. 1992. *The Cage of Melancholy: Identity and Metamorphosis in the Mexican Character*. New Brunswick, NJ: Rutgers University Press.

Beebe, James. 2001. *Rapid Assessment Process: An Introduction*. Walnut Creek, CA: AltaMira.

Benería, Lourdes, and Martha Roldán. 1986. *The Crossroads of Class and Gender: Industrial Homework, Subcontracting, and Household Dynamics in Mexico City*. Chicago: University of Chicago Press.

Benford, Robert D. 1997. "An Insider's Critique of the Social Movement Framing Perspective." *Sociological Inquiry* 67 (4): 409–430.

Bensinger, Ken. 2003. "Film Companies Take to Mexico's Streets to Fight Piracy." *New York Times* December 17, B1.

Bergareche, Ana. 2002. *Tiempos de ambivalencia: violencia sexual, religión e identidad en las trabajadoras de la maquiladora*. (unpublished manuscript)

Bhabha, Homi. 1994. "Narrating the Nation." In *Nationalism*, eds. John Hutchison and Anthony D. Smith. New York: Oxford University Press.

Billeaud, Jacques. 2007. "Smuggling Could Be Behind Arizona Killings." *Associated Press Online* February 14.

Binion, Gayle. 2006. "Human Rights: A Feminist Perspective." In Lockwood 2006, 70–87.

Birns, Larry, and Alex Sánchez. 2007. "The Government and Drug Lords: Who Rules Mexico?" Council on Hemispheric Affairs, States News Service, April 10.

Bishop, Jack. 2004. "Who Are the Pirates? The Politics of Piracy, Poverty, and Greed in the Globalized Music Market." *Popular Music and Society* 27 (1): 104–105.

Bouvard, Marguerite Guzman. 1994. *Revolutionizing Motherhood: The Mothers of the Plaza de Mayo*. Wilmington, DE: Scholarly Books.

Braine, Theresa. 2007. "Governor Promises Thorough Investigation into Migrant shooting deaths." *Associated Press State & Local Wire* February 10.

Brickman J. 1996. "Female Lives, Feminist Deaths: The Relationship of the Montreal Massacre to Dissociation, Incest, and Violence against Women." In *States of Rage: Emotional Eruption, Violence and Social Change*, eds. Reneé R Curry and Terry L. Allison. New York: New York University Press.

Brison S. 2002. *Violence and the Remaking of a Self*. Princeton, NJ: Princeton University Press.

Brotherton, David, and Philip Kretsedemas, eds. 2008. *Keeping Out the Other: A Critical Introduction to Immigration Enforcement Today*. New York: Columbia University Press.

Bunch, Charlotte. 2006. "Women's Rights as Human Rights: Toward a Re-Vision of Human Rights." In Lockwood 2006, 57–69.

Burgen, Stephen. 2006. "Pirates of the Mediterranean," *Sunday Times* (London) July 30.

Bustamante, J. A. 2002. "Immigrants' Vulnerability as Subjects of Human Rights." *International Migration Review* 36:333–354.

———. 2006. "La migración indocumentada de México a Estados Unidos; la dialéctica de la vulnerabilidad y los derechos humanos." Paper presented at the Simposio Internacional sobre la vulnerabilidad de los migrantes internacionales, November 3–4, Monterrey, México. http://www.comitenorte.org.mx/simposio/ponencias/jorgeb.pdf (accessed June 20, 2007).

Butterfield, F. 1996. *All God's Children: The Boskett Family and the American Tradition of Violence.* New York: Avon Books.

Buzzelle, Stanley, and Carol Mueller. 2005. "Feminism Meets Human Rights: The International Campaign to Stop Femicide in Juárez." Presented at the annual meetings of the International Studies Association. Honolulu, Hawaii.

Camacho, Alicia Schmidt. 2004. "Body Counts on the Mexico–U.S. Border: Feminicidio, Reification and the Theft of Mexicana Subjectivity." *Chicana/Latina Studies* 4 (1): 22–62.

Cámara de Diputados del H. Congreso de la Unión. 2006. *Reglamento de la Ley General de Población.* México Centro de Documentación, Información y Análisis de la Secretaría de Servicios Parlamentarios.

———. 2009. *Ley General de Población.* México. Centro de Documentación, Información y Análisis de la Secretaría de Servicios Parlamentarios.

Campbell, Howard. 2005. "Drug Trafficking Stories: Everyday Forms of Narco-Folklore on the U.S.–Mexico Border." *International Journal of Drug Policy* 16 (5): 326–333.

Carlsen, Laura. 2007. "NAFTA Free Trade Myths Lead to Farm Failure in Mexico." *Americas Program Policy Report.* December 5. http://americas.irc-online.org/am/4794.html (accessed February 2, 2008)

Carruthers, Ian, and Robert Chambers. 1981. "Rapid Appraisal for Rural Development." *Agricultural Administration* 8:407–22.

Casillas, R. 1996. "Un viaje mas allá de la frontera. Los migrantes centroamericanos en México." *Perfiles Latinoamericanos* 8:141–171.

Castillo, M. A. 2000. "Las políticas hacia la migración centroamericana en países de origen, de destino y de tránsito." *Papeles de Población* 24:133–157.

———. 2003. "Los desafíos de la emigración centroamericana en el Siglo XXI." *Amérique Latine Histoire et Mémoire* no. 7. http://alhim.revues.org/document369.html (accessed April 14, 2007).

Castles, S., and M. J. Miller. 2003. *The Age of Migration. International Population Movements in the Modern World.* New York: Guilford Press.

Castro Luque, Ana Lucía, Jaime Olea Miranda, and Blanca E. Zepeda Bracamonte. 2006. *Cruzando el Desierto: Construcción de una Tipología para el Análisis de la Migración en Sonora.* Hermosillo, Sonora: El Colegio de Sonora.

CDHNU. *See* Comisión de Derechos Humanos de las Naciones Unidas.

Cerrutti, Marcela, and Douglas S. Massey. 2001. "On the Auspices of Female Migration from Mexico to the United States." *Demography* 38 (2): 187–201.

Charlton, Sue Ellen, Jana Everett, and Kathleen Staudt, eds. 1989. *Women, the State, and Development.* Albany, NY: SUNY Press.

Chávez Cano, Esther. 2002. "Murdered Women of Juárez." In *Puro Border: Dispatches, Snapshots, and Graffiti from La Frontera,* eds. Luis Humberto Crosthaite, John William Byrd, and Bobby Byrd, 153–158. El Paso: Cinco Puntos Press.

Cieslak, David J. 2000. "Border Patrol Agent Accused of Sex Abuse." *Tucson Citizen* August 12, 1-C.

Cimacnoticias. 1999. "Solicitan a la Relatora de Ejecuciones Extrajudiciales recomendación para gobierno mexicano." 15 de julio. http://www.cimacnoticias.com/especiales/ciudadjuarez (visitada en diciembre 2005).

CNN.COM U.S. News. 2000. "Migration on Rise Worldwide, Especially Among Women, IOM says." November 11.

Coetzee, J. M. 1982. *Waiting for the Barbarians.* New York: Penguin.

Cohn, Carol, and Cynthia Enloe. 2003. "A Conversation with Cynthia Enloe: Feminists Look at Masculinity and the Men Who Wage War." *Signs: Journal of Women in Culture and Society* 28 (4): 1187–1207.

Coleman, Mathew. 2007. "Immigration Geopolitics Beyond the Mexico–U.S. Border." *Antipode* 39 (1): 54–76.

Comisión de Derechos Humanos de las Naciones Unidas (CDHNU). 2002. *Informe presentado por la Relatora Especial, Sra. Gabriela Rodríguez Pizarro, de conformidad con la resolución 2002/62 de la Comisión de Derechos Humanos.* Adición Visita a México. http://daccessdds.un.org/doc/UNDOC/GEN/G02/154/09/PDF/G0215409.pdf?OpenElement (accessed March 12, 2007).

Comisión Nacional de Derechos Humanos. 1998. Recomendación Núm. 44/98. *Caso de las mujeres asesinadas en Ciudad Juárez y sobre la falta de colaboración de las autoridades de la Procuraduría General de Justicia del Estado de Chihuahua.* http://www.cndh.org (accessed October 2005).

Corchado, Alfredo. 2004. "Mexico to Release Report on Juarez Killings." *Dallas Morning News* October 10.

———. 2007. "Mexican Cartel's Enforcers Outpower Their Boss," *Dallas Morning News* June 11.

Cornelius, Wayne A. 2001. "Death at the Border: Efficacy and Unintended Consequences of U.S. Immigration Control Policy." *Population and Development Review* 27 (4): 661–685.

Cornelius, Wayne, and Jessica Lewis, eds. 2007. *Impacts of Border Enforcement on Mexican Migration: The View from Sending Communities.* Anthology #3. La Jolla: University of California Center for Comparative Migration Studies.

Cornelius, Wayne A., and David A. Shirk, eds. 2007. *Reforming the Administration of Jusice in Mexico.* Notre Dame: University of Notre Dame Press; La Jolla: University of California at San Diego Center for U.S.–Mexican Studies.

Coronado, Roberto, and Pia Orrenius. 2006. "Border Crime and Enforcement." In *Basic Border Econometrics,* ed. Martha Patricia Barraza and Thomas M. Fullerton, 38–56. Ciudad Juárez: la Universidad de Ciudad Juárez.

Council on Foreign Relations. 2005. *Building a North American Community.* New York: Council on Foreign Relations Press.

CQ Press. 2007. *City Crime Rankings,* 14th ed. http://www.cqpress.com.

Cunningham, Hilary, and Josiah McC. Heyman. 2004. "Introduction: Mobilities and Enclosures at Borders." *Identities: Global Studies in Culture and Power* 11:289–302.

De Genova, Nicholas P. 2002. "Migrant 'Illegality' and Deportability in Everyday Life." *Annual Review of Anthropology* 31:419–47.

De León, Arnoldo. 1983. *They Called Them Greasers: Anglo Attitudes Toward Mexicans in Texas, 1821–1900.* Austin: University of Texas Press.

Democracy Now. 2007. Interview with Jodi Goodwin. February 23. http://www.democracynow.org (accessed 12/1/08).

Demos, Telis. 2006. "A Compendium of Revealing Stats." *Fortune* 154 (8). money.cnn.com/magazines/fortune/fortune_archive/2006/10/16/8388652/index.htm

Department of Homeland Security. 2005. Yearbook of Immigration Statistics: 2005, Data on Enforcement Actions. http://www.dhs.gov/ximgtn/statistics/ (accessed March 11, 2007).

Dobles, I. 1990. "Psicología de la Tortura." In *Aportes Críticos a la Psicología en Latinoamérica,* coord. Bernardo Jiménez-Domínguez. Guadalajara Mexico: Universidad de Guadalajara:.

Donato, Katherine M. 1994. "U.S. Policy and Mexican Migration to the United States 1942–92." *Social Science Quarterly* 75 (4): 705–29.

Donohue, Brian. 2007. "Fear Grips a Border Crossing." *Newhouse News Service* February 19.

Dunn, Timothy. 1996. *The Militarization of the U.S.–Mexico Border 1978–1992.* Austin: University of Texas, Center for Mexican American Studies.

———. 2009. *Blockading the Border and Human Rights: The El Paso Operation that Remade U.S. Border Enforcement.* Austin: University of Texas Press.

Ensler, Eve. 1998. *The Vagina Monologues.* New York: Random House.

Eschbach, Karl, Jacqueline Hagan, Nestor Rodríguez, Rubén Hernández-León, and Stanley Bailey. 1999. "Death at the Border." *International Migration Review* 33 (2): 430–454.

Evans, Sara. 2003. *Tidal Wave: How Women Changed America at Century's End.* New York: Free Press.

Falcon, Sylvanna. 2001. "Rape as a Weapon of War: Advancing Human Rights for Women at the U.S.–Mexico Border." *Social Justice* 28 (2): 31–51.

Faludi, Susan. 1991. *Backlash: The Undeclared War Against American Women.* New York: Crown.

FDA Consumer. 2005. "Counterfeit Drug Warning." 39 (4).

Finnemore, Martha. 1996. "Norms, Culture and World Politics: Insights from Sociology's Institutionalism." *International Organization* 50 (2): 325–347.

Free the Slaves and Human Rights Center. 2004. "Hidden Slaves: Forced Labor in the United States." Cornell University ILR School. http://www.digitalcommonsilr.cornell.edu/forcedlabor/8 (accessed May 10, 2009).

Friedman, Amy. 1992. "Rape and Domestic Violence: The Experience of Refugee Women." In *Refugee Women and Their Mental Health*, ed. Ellen Cole, Esther D. Rothblum, and Oliva M. Espin. New York: Harrington Park Press.

Fuentes, Marío Luis. 2005. "Urge combatir la esclavitud en México." Centro de Estudios e Investigación en Desarrollo y Asistencia Social (CEIDAS), México. http://www.iesam.csic.es/doctrab2/dt-0506.pdf.

Fuentes, Francisco Javier Moreno. 2006. "The Regularisation of Undocumented Migrants as a Mechanism for the 'Emerging' of the Spanish Underground Economy." Working paper 05-06. Madrid: Unidad de Políticas Comparadas.

García, M. C. 2006. *Seeking Refuge: Central American Migration to Mexico, the United States, and Canada*. Los Angeles: University of California Press.

García, Mia R. 2004. "Interview: Gloria Terry." *El Paso Inc.* 14ª–15ª. July 11–17.

García, Sean. 2005. "Scapegoats of Juárez: The Misuse of Justice in Prosecuting Women's Murders in Chihuahua, Mexico." Washington, DC: Latin American Working Group Education Fund. http://www.lawg.org/storage/lawg/documents/scapegoats%20of%20juarez.pdf (accessed May 10, 2009).

Gaspar de Alba, Alicia. 2003. "The Maquiladora Murders 1993–2003." *Aztlán: A Journal of Chicano Studies* 28 (3): 1–17.

Giugale, Marcelo, Oliver Lafourcade, and Vinh Nguyen. 2001. *Mexico: A Comprehensive Agenda for the New Era*. Washington, DC: World Bank.

Glassner, Barry. 1999. *The Culture of Fear: Why Americans Are Afraid of the Wrong Things*. New York: Basic Books.

Gori, Graham. 2002. "In Mexico, Pirated Music Outsells the Legal Kind," *New York Times* April 1.

Greenlees, Clyde S., and Rogelio Saenz. 1999. "Determinants of Employment of Recently Arrived Mexican Immigrant Wives." *International Migration Review* 33 (2): 354–78.

Grillo, Ioan. 2007. "Slain Councilman's Severed Head Left Outside Mexican Newspaper Office." *Associated Press Worldstream* May 27.

Grissom, Brandi. 2008. "Homeland Security Secretary Chertoff to Border: 'Grow up.' Critics of New ID Rules Find Comments Insulting." *El Paso Times* 1A, January 18.

Guerette, Rob T. 2007. "Immigration Policy, Border Security, and Migrant Deaths: An Impact Evaluation of Life-Saving Efforts Under the Border Safety Initiative." *Criminology and Public Policy* 6 (2): 245–66.

Hannerz, Ulf. 1998. "Transnational Research." In *Handbook of Methods in Cultural Anthropology*, ed. H. Russell Bernard, 235–256. London: Sage.

Hanson, Stephanie. 2007. "Backgrounder: Mexico's Drug War." Council on Foreign Relations, June 28.

Heilbroner, Robert. 1989. "Reflections: The Triumph of Capitalism." *New Yorker* January 23.

Hero, Rodney. 1992. *Latinos and the U.S. Political System: Two-Tiered Pluralism*. Philadelphia: Temple University Press.

Hester, Marianne. 1992. "The Witch-craze in Sixteenth and Seventeenth Century England as Social Control of Women." In *Femicide: The Politics of Woman Killing*, eds. Jill Radford and Diana E. H. Russell, 27–39. New York: Twayne.

Heyman, Josiah. 1998. *Finding a Moral Heart for U.S. Immigration Policy: An Anthropological Perspective*. Arlington, VA: American Anthropological Association.

Hirsch, Jennifer S. 2002. "'Que, pues, con el pinche NAFTA?': Gender, Power and Migration between Western Mexico and Atlanta." *Urban Anthropology & Studies of Cultural Systems & World Economic Development* 31 (3/4): 351–89.

Hise, Steve. [2006] "On the Edge: The Femicide in Ciudad Juárez." http://www.illegalart.net.

Hondagneu-Sotelo, Pierrette. 2002. "Families on the Frontier: From Braceros in the Fields to Braceras in the Home." In *Latinos: Remaking America*, eds. Marcelo M. Suárez-Orozco and Mariela M. Páez, 259–274. Berkeley: University of California Press and David Rockefeller Center for Latin American Studies.

Hsu, Spencer W. 2007. "Border Crackdown Has El Paso Caught in Middle." *Washington Post* A1.

Hsu, Spencer W., and Sylvia Moreno. 2007. "Border Policy's Success Strains Resources." *Washington Post* February 2.

Hull, Elizabeth. 1983. "The Rights of Aliens: National and International Issues." In *The Unavoidable Issue: U.S. Immigration Policy in the 1980s*, eds. Demetrios G. Papademetriou and Mark J. Miller, 215–249. Philadelphia: Institute for the Study of Human Issues.

Ibarra, María de la Luz. 2003. "The Tender Trap: Mexican Immigrant Women and the Ethics of Elder Care Work." *Aztlán: A Journal of Chicano Studies* 28 (2): 87–112.

IFPI. *See* International Federation of Phonographic Industry.

IIPA. *See* International Intellectual Property Alliance.

Iliff, Laurence. 2007. "Police in Mexico Protest Low Pay, High Risks." *Dallas Morning News* May 21.

Inda, Jonathan Xavier. 2007. "The Value of Immigrant Life." In *Women and Migration at the U.S.–Mexico Borderlands*, eds. Denise A. Segura and Patricia Zavella, 134–137. Durham, NC: Duke University Press.

Instituto Nacional de las Mujeres (INMUJERES), Instituto Nacional de Estadística Geografía e Informática (INEGI), and the United Nations Development Fund for Women (UNIFEM). 2004. *Encuesta nacional sobre la dinámica de las relaciones en los hogares*. http://www.inmujeres.gob.mx.

Intergovernmental Parliamentary Union. 2007. "Women in National Parliaments." http://www.ipu.org.

International Federation of Phonographic Industry (IFPI). 2005. "The Recording Industry 2005 Commercial Piracy Report." London: IFPI. http://www.ifpi.org/content/library/piracy2005.pdf.

International Intellectual Property Alliance (IIPA). 2006. "2006 Special 301 Report, Mexico." http://www.iipa.com/rbc/2006/2006SPEC301MEXICO.pdf.

International Rescue Committee. 2004. "ORR Trafficking in Persons Program." *Trafficking Watch* no. 3 (Winter).

Jaggar, Alison. 1983. *Feminist Politics and Human Nature.* Totowa, NJ: Roman and Allanheld.

Jahangir, Asma. 1999. Informe relativo a las ejecuciones extrajudiciales, sumarias o y abitrarias. Naciones Unidas, Relatoría sobre ejecuciones extrajudiciales, sumarias y arbitrarias. http://www.cinu.rg.mx/biblioteca/documentos/dh/eesa.htm (visitada enero 2006).

Joachim, Jutta. 1999. "Shaping the Human Rights Agenda: The Case of Violence Against Women." In *Gender Politics in Global Governance,* ed. Mary K. Meyer and Elisabeth Prügl, 142–160. Lanham, Maryland: Rowman and Littlefield.

Johnson, Kevin R. 2004. *The "Huddled Masses" Myth: Immigration and Civil Rights.* Philadelphia: Temple University Press.

Jones, David. 2004. "Costa del Fear." *Daily Mail,* May 8, 2nd ed., 36–37.

Kauffer, Michel E. F. 2003. Entre peligros y polleros: la travesía de los indocumentados centroamericanos. *Ecofronteras* 19:9–11.

Keck, Margaret E., and Kathryn Sikkink. 1998. *Activists Beyond Borders: Advocacy Networks in International Politics.* Ithaca: Cornell University Press.

Kelly, Kate, Ethan Smith, and Peter Wonacott. 2005. "Movie, Music Giants Try New Weapon Against Pirates: Price." *Wall Street Journal* March 7, B1.

Kerr, Joanna, Ellen Sprenger, and Alison Symington. 2004. *The Future of Women's Rights: Global Visions and Strategies.* London: Zed and AWID.

Kidd, Dorothy. 2003. "Indymedia.org: A New Communications Common." In *Cyberactivism: Online Activism in Theory and Practice,* ed. Martha McCaughey and Michael D. Ayers, 47–69. New York: Routledge.

Kirana, Karina. 2005. VETA Staff Attorney Boat People SOS, electronic correspondence with Alexandra Webber. August 18.

Kopinak, Kathryn, ed. 2004. *The Social Costs of Industrial Growth in Northern Mexico.* La Jolla: University of California at San Diego Center for U.S.–Mexican Studies.

Kravetz, Diane. 2004. *Tales from the Trenches: Politics and Practice in Feminist Service Organizations.* Lanham, MD: University Press of America.

La Jornada. 2000. "Creció el número de mujeres migrantes desde 1997." September 17.

La Jornada. 2003. "México, frontera de represión y sufrimiento para migrantes indocumentados." October 3.

La Jornada. 2006. "Mujeres, casi 50 percent del total de la población mundial migrante." September 6.

La Opinión. 1997a. "Mujeres, sureños e indígenas, víctimas usuales." April 16.

La Opinión. 1997b. "Reportan abusos en la frontera." May 2. http://daccessdds.un.org/doc/UNDOC/GEN/G02/154/09/PDF/G0215409.pdf?OpenElement (accessed March 12, 2007).

Lichtblau, Eric. 2002. "New Hiding Place for Drug Profits: Insurance Policies." *New York Times* December 6, A1.

Lipsky, Michael. 1980. *Street-Level Bureaucracy: Dilemmas of the Individual in Public Services.* New York: Russell Sage.

Lockwood, Bert B. 2006. *Women's Rights: A Human Rights Quarterly Reader.* Baltimore: Johns Hopkins University Press.

López Urbina, María. 2004. *Report of the Special Prosecutor's Unit for Crimes Related to the Homicides of Women in the Municipality of Juárez, Chihuahua.* June and October. Mexico City: Office of the Assistant Attorney General for Human Rights, Attention to Victims and Community Services.

Lorber, J. 1994. *Paradoxes of Gender.* New Haven: Yale University Press.

Lovenduski, Joni. 1998. "Gendering Research in Political Science." *Annual Review of Political Science,* 1 (1): 333–356.

Lyotard, J. F. 1984. *The Postmodern Condition: A Report on Knowledge.* Minneapolis: University of Minnesota Press.

MacKinnon, C. 1982. "Feminism, Marxism, Method, and the State: An Agenda for Theory." *Signs: Journal of Women and Culture in Society* 7.

Magaloni, Beatriz, and Guillermo Zepeda. 2004. "Democratization, Judicial and Law Enforcement Institutions, and the Rule of Law in Mexico." In *Dilemmas of Political Change in Mexico,* ed. Kevin Middlebrook. La Jolla: University of California at San Diego Center for U.S.–Mexican Studies and Institute of Latin American Studies; London: University of London.

Mahler, S. J. 2000. "Migration and Transnational Issues. Recent Trends and Prospects for 2020," CA 2020: Working Paper #4 Institut für Iberoamerika-Kunde. http://www1.uni-hamburg.de/IIK/za2020/mahler.pdf (accessed March 10, 2007).

Maier, E. 2001. "Deconstruyendo las violencias de género." In *Los Rostros de la Violencia.* Tijuana, Mexico: El Colegio de la Frontera Norte.

Márquez, Raquel R., and Yolanda C. Padilla. 2003. "Migration in the Life Course of Women in the Border City of Matamoros, Tamaulipas: Links to Educational, Family and Labor Trajectories." *Journal of Borderlands Studies* 18 (2): 87–104.

Martínez, Oscar. 1996. *Border People.* Tucson: University of Arizona Press.

Martínez, Ramiro, Jr., and Abel Valenzuela Jr., eds. 2006. *Race, Ethnicity, and Violence.* New York: New York University Press.

Massey, Douglas S., Jorge Durand, and Nolan J. Malone. 2002. *Beyond Smoke and Mirrors: Mexican Immigration in an Era of Economic Integration.* New York: Russell Sage Foundation.

McAdam, Doug, John D. McCarthy, and Mayer N. Zald, eds. 1996. *Comparative Perspectives on Social Movements: Political Opportunities, Mobilizing Structures, and Cultural Framings.* New York: Cambridge University Press.

McCarthy, John D., Clark McPhail, and Jackie Smith. 1996. "Images of Protest: Estimating Selection Bias in Media Coverage of Washington Demonstrations 1982 and 1991." *American Sociological Review* 61:478–99.

Meikle, Graham. 2002. *Future Active: Media Activism and the Internet.* New York: Routledge.

Méndez, J. E., G. O'Donnell, and P. S. Pinheiro. 2002. *La inefectividad de la ley y la exclusión en América Latina*. Barcelona: Paidós.

Merry, Sally Engle. 2006. *Human Rights & Gender Violence: Translating International Law into Local Justice*. Chicago: University of Chicago Press.

Mexico Solidarity Network (MSN). 2004. "Femicides of Ciudad Juárez and Chihuahua." http://MSN@MexicoSolidarity.org.

Meyer, David, Nancy Whittier, and Belinda Robnett, eds. 2002. *Social Movements, Identity, Culture and the State*. New York: Oxford University Press.

Millett K. 1970. *Sexual Politics*. Garden City, NY: Doubleday.

Milovanovic, Dragan, and Katheryn K. Russell, eds. 2001. "Introduction: Petit Apartheid." In *Petit Apartheid in the U.S. Criminal Justice System*, xv–xxiii. Durham, NC: Carolina Academic Press.

Monárrez Fragoso, Julia. 2002. "Feminicidio sexual serial en Ciudad Juárez: 1993–2001." *Debate Feminista* 13:25.

———. 2003. "El feminicidio es el exterminio de la mujer en el patriarcado." Entrevista de 19 octubre.http://www.webmujeractual.com/noticias/femicidio.htm (visitado en marzo 2006).

———. 2005. "Violencia e (in)seguridad ciudadana en Ciudad Juárez." *Diagnóstico geo-socio-económico de Ciudad Juárez*, coor. Luis Cervera Gómez. Ciudad Juárez: COLEF (El Colegio de la Frontera Norte), capitulo IX.

Monteverde García, Ana María. 2004. "Propuesta de campaña preventiva contra la violencia hacia la mujer inmigrante y operadora de la industria maquiladora en la ciudad de Nogales Sonora." Tesis profesional, Universidad de las Américas, Escuela de Ciencias Sociales, Departamento de Ciencias de la Comunicación, Cholula, Puebla, México. http://140.148.3.250/u_dl_a/servlet/mx.udlap.ict.tales.html.Block?Thesis=2074&Type=O (accessed June 19, 2005).

Moreno Fuentes, Francisco Javier. 2005. "The Regularization of Undocumented Migrants as a Mechanism for the 'Emerging' of the Spanish Underground Economy." Working Paper 05–06. Madrid: Unidad de Políticas Comparadas.

Morfín, Guadalupe. 2004. *Informe de gestión: Noviembre 2003–abril 2004*. Cd. Juárez: Comisión para Prevenir y Eradicar la Violencia Contra las Mujeres in Ciudad Juárez. Secretaría de Gobernación (SEGOB).

Moulson, Geir. 2007. "'Bordertown' Shown at Berlin Film Fest." Associated Press Release. February 15.

MPI Staff. 2006. "The U.S.–Mexico Border." Migration Information Source: Fresh Thought, Authoritative Data, Global Reach. Migration Policy Institute (MPI). June. http://www.migrationinformation.org/Feature/display.cfm?id= 407.

MSN. *See* Mexico Solidarity Network.

Mueller, Carol. 1997. "International Press Coverage of East German Protest Events 1989." *American Sociological Review* 62:820–832.

Mueller, Carol, Michelle Hansen, and Karen Qualtire. 2006. "A Grassroots Caravan for Justice Targets Femicide in Cuidad Juárez." Paper presented at the Lineae

Terrarum: International Borders Conference and the International Studies Association, San Diego.

Murphy Erfani, Julie A. 2007. "Whose Security? Dilemmas of U.S. Border Security in the Arizona-Sonora Borderlands." In *Comparing Border Security in North America and Europe*, ed. Emmanuel Brunet-Jailly. Ottawa: University of Ottawa Press.

Nadelmann, Ethan. 2007. "Think Again: The War on Drugs." *Foreign Policy* 162 (September–October).

Naím, Moisés. 2005. *Illicit*. New York: Random House.

Nevárez, Oman. 2007. "State Governor Says Deadly Mexico Attack Was Revenge by Drug Cartel for Police Betrayal." *Associate Press Worldstream* May 19.

Neville, Sheila. Staff Attorney Los Angeles Legal Aid Foundation, electronic correspondence, August 22, 2005.

Newman, Paul. 2007. Panel presentation at the "Building a New Vision of the Border: A Conference on Border Policy." Convened by the Border Human Rights Collaborative and the U.S.–Mexico Border and Immigration Task Force. El Paso, Texas, November 29–30.

Nordstrum, Carolyn. 2006. *Global Outlaws*. Berkeley: University of California Press.

Nuñez, Guillermina Gina, and Josiah McC. Heyman. 2007. "Entrapment Processes and Immigrant Communities in a Time of Heightened Border Vigilance." *Human Organization* 66 (4): 354–365.

Nye, Joseph S., Jr. 2005. *Soft Power: The Means to Success in World Politics*. New York: Perseus.

O'Connor, Anne-Marie. 2002. "Gathering Fights Those Who Deal in Human Lives." *Los Angeles Times* August 25, B–10.

O'Day, Patrick, and Angelina López. 2001. "Organizing the Underground NAFTA: Fayuqueros and the El Arreglo." *Journal of Contemporary Criminal Justice* 17 (3): 232–242.

Oficina del Alto Comisionado de las Naciones Unidas para los Derechos Humanos en México. 2003. *Diagnostico sobre la situación de los derechos humanos en México*. http://www.cinu.org.mx/prensa/especiales/2003/dh_2003/ (accessed January 10, 2007).

———. 2009. "The ABCs of Unauthorized Border Crossing Costs: Assembling, *Bajadores*, and Coyotes." *Migration Letters* 6 (1): 27–36.

O'Leary, Anna Ochoa. Forthcoming. "*Mujeres en el Cruce*: Mapping Family Separation/Reunification at a Time of Border (In)Security." *Journal of the Southwest*.

Olmos, C. 2003. "América Central: Situación migratoria después de los conflictos." *Amérique Latine Histoire et Mémoire* no. 7. http://alhim.revues.org/document366.html (accessed April 14, 2007).

Omi, M. and Howard Winant. 1994. *Racial Formation in the United States, from the 1960s to the 1990s*. New York: Routledge.

Orrenius, Pia M., and Roberto Coronado. 2005. *The Effect of Illegal Immigration and Border Enforcement on Crime Rates along the U.S.–Mexico Border*. Working paper 131. La Jolla: University of California at San Diego Center for Comparative Immigration Studies.

Parkerson, Chris. "The Challenges and Successes of Conducting Reliable Threat Assessment along the U.S. Mexico Border." http://www.securitydriver.com/aic .stories/article-90.html (accessed December 4, 2007).

Parpademetriou, Demetrios G., and Mark J. Miller, eds. 1983. The Rights of Aliens: National and International Issues. In *The Unavoidable Issue: U.S. Immigration Policy in the 1980s*, 215–249. Philadelphia: Institute for the Study of Human Issues.

Parrot, Andrea, and Nina Cummings. 2006. *Forsaken Females: The Global Brutalization of Women*. Lanham, MD: Rowman and Littlefield.

Payán Alvarado, Luis Antonio. 2004. "Ciudad Juárez y El Paso: Tan cerca y tan lejos. Estudio sobre las estadísticas delictivas en la región." In *Gobernabilidad o Ingobernabilidad en la Region Paso del Norte*, coord. Luis Antonio Payán Alvarado y María Socorro Tabuenca Córdoba, 219–252. Tijuana: COLEF.

Payan, Tony. 2006. *The Three U.S.–Mexico Border Wars: Drugs, Immigration, and Homeland Security*. New York: Praeger.

Paz, Octavio. 1961. *The Labyrinth of Solitude: Life and Thought in Mexico*. New York: Grove Press.

Pécoud, Antoine. 2008. "Toward a Right to Mobility: International Migration, Border Controls, and Human Rights." Presented at the annual BRIT Conference, Victoria, British Columbia.

Pérez, C. 2007. "La frontera sur es una coladera, entra quien quiere hacerlo." *La Jornada* April 24, Sociedad y Justicia section. http://www.jornada.unam.mx/ 2007/04/24/index.

PGR. *See* Procuraduría General de la República.

Pinheiro, P. S. 1996. Democracies without Citizenship. *NACLA Report on the Americas* 30:17–23.

Polaski, Sandra. 2006. "NAFTA at Year 12." Testimony at the U.S. Senate International Trade Subcommittee Hearing, September 11. Carnegie Endowment for International Peace. http://www.carnegieendowment.org/publications/index .cfm?fa=view&id=18703&prog=zgp (accessed February 2, 2008).

Preston, Julia. 2007. "Tighter Border Delays Re-entry by U.S. Citizens." *New York Times* October 21, A1.

Procuraduría General de la República (PGR). 2004a. Palabras del Lic. Macedo de la Concha, Procurador General de la República, durante la presentación de la Campaña Nacional de Equidad y Seguridad Integral de la Mujer y del Lic. Peñaloza, Director General de Prevención del delito y servicios a la comunidad, de la PGR, 8 de marzo 2004. http://www.pgr.gob.mx (visitada en marzo 2006).

———. 2004b. Comparecencia de la Lic. María López Urbina, Fiscal Especial para la Atención de Delitos Relacionados con los Homicidios de Mujeres en el Municipio de Juárez y del Dr. Álvarez Ledesma, Subprocurador de Derechos Humanos, Atención a Víctimas y Servicios a la Comunidad de la PGR, ante las Comisiones

Especiales Unidas de la Cámara de Diputados y de la Cámara de Senadores, 20 julio 2004. http://www.pgr.gob.mx (visitada en marzo 2006).

———— 2006. Comparecencia del Procurador General de la República, Daniel Cabeza de Vaca ante la Comisión del Feminicidio y las Comisiones Unidas de Equidad y Género del Congreso y del Senado, 7 de marzo del 2006. http://www.pgr.gob .mx (visitado el 5 de abril 2006).

Rai, Shirin, ed. 2003. *Mainstreaming Gender, Democratizing the State? Institutional Mechanisms for the Advancement of Women.* Manchester and New York: Manchester University Press.

Rainier, Chris. 2003. "In Sahara, Salt-Hauling Camel Trains Struggle On." *National Geographic News* May 28. http://news.nationalgeographic.com/ news/2003/05/0528_030528_saltcaravan.html.

Ramshaw, Emily. 2006. "Losing Track of Sex Offenders." *Dallas Morning News* October 3.

Reforma. 1997. "Reporta ONG denuncias en frontera Tijuana." July 23.

Reporters Without Borders. 2007. "The Deadliest Year since 1994." http://www.rsf .org/article.php3?id_article=20286.

Reyes-Rubi, Nancy J. 2005. Attorney, Legal Aid Foundation of Los Angeles, email interview with Alexandra Webber, August 8.

Richard, Amy O'Neill. 2000. *International Trafficking in Women to the United States: A Contemporary Manifestation of Slavery and Organized Crime.* Washington, DC: Center for the Study of Intelligence, U.S. Central Intelligence Agency.

Risse, Thomas. 2000a. "The Power of Norms versus the Norms of Power: Transnational Civil Society and Human Rights Norms." In *The Third Force. The Rise of Transnational Civil Society,* ed. Ann Florini. Washington, DC: Japan Center for International Exchange and Carnegie Endowment for International Peace.

————. 2000b. "Let's Argue: Communicative Action in World Politics." *International Organization* 54:1–39.

Risse, Thomas, and Kathryn Sikkink. 1999. "The Socialization of International Human Rights Norms into Domestic Practices: Introduction." In *The Power of Human Rights. International Norms and Domestic Change,* ed. Thomas Risse, Stephen Ropp, and Kathryn Sikkink. Cambridge: Cambridge University Press.

Risse, Thomas, Stephen Ropp, and Kathryn Sikkink. 1999. *The Power of Human Rights: International Norms and Domestic Change.* Cambridge: Cambridge University Press.

Rodríguez, Olga R. 2007. "Drug Lords Seize People-Smuggling Routes." *Associated Press Online* May 1.

Rodríguez, Teresa. 2007. *The Daughters of Juárez.* New York: Simon and Schuster.

Rodríguez, Victoria. 1997. *Decentralization in Mexico: From Reforma Municipal to Solidaridad to Nuevo Federalismo.* Boulder, CO: Westview Press.

Rojas Blanco, Clara. 2005. "Voces que silencian y silencios que enuncian." *Noésis* 15 (28): 15–32.

Romero, Manuela, and Tracy Yellen. 2004. "El Paso Portraits: Women's Lives, Potential & Opportunities: A Report on the State of Women in El Paso, Texas." El Paso: YWCA El Paso Del Norte Region and the University of Texas at El Paso. Monograph available at www.womensfundofelpaso.org/NeedsReport.pdf (accessed December 1, 2007).

Romo, David. 2005. *Ringside Seat to a Revolution: An Underground Cultural History of El Paso and Juárez: 1893–1923.* El Paso: Cinco Puntos Press.

Rosaldo, Renato. 1989. *Culture and Truth.* Stanford: Stanford University Press.

Rotstein, Arthur H. 2007a. "Two Dead in Attack on Migrants in Arizona." *Associated Press Online* March 31.

———. 2007b. "Two Suspects in Green Valley Migrant Killings Indicted." *Associated Press State & Local Wire* April 19.

Rubio-Goldsmith, Raquel, M. Melissa McCormick, Daniel Martínez, and Inez Magdalena Duarte. 2006. *"The Funnel Effect" and Recovered Bodies of Unauthorized Migrants Processed by the Pima County Office of the Medical Examiner 1990–2005.* Immigration Policy Center Brief, available at http://immigration.server263 .com/index.php?content=B070201 (accessed May 3, 2009).

Rucht, Dieter, Ruud Koopmans, Friedhelm Neidhardt, eds. 1998. *Acts of Dissent: New Developments in the Study of Protest.* Berlin: Sigma.

Ruiz, O. 2003. La migración centroamericana en la frontera sur: Un perfil de riesgo en la migración indocumentada internacional. *Center for U.S.–Mexican Studies,* Paper Ruiz, http://repositories.cdlib.org/usmex/ruiz (accessed March 8, 2007).

Ruiz, O. 2008. "The Gender of Risk: Sexual Violence Against Undocumented Women." In *A Promised Land, A Perilous Journey: Theological Perspectives on Migration.* eds. Daniel Groody and Gioacchino Campese, 225–239. Notre Dame, IN: Notre Dame Press.

Ruiz, O., and Red de las Casas del Migrante Scalabrini. 2001. "Los riesgos de cruzar: La migración centroamericana en la frontera México–Guatemala." *Frontera Norte* 25:7–33.

Rumbaut, Rubén, and Walter Ewing. 2007. *The Myth of Immigrant Criminality and the Paradox of Assimilation: Incarceration Rates Among Native and Foreign-born Men.* Washington, DC: Immigration Policy Center.

Russell, Diana E. H. 2001. "Introduction: The Politics of Femicide." In *Femicide in Global Perspective,* ed. Diana E. H. Russell and Roberta A. Harmes, 3–11. New York: College Teachers Press.

Russell, Diana E. H., and Roberta A. Harmes, eds. 2001. *Femicide in Global Perspective.* New York: College Teachers Press.

Salzinger, Leslie. 2003. *Gender in Production: Making Women Workers in Mexico's Global Factories.* Berkeley: University of California Press.

San Diego Union-Tribune. 2006 "More Female Migrants Give Birth, Face Rape and Robbery, on Illegal Journey to U.S." April 27.

Schafer C., and M. Frye. 1986. "Rape and respect." In *Women and Values,* ed. Marilyn Pearsall. Belmont, CA: Wadsworth.

Scott, James. 1990. *Domination and the Arts of Resistance: Hidden Transcripts.* New Haven: Yale University Press.

Scully, D. 1990. *Understanding Sexual Violence: A Study of Convicted Rapists.* Boston: Unwin Hyman.

Secretaría de Relaciones Exteriores. 2007. *Ley General de Acceso de las Mujeres a Una Vida Libre de Violencia.* México D.F.: Gobierno de México.

Segal, L. 1990. *Slow Motion: Changing Masculinities, Changing Men.* New Brunswick, NJ: Rutgers University Press.

Shirk, David, and Alexandra Webber. 2004. "Slavery Without Borders: Human Trafficking in the U.S.–Mexican Context." *Hemisphere Focus* 7 (5): 2–3.

Sinikka, Tarvainen. 2006. "Corruption Scandals Rock Spain," *Deutsche Presse-Agentur* November 10.

Small, Jim. 2007. "Arizona Lawmakers Say Immigration Bill Targeting Businesses Better Than Ballot Measure." *Arizona Capitol Times* March 23.

Spagat, Elliot. 2006. "Border Crackdown Fuels Smugglers' Boom on U.S.–Mexico Border." Associated Press State & Local Wire, December 27.

Spener, D. 2001. El contrabando de migrantes en la frontera de Texas con el Nordeste de México: Mecanismo para la integración del mercado laboral de América del Norte. *Espiral* 21:201–247.

Staudt, Kathleen. 1998. *Free Trade? Informal Economies at the U.S.–Mexico Border.* Philadelphia: Temple University Press.

———. 2008a. "Bordering the Other in the U.S. Southwest: El Pasoans Confront the Local Sheriff on Immigration Enforcement." In Brotherton and Kretsedemas 2008, 291–313.

———. 2008b. *Violence and Activism at the Border: Gender, Fear and Everyday Life in Ciudad Juárez.* Austin: University of Texas Press.

Staudt, Kathleen, and Irasema Coronado. 2002. *Fronteras no más: Toward Social Justice at the U.S.–Mexico Border.* New York: Palgrave USA.

Staudt, Kathleen, and Gabriela Montoya. 2009. "Violence and Activism at the U.S.–Mexico Border: Women, Migration, and Obstacles to Justice." In *Feminist Agendas and the Challenges of Democracy in Latin America*, ed. Jane S. Jaquette. Durham, NC: Duke University Press.

Staudt, Kathleen, and Beatriz Vera. 2006. "Mujeres, políticas públicas y política: Los caminos globales de Ciudad Juárez, Chihuahua-El Paso, Texas." *Región y sociedad.* 18 (37): 127–172.

Steller, Tim. 2001. "Border Unit Fights an Enemy Within." *Arizona Daily Star* June 16, A1.

Stone, Deborah. 1997. *Policy Paradox: The Art of Political Decision-Making.* New York: W. W. Norton.

Tarrow, Sidney. 1998. *Power in Movement: Social Movements and Contentious Politics.* New York: Cambridge University Press.

Tarvainen, Sinnikka. 2006. "Corruption Scandal Rocks Spain." *Deutsche Presse-Agentur* November 10.

Teicher, Martin H. 2002. "Scars That Won't Heal: The Neurobiology of Child Abuse." *Scientific American* 286 (3): 68.

Tenorio, Christopher. 2005. Assistant United States Attorney, electronic correspondence, August 12.

Tertulia. 2000. "Frontera con México: Ultrajan a 22 mujeres indocumentadas." June 12.

Tickner, J. Ann. 2002. "Feminist Perspectives on 9/11." *International Studies Perspectives* 3:333–350.

Tilly, Charles. 1983. "Speaking Your Mind without Elections, Surveys, or Social Movements." *Public Opinion Quarterly* 47:461–78.

———. 1995. *Popular Contention in Great Britain, 1758–1834.* Cambridge, MA: Harvard University Press.

———. 1999. "From Interactions to Outcomes in Social Movements." In *How Social Movements Matter,* ed. Marco Giugni, Doug McAdam, and Charles Tilly, 253–270. Minneapolis: University of Minnesota Press.

———. 2004. *Social Movements, 1768–2004.* Boulder, CO: Paradigm Publishers.

Timewell, Stephen. 2006. "The World's Most Lucrative Money Trail." *Financial Times Business Limited,* September 1.

Tobar, Héctor, and Cecilia Sánchez. 2007. "In Mexico's Drug Trade, No Glitter for Grunts." *Los Angeles Times.* December 1, sec. 1,1.

Tong, Rosemarie Putnam. 1989. *Feminist Thought: A More Comprehensive Introduction,* Boulder, CO: Westview Press.

———. 1998. *Feminist Thought: A More Comprehensive Introduction.* 2nd ed. Boulder, CO: Westview Press.

Trafficking Victims Protection Reauthorization Act (TVPA) 2005, H.R. 972.

United Nations. 2000. United Nations Millennium Declaration. http://www.un .org/millennium/declaration/ares552e.htm (accessed May 10, 2009).

———. 2003. *Eighth United Nations Survey on Crime Trends and the Operations of Criminal Justice Systems, 2001–2.* New York: United Nations Office on Drugs and Crime.

United Nations Committee on the Protection of the Rights of All Migrant Workers and Members of their Families. 2006. Concluding Observations of the Committee on the Protection of the Rights of All Migrant Workers and Members of Their Families. Mexico. http://www.ohchr.org/english/countries/mx/index .htm (accessed May 2, 2007).

United Nations Development Programme. 2009. "About the Millennium Development Goals." Millennium Campaign. http://www.endpoverty2015.org/goals (accessed May 10, 2009).

United Press International (UPI). 2007a. "Crime Increases along Mexican Border." April 24.

———. 2007b. "Mexico Drug Gangs Buy at U.S. Gun Shows." January 17.

———. 2007c. "Violence Prompts Mexican Papers to Close." June 8.

U.S. Customs and Border Protection. 2007. "Operation Jumpstart." http://www .asisonline.org/newsroom/051506operationjumpstart.pdf (accessed January 20, 2008).

U.S. Department of Health and Human Services, Administration for Children and Families, Campaign to Rescue and Restore Victims of Human Trafficking. 2004. "Victim Assistance Fact Sheet."

U.S. Department of Justice (USDOJ). 2001. *Intimate Partner Violence and Age of Victim.* Special report, NCJ 187635. Washington, DC: USDOJ.

———. 2005. Report to Congress from Attorney General Alberto R. Gonzáles on U.S. Government Efforts to Combat Trafficking in Persons in Fiscal Year 2004. July.

U.S. Department of Justice, Civil Rights Division. 2005. "US/Mexico: Cross-Border Dialogue on Trafficking Enforcemnt Efforts," *Anti-Trafficking News Bulletin,* vol. 2, issue 2. August 2005.

U.S. Department of Justice, Immigration and Naturalization Service. 2002. "'T' Visa Regulations." January 31, 4, 5–13.

U.S. Department of State (USDOS). 2000. Victims of Trafficking and Violence Protection Act of 2000. Publication L. no. 106-386. October 28. http://www.state.gov/g/tip/laws/61124.htm (accessed April 23, 2009).

———. 2003. Trafficking Victims Protection Reauthorization Act of 2003. H.R. 2620. http://www.state.gov/g/tip/laws/61130.htm (accessed April 23, 2009).

———. 2004. *Trafficking in Persons Report.* June.

———. 2005. *Trafficking in Persons Report.* June.

USDOJ. *See* U.S. Department of Justice.

USDOS. *See* U.S. Department of State.

U.S. Government Accountability Office. 2006. *Illegal Immigration: Border Crossing Deaths Have Doubled Since 1995.* Washington, DC: GAO 06:770, August 15.

UPI. *See* United Press International.

Urquijo-Ruiz, Rita E. 2004. "Police Brutality Against an Undocumented Mexican Woman." *Chicana/Latina Studies* 4 (1): 62–84.

Van der Wel, Mariette. 2006. "Radio Netherlands and Novib Expose Mexican Murders of Women." Oxfam Novib Network. http://www.oxfamnovib.nl/id7851.html?lang=en&from=4285.

Velasco, José Luis. 2005. "Insurgency, Authoritarianism, and Drug Trafficking in Mexico's Democratization." New York: Routledge.

Vélez-Ibáñez, Carlos. 1996. *Border Visions.* Tucson: University of Arizona Press.

Violence Against Women Act Reauthorization. 2005. H.R. 3402/S. 1197.

Vital Voices Global Partnership. 2005. Trafficking Alert, International Edition, August.

Wagner, Steve. 2005. Coordinator, Trafficking in Persons Program, Office of Refugee Resettlement, telephone interview, June 28.

Wallace-Wells, Ben. 2007. "How America Lost the War on Drugs. After 35 Years and $500 Billion, Drugs Are as Cheap and Plentiful as Ever: An Anatomy of a Failure." *Rolling Stone.* (November): 90–119.

Washington Valdez, Diana. 2002. "Death Stalks the Border." *El Paso Times* June 24, Special Insert.

————. 2005. *Cosecha de mujeres: Safari en el desierto mexicano.* Mexico City: Oceana.

————. 2006. *The Killing Fields: Harvest of Women.* Los Angeles: Peace at the Border Publishing.

Weldon, S. Laurel. 2002. *Protest, Policy, and the Problem of Violence Against Women: A Cross-National Comparison.* Pittsburgh: University of Pittsburgh Press.

————. 2006. "The Structure of Intersectionality: A Comparative Politics of Gender." *Politics & Gender* 2 (2): 235–248.

Wetmore, Jennifer M. 2003. "The New T-Visa: Is the Higher Extreme Hardship Standard Too High for Bona Fide Trafficking Victims?" *New England International and Comparative Law Annual* 9 (1): 161.

White House. 2007. "Fact Sheet: A Record of Achievement on Border Security and Worksite Enforcement." States News Service, May 23.

Winders, Jamie. 2007. "Bringing Back the (B)order: Post-9/11 Politics of Immigration, Borders, and Belonging in the Contemporary U.S. South." *Antipode* 39 (5): 920–942.

Wright, Melissa W. 2006. "Public Women, Profit, and Femicide in Northern Mexico." *South Atlantic Quarterly* 105 (4): 684–698.

Zepeda Lecuona, Guillermo. 2002. "Inefficiency at the Service of Impunity: Criminal Justice Organizations in Mexico." In *Transnational Crime and Public Security*, ed. John Bailey and Jorge Chabat, 71–107. La Jolla: University of California at San Diego Center for U.S.–Mexican Studies.

Zlotnik, Hania. 2003. "The Global Dimensions of Female Migration." Migration Policy Institute. http://www.migrationinformation.org/Feature/display.cfm?id=109.

About the Editors

Kathleen (Kathy) Staudt, PhD (University of Wisconsin), lead editor, is professor of political science at the University of Texas at El Paso. She has published more than a dozen books, five of which focus on the U.S.–Mexico border, including *Violence and Activism at the Border: Gender, Fear and Everyday Life in Ciudad Juárez; Free Trade? Informal Economies at the U.S.–Mexico Border; The U.S.–Mexico Border: Contesting Divisions, Transcending Identities*, with David Spener, coeditor; *Ni Una Más: Toward Social Justice at the U.S.–Mexico Border*, with Irasema Coronado; and *Pledging Allegiance: Learning Nationalism in El Paso-Juárez*. Kathy is active in border community-based and nonprofit organizations including the Coalition Against Violence, Border Interfaith, the Women's Fund of El Paso, the Nonprofit Congress, and the Paso del Norte Civil Rights Project. She has also provided public service on city boards, the Empowerment Zone, the Domestic Violence Fatalities Review Commission, and the Victims' Services Response Team of the El Paso Police Department.

Tony Payan, PhD, and **Z. Anthony (Tony) Kruszewski,** PhD, are political science professors at the University of Texas at El Paso. They coorganized the four-day Lineae Terrarum conference of March 2006 at the U.S.–Mexico border with the collaboration of UTEP, the Universidad Autónoma de Ciudad Juárez, New Mexico State University, and the Colegio de la Frontera Norte (COLEF), Mexico's leading think tank associated with El Colegio de México. Over six hundred scholars attended this largest-ever conference on international borders, and several chapters in this volume were originally presented at the conference. Payan is the author of two recent books on the U.S.–Mexico border: *Cops, Soldiers, and Diplomats: Exlaining Agency Behavior in the War on Drugs;* and *Three U.S.–Mexico Border Wars: Drugs, Immigration, and Homeland Security*. Kruszewski, one of the founders of the Association of Borderlands Studies, specializes in European and post-Soviet international borders. He is a co-editor of *Politics and Society in the Southwest : Ethnicity and Chicano Pluralism*, with Richard L. Hough and Jacob Ornstein-Galicia; and *Chicanos and Native Americans: The Territorial Minorities*, with Rudolph O. de la Garza and Tomás A. Arciniega.

About the Contributors

Olga Aikin Araluce is a professor/researcher at the Instituto Tecnológico de Estudios Superiores de Occidente (ITESO), Guadalajara, México. She has a master's degree in international relations, from the Instituto Tecnológico de Estudios Superiores de Monterrey (ITESM), and received her PhD in the International Relations program at the Universidad Complutense de Madrid, Spain in 2009. Her areas of interest and research are transnational activism, gender, femicide, human rights, and international relations theory.

Timothy Dunn (University of Texas) is an associate professor of sociology at Salisbury University in Salisbury, Maryland. He wrote the pathbreaking book on the militarization of the U.S.–Mexico border in 1996. Dunn's 2009 book from the University of Texas Press is titled *Blockading the Border and Human Rights: The El Paso Texas Operation that Remade U.S. Border Enforcement.*

Ana Fernández Zubieta has a doctorate in humanities from the Carlos III University of Madrid. Her main research topics are violence and the sociology of science. She has several publications addressing the relationship between violence and globalization. She was a researcher at the Autonomous University of Tamaulipas (Mexico). Currently, she is a visiting fellow at University of Sussex (United Kingdom).

Michelle Hansen, a former student of Carol Mueller, received her bachelor's degree from Arizona State University.

Alberto Martín Alvarez has a PhD in political science from the Universidad Complutense of Madrid (Spain). His main research topics are political violence, human rights, and the quality of democracy in Latin America, and collective action in the Central American area. He has published several works addressing these topics in Spain, Mexico, and El Salvador. He is currently a researcher at the Autonomous University of Tamaulipas (Mexico).

Carol Mueller is professor of political sociology in the Department of Social and Behavioral Sciences at the New College of Interdisciplinary Arts and Sciences, Arizona State University. Her work focuses on the global women's movement and social movement theory. Previous publications include *Repression and Mobilization*, edited with Charles Davenport and Hank Johnston (Minnesota); *Frontiers in Social*

Movement Theory, edited with Aldon Morris; *Politics of the Gender Gap*; and *The Women's Movements of the U.S. and Western Europe*, edited with Mary Katzenstein; as well as numerous journal articles and book chapters.

Karen Qualtire, a former student of Carol Mueller, graduated summa cum laude with a B.S. in political science from Arizona State University. She and her husband operate a small business in the Phoenix area.

Julie Murphy Erfani is an associate professor in the Department of Social & Behavioral Sciences at Arizona State University. Her current research focuses on fair trade, illicit trade, and processes of integration in North America. Her most recent work is entitled, "Whose Security? Dilemmas of U.S. Border Security in the Arizona-Sonora Borderlands," in *Borderlands: Comparing Border Security in North America and Europe*, edited by Emmanuel Brunet-Jailly.

Anna Ochoa O'Leary, with a PhD in anthropology from the University of Arizona, teaches at the Mexican American Studies and Research Center (MASRC) of the University of Arizona and is affiliated with the Binational Migration Institution, an association of scholars dedicated to the study of how immigration enforcement affects Latino populations regardless of legal status. Her research and teaching interests continue to focus on immigration, gender issues, education, and culture on the U.S.–Mexico border. In 2007, she completed Fulbright-sponsored research of migrant women's encounters with immigration enforcement agents.

Olivia T. Ruiz Marrujo is a cultural anthropologist and researcher at El Colegio de la Frontera Norte (COLEF) in Tijuana, Baja California, Mexico. Her research focuses on risk in international migration in Mexico's northern and southern borders. She is especially interested in the links between risk and poverty, gender, ethnicity and race.

David A. Shirk has been the director of the Trans-Border Institute at the University of San Diego since 2003. He is an assistant professor in the Political Science Department and received his PhD in political science at the University of California, San Diego. Shirk conducts research and publishes on topics related to Mexican politics, U.S.–Mexican relations, and law enforcement and security issues along the U.S.–Mexico border. Some of his most recent publications are *Mexico's New Politics: The PAN and Democratic Change* and a coedited volume with Wayne Cornelius, *Reforming the Administration of Justice in Mexico*.

Alexandra Webber, a practicing attorney and a former Fulbright Fellow, 2004–5, has done extensive research in Mexico on human trafficking in the national context.

Index